THE
DATA
GAME

THE DATA GAME

Controversies in Social Science Statistics

Mark H. Maier

SECOND EDITION

M.E. Sharpe
Armonk, New York
London, England

First edition 1991. Second edition 1995

Library of Congress Cataloging-in-Publication Data

Maier, Mark.
The data game : controversies in social science statistics / Mark H. Maier.—2nd ed.
p.   cm.
Includes bibliographical references and index.
ISBN 1-56324-481-0.—ISBN 1-56324-482-9 (pbk.)
1. Social sciences—Statistical methods.
2. Social problems—Statistics.
I. Title.
HA29.M236   1995
300′.1′5195—dc20
94-47648
CIP

Printed in the United States of America

BM (c)   10   9   8   7   6   5   4   3   2   1
BM (p)   10   9   8   7   6   5   4   3   2   1

Contents

Figures, Tables, and Boxes

Preface to the Second Edition

This book fills the need for a companion text to introductory statistics courses on the collection and use of social science data. It is suitable for undergraduate courses in statistics and research methods, as well as for first courses in statistics offered in many social science graduate programs.

An analysis of statistical source material is readily justified and often called for by social science practitioners. As illustrated throughout this book, many public policy debates arise because of different interpretations of the underlying data. For topics as diverse as the size of the middle class and the crime rate, ambiguities in the data produce statistics that appear to support opposite positions. Cases such as those included here bring statistics to the real world, demonstrating to students the critical role that data play in a wide variety of social issues.

The subject areas in this book include demography, housing, health, education, crime, the national economy, wealth and poverty, labor, business, and government. New to this edition is a chapter on public opinion polling. All the data sources and controversy sections have been revised and updated where necessary, and many new figures have been added. Students in all disciplines will benefit from this wide coverage because much research involves social statistics that transcend narrow disciplinary confines, and because almost every example teaches a lesson that has relevance for all the social sciences. Several common questions recur across the disciplinary spectrum represented in this book. How do the popular media misinterpret social statistics? Why are some social statistics continually cited, even though they are widely known to be misleading? Why are some data collected in abundance, while many critically needed data are missing? Why are the categories into which data are organized so critical for statistical analysis? In addition, fundamental statistical techniques are reviewed, including the difference between surveys and complete counts, index numbers, the use of means and medians, and the use of absolute and relative measures. These issues are probed further in case study questions at the end of each chapter, and they are summarized in the final chapter.

In brief, this book is an invitation to social science research for students, whether as future practitioners in social science or as enlightened citizens. *The Data Game* demonstrates the excitement, the frustrations, and always the importance of social statistics as an instrument for understanding and changing the world in which we live.

Acknowledgments

I owe profound thanks to the many specialists who offered guidance in their respective fields of expertise. These generous individuals include Randy Albelda, James Campen, Robert Carson, Todd Easton, Matthew Edel, Mona Field, Theodore Joyce, Peter L. Maier, Scott R. Maier, Richard McGahey, William D. Mosher, Michelle Naples, Robert Pollin, John Queen, Michael Schiller, David Stern, Michael Swerdlow, Robert Untermann, Thomas E. Weisskopf, and Steven White. Many others provided encouragement and professional advice at key points during this project. In particular, I thank David M. Gordon and members of the Greater Los Angeles Political Economy Seminar. The entire project benefited from the assistance of Lou Ferleger, who read every chapter. Lou's political acumen and good sense of pedagogy provided sound advice when it was much needed. For library assistance, gratitude is due in particular to Brenda Jones, Janet Naumer, and Linda Winters. At M.E. Sharpe, I thank Barbara Leffel for her enthusiasm during the book's early stages and Michael Weber, whose persistent care and interest guided the book to completion. The Glendale College Faculty Development Fund provided much-appreciated release time. And finally, greetings to Sam and Julia, who now can read their names, and thank you to Anne, my life partner, for whom words are not enough.

Chapter 1

Introduction

The Purpose of This Book

Social statistics can be frustrating. It seems as if there are numbers to prove anything—even entirely opposite points of view. For example, there are statistics to "prove" that the average U.S. family is becoming richer *and* that it is becoming poorer; that the crime rate is up *and* the crime rate is down; that illegal immigration is increasing *and* that it is decreasing; and that the traditional family is both disappearing *and* returning.

A quite natural inclination is to reject all statistical results. After all, why trust any number if equally convincing numbers prove precisely the opposite conclusion? This cynical view was summed up by Benjamin Disraeli, who according to Mark Twain listed, in descending order of credibility, "lies, damn lies, and statistics." Indeed, examples abound in which politicians, journalists, and policy makers fit statistics to their preconceived ideas. This book provides hints to alert readers to ways in which statistics can be misused.

But statistics are more than just sophisticated lies. In most cases the source of contradictory numbers is sincere disagreement between experts. If we can find out why the experts reach different conclusions, we will understand much more about the problem being analyzed. Consider, for example, data on cancer.

The National Cancer Institute maintains the United States is winning the war on cancer because of increases in cancer survival rates and a decline in the cancer death rate for all but the elderly. In contrast, well-respected health statisticians argue that the war on cancer has failed because the overall cancer death rate has not fallen. As described in chapter 4, the statistics each side marshals in its favor are neither right nor wrong; instead, they are based on differing assumptions about which cancers should be counted and what should be expected from a population that is getting older on average and is thus more likely to suffer from such diseases. At stake in this statistical debate are billions of dollars in research funds as well as potentially costly regulations aimed at controlling the incidence of environmentally caused cancers.

Other statistical controversies presented in this book teach a similar lesson. For example, experts disagree about whether the death penalty deters murder, whether rent control causes housing shortages, and whether taxes are becoming more unfair. No book of reasonable length could presuppose to answer these or any of the many other policy questions raised in the following chapters. Instead, the intent here is to show *why* well-respected researchers are able to reach such contradictory results. In some cases such understanding will help us decide which side is correct; often it is less important to decide which side is correct than to uncover the complex measurement problems that underlie the issue.

Another purpose of this book is to help researchers, both students and more experienced practitioners, in using social statistics. Consider the following hapless case:

A social science researcher wanted to study the effect of military spending on jobs. Do communities with large military contractors benefit from increased employment, as advocates of military spending argue, or does military spending create relatively fewer jobs than other kinds of government spending, as critics of military spending have charged? To answer this question, the researcher obtained records of military contracts from the U.S. Defense Department arranged by the city where the contractor was located. To measure the number of jobs, the researcher obtained publications of the U.S. Labor Department's Bureau of Labor Statistics, listing employment by location. Armed with a microcomputer statistical package and all the latest knowledge about statistical probability, the researcher was ready to punch in the numbers and find the answer to his question.

But suddenly the project stalled: just about everything was wrong. The Defense Department data were unusable because they listed contracts by the year in which they were awarded, which was not necessarily the year in which they were spent. To make matters worse, the location where the contract was awarded was not necessarily the location where people were hired. In fact, many contracts were subcontracted to other companies of unknown locale. There were problems with the employment data as well. When one employer dominated the industry, the data were not available on the grounds that the information would betray that company's trade secrets. Finally, data from the Defense and Labor departments were incompatible because of different definitions of location. The "city" or "metropolitan area" in each survey was not necessarily the same.

I was the ill-informed researcher in this case. But I was not the first researcher whose good idea floundered because of unusable data. It is a recurring complaint in the social sciences that researchers, from the student in training to the advanced scholar, do not know enough about the data they use. By examining the pitfalls encountered by previous researchers, this book will help today's users of social statistics be more aware of which data sources are available and of the limitations of these data. Had I been aware of the problem of Census Bureau confidentiality frequently encountered by research on business corporations (see chapter 10) before undertaking my failed research on military spending, I would not have expected to find employment data for large firms that dominate a single city's industry. Similar examples will serve as cautionary tales for other researchers.

In summary, this book is written for two groups of readers. First, it will help everyone who is confused by statistics that seem to prove everything and anything. By sorting out the reasons behind seemingly contradictory statistics, we can better understand the issues under debate. Second, this book will assist researchers in assessing the problems of the underlying data. Without such knowledge, many social science projects will fail, as in the case of my military spending research, or worse, projects will proceed without sufficient caution as to the data's limitations.

How to Use This Book

Each of the chapters in this book is devoted to a single subject: demography; housing; health; education; crime; national economy; wealth, income, and poverty; labor statistics; business statistics; government; and public opinion polling. Although students of a particular field will find the chapter in that area most useful, the book is intended to be read as a whole. Social scientists work within their own narrow specialty at considerable cost. Most projects use data from outside a narrow discipline, and the data may have limitations that are unknown to the researcher. For example, almost every area in social science measures variables on a per-person basis, a calculation that presupposes accurate population data, which is not necessarily a warranted assumption (as is discussed in chapter 2 on demography). Similarly, geographic units such as Metropolitan Statistical Areas (chapter 3) and corrections of price data for inflation (chapter 11) are common throughout social science research. Thus it is useful for researchers to consult chapters beyond their narrow specialization.

Each chapter opens with a brief overview of the data sources for that area of social science. These sections will acquaint readers with the names of the most important government and private-sector data sources, which statistics they publish, and in many cases an illustrative "data sample." The names and major publications of these data sources are listed in a table at the opening of each chapter.

Following the "Data Sources" section are "Controversies," a series of debates about the use of statistics in each area. No attempt is made to cover every debate in each field. Instead, controversies have been selected primarily because they form the basis of recent public policy disputes. These include controversies "in the news," such as the U.S. Census population undercount, the disappearing middle class, and the number of homeless individuals in the United States. A second criterion for including a controversy was its use as an instructive illustration of a statistical issue. For example, while the rating of individual cities as the best places to live or the lists of the nation's largest corporations are not particularly critical policy questions, debates about these numbers teach important lessons about the use and misuse of ranking in social statistics.

All the controversies obviously predate the publication of this Second Edition in 1995. But readers should resist the temptation to reject the examples from past years as out of date. Almost all the debates are ongoing, perhaps with different individuals or institutions, but still involving the same issues. As long as the underlying social and economic system remains the same, controversies based on fundamental measurement problems will stay with us.

Finally, each chapter concludes with "Case Study Questions," which instructors may assign to students as a means for further learning. These questions are designed to stimulate thought about the issues raised in each chapter. In most cases there is no single "correct" answer; instead, the questions pose problems frequently encountered by researchers. In many instances citations are given for those who want to explore the question in greater depth.

Finally, readers should not overlook the Notes section. There may be found for each subject area recommended guides to data sources, including both official government handbooks and privately published works. For each controversy, references include popular presentations in magazines and newspapers, which are often the most accessible sources and are worth consulting to see how the topic was generally understood—or misunderstood. In addition, there are references to summary reviews of each public policy debate that often appear in academic journals, as well as citations for the key technical articles for each controversy.

Chapter 2

Demography

Demography, the scientific study of population, provides some of the most fundamental social statistics. This chapter looks at demographic controversies about the size of the population, the birthrate, the classification of individuals by race and ethnicity, household characteristics, and the trend in marriage and divorce. These controversies have public policy implications for congressional representation, social security financing, affirmative action, and family law. In addition, because demographic data are used in so many areas of social science, the potential problems described here have implications for research outside the field of demography itself.

In the United States, the major source of demographic data is the U.S. Census, an attempt made every ten years to count each individual, citizen or noncitizen, with or without legal documentation, who resides in the country. Less well known but similarly comprehensive are U.S. Vital Statistics that tabulate most births, deaths, marriages, and divorces. Researchers accustomed to surveys and the problem of sampling error might wonder how there can be controversies about statistics based on complete data. This chapter identifies four major problems: (1) despite valiant efforts to be inclusive, not everyone is counted; (2) the categories used to classify race, ethnicity, and type of household are arbitrary and are therefore subject to debate; (3) the most commonly used categories to describe households leave out significant parts of the population; and (4) demographic data on births, marriage, and divorce sometimes lead to misleading predictions.

Where the Numbers Come From

Organizations	Data sources	Key publications
Bureau of the Census, U.S. Department of Commerce	U.S. Census	*U.S. Census of Population; Statistical Abstract of the United States*
National Center for Health Statistics, U.S. Department of Health and Human Services	U.S. Vital Statistics	*Vital Statistics of the United States; Monthly Vital Statistics Report*
Statistics Branch, Immigration and Naturalization Service, U.S. Department of Justice	Records of border crossing and naturalization	*Statistical Yearbook of the Immigration and Naturalization Service*

Data Sources

U.S. Census

Collected every ten years since 1790, the U.S. Census is the longest-running consecutive data set in the world. It is also the world's largest data set, compiling information about the sex, age, marital status, and race of nearly every individual residing in the United States. In addition, about one in six households receives a "long form" asking forty-five additional questions on such diverse matters as number of motor vehicles owned and level of education. A number of surveys sponsored by the U.S. government use the census as a statistical base, most notably the Current Population Survey (see chapter 9).

> *Data Sample:* In the 1990 U.S. Census for Hazard, Kentucky, of 5,416 inhabitants, 912 listed English as their ancestry group, 11 listed Hungarian, and 44 listed Swedish.

Vital Statistics

Most countries have a system for recording births, deaths, marriages, and divorces, called vital statistics. These data were among the first ever collected and thus are used by historians to estimate population for time periods before governments began national censuses. For the United States, Vital Statistics are more recent and in some cases are still incomplete. Data are collected by individual counties and states and are assembled on a national basis by the U.S. National Center for Health Statistics. Hospital records and doctors' reports provide a nearly complete count of births and deaths. (Death rates are discussed in chapter 4 on health.) Local information provides a nearly complete count of marriages and divorces for the entire nation. Because of inadequate records in some states, however, as of 1989 detailed statistics in the official Marriage Registration Area omitted eight states, while the Divorce Registration Area omitted nineteen states, including California, where one-eighth of all divorces occur.

> *Data Sample:* In 1987, U.S. Vital Statistics recorded 3,809,394 live births, for which 1,375 mothers reported their age to be between 45 and 49 years.

Controversies

The Population Undercount

Since 1960, the U.S. Census has relied on self-enumeration, that is, voluntary completion of forms mailed to individual households. Finding those who fail to return the forms is the Census Bureau's major expense, involving nearly half a million employees recruited for the 1990 census. The homeless, migrants, and transients were counted in a "shelter and street night" visit to inexpensive hotels, shelters, parks, train stations, and abandoned buildings.

For all its efforts, the Census Bureau admits that it misses some individuals. In 1990, the shortfall was between 3 and 5 million, or between 1 and 2 percent of the population. Although this error seems small, it was unevenly divided across the country. The undercount was estimated to be four times as high for blacks as for whites and nine times as high for inner-city residents as for the general population. Research on the undercount suggests that most minority households were successfully contacted but that distrust of government officials caused some household's individuals not to be counted. In one study, more than 12 percent of young black men were omitted from the census.

Box 2.1. **Undercount in History**

Concern about census undercount dates back to 1790 when 3,929,326 individuals were counted, but, as Thomas Jefferson wrote to George Washington, the omissions were "very great," and "we are certainly above four million." Following the 1870 census, New York City and Philadelphia successfully demanded recounts, increasing their census population by just over 2 percent. Indianapolis, home of powerful Senator Oliver Morton, obtained a recount based on land annexed *after* the census date so that the city could reach the prestigious 50,000 level. Subsequent research suggests that the biggest error in the 1870 census went uncorrected, an undercount by 10 percent of recently freed southern blacks.

The undercount has important implications for congressional representation and dispersal of government funds. According to New York City officials, the 1980 undercount cost the city one lost congressional representative and a $50 million reduction in federal funds for each year. When New York and other large cities filed a lawsuit to force adjustment of the 1990 census, the Census Bureau agreed to an experimental recount in some areas, but only after bitter dispute.

During the mid-1980s, census officials devised a plan to survey an additional 300,000 housing units and then compare the data with the original census. The proportion of individuals in this sample that was missed in the original census could be used to provide a minimum estimate of the entire census undercount. In late 1987, however, U.S. Department of Commerce officials who oversee the Census Bureau canceled the plan on the grounds that any manipulation of the numbers would undermine public confidence in the census. Many experts objected strenuously to the decision not to correct the census. Barbara Bailar, the head of Census Bureau statistical research, resigned in protest, charging that "the decision was politically motivated because Republicans would lose from an adjustment." Stephen Feinberg, chair of a National Academy of Sciences panel appointed to study the issue, agreed that the "[Department of] Commerce canned the project" because it "will mean more funds and more votes in areas heavily black and urban." Five years after the 1990 census, the dispute remained unresolved and is likely to go to the U.S. Supreme Court.

Implications

No population count will ever be completely accurate. When the undercount is higher for some part of the population than for others, there can be significant error in electoral misrepresentation. The 1990 census provides the first test case to see whether it is technically possible to make an accurate adjustment for the undercount—and whether that adjustment will be accepted by all the political groups involved.

For researchers, the problem of the undercount presents a major challenge. Official population data may be misleading, especially for research that focuses on minority groups or inner-city residents, who are most likely to be undercounted. For example, in 1987, sociologists Reynolds Farley and Walter R. Allen recomputed census data to take into account the maximum effect the undercount might have on important social and economic variables for black men aged 20 to 34. This change eliminated the apparent shortage of men relative to women and, according to Farley and Allen, disproved the thesis that black women remain single because there are relatively few black men in their age group.

Farley and Allen found that other important social statistics were affected in a less dramatic manner. The pay gap between young white men and young black men, measured at 36 percent with traditional statistics, increased only slightly to 39 percent, assuming uncounted black men had extremely low earnings. Similarly, the difference in unemployment rates between black and white men, measured at 5.6 percent, increased to 7.1 percent, assuming the uncounted have very high unemployment rates. Thus, correcting for the undercount caused only a small increase in the measurement of the already severe economic deprivation for young black men.

The lesson for researchers is that population data should be analyzed for the effect of the potential population undercount. Even if the correction is relatively minor, as was the case with income and unemployment, such adjustment adds credibility to research results. Farley and Allen calculated their own estimates of the potential undercount. The availability of official Census Bureau adjustments will simplify the task for researchers, although debate will likely continue about the accuracy of the revised numbers as well.

Undocumented Immigrants

How many immigrants enter the United States without legal status? No one knows for certain. At stake is political representation in areas with large numbers of undocumented immigrant populations. Even though noncitizens cannot vote, they are counted in the U.S. Census and therefore contribute to the apportionment of congressional representation. In 1988, a lobbying group called the Federation for American Immigration Reform, joined by forty members of Congress and the states of Pennsylvania and Kansas, filed a lawsuit to exclude illegal aliens from the U.S. Census. The executive director of the federation, Roger L. Conner, compared the current system to counting "an army of Russian troops in Oregon." Critics of this position point out that the U.S. Constitution specifically mandates a complete count of all inhabitants, including all nonvoting residents, as the basis for representation.

One problem in the debate about apportionment is that there is wide disagreement about the number of undocumented aliens, who, not surprisingly, are reluctant to report their status to survey takers. Research based on analysis of the U.S. and Mexican censuses suggest that the total undocumented population was over 3 million in 1992, about half from Mexico. This is far less than figures as high as 12 million that appear in popular accounts. The perception of large numbers of undocumented immigrants likely is prompted by U.S. Immigration and Naturalization Service reports of more than a million border arrests every year. These statistics are deceptive because they include multiple arrests of the same individuals who cross repeatedly until successful. Also, most illegal border crossers plan to work only temporarily in the United States; the large return flow to Mexico goes unnoticed. The majority of undocumented residents who remain in the United States had crossed the border legally with visas and then failed to return when the visas expired. The U.S. Census Bureau estimates average illegal immigration between 200,000 and 300,000 per year during the early 1990s.

Costly Immigrants?

Do immigrants pay their way in taxes, or do they overuse social programs? One widely cited study by Rice University economist Donald L. Huddle for the Carrying Capacity Network, a nonprofit group that advocates reductions in immigration, estimated the 1992 cost of immigrants at $42.5 billion more than they pay in taxes. Urban Institute researcher Jeffrey S. Passel challenged Huddle's estimate on the grounds that it overstated immigrant use of public services and understated immigrant contributions by leaving out social security and gasoline taxes. By Passel's accounting, immigrants pay $25 billion more in taxes than they use in services.

Both Huddle and Passel studied the net cost of all immigrants, legal and illegal. Researchers are more uncertain about the impact of undocumented immigrants because their precise numbers are unknown. One study by the Texas Office of Immigration and Refugee Affairs measured a $166 million deficit primarily because illegal immigrants were assumed to pay relatively little in taxes. In a report for the Urban Institute, however, Passel and Michael Fix point out that it would be poor public policy to reduce government benefits to match any group's tax payments. In the case of illegal immigrants, the largest single cost to government is education, an expenditure that creates a better-trained future workforce. Such benefits are omitted by those who argue that immigrants are a net drain on the economy.

A Birth Dearth?

According to Ben J. Wattenberg of the American Enterprise Institute, the United States will face a population shortage during the next century. Today's low birthrate will produce too few young workers to pay for the elderly's pensions and medical care when the relative size of what he calls the "Western Community" shrinks from its current 15 percent of the world population to 5 percent in the year 2085. Wattenberg asks: "Is it possible that the spread of democratic values may be slowed? Or stopped? Or reversed?" Wattenberg's argument received front-cover attention in national magazines and newspapers and was adopted by Republican presidential hopefuls Jack Kemp and Pat Robertson.

Critics charge that Wattenberg's vision is subtly racist because the fast-growing nations he is afraid will dominate the United States are primarily nonwhite. In addition, others argue that it is impossible to predict future populations as accurately as Wattenberg claims. Past experience demonstrates the difficulty in making such projections. For example, after World War II, most demographers failed to predict the

U.S. baby boom. In 1945, the U.S. Census Bureau underestimated by more than 25 percent the population growth for the following twenty-five years. Today's Census Bureau predictions for the next century are already disputed. Population experts Dennis A. Ahlburg and James W. Vaupel argue that the Census Bureau's *highest* projections for the year 2080 are 300 million too low because they discount the possibility of another baby boom, greater longevity, and more immigration.

Demographer Nathan Keyfitz, who studied the error in 1,000 population growth predictions using modern methods, concludes: "We know virtually nothing about the population fifty years from now. We could not risk better than two to one odds on any range narrower than 285 million to 380 million for the year 2030." In other words, the margin of error encompasses both Wattenberg's scenario of too few Americans and those who argue that the United States will suffer from *over*population. Keyfitz advises researchers to be modest. Rather than attempt to predict population size far into the future, Keyfitz would like to see social scientists study problems for the population *already* born. For example, schools need assistance in planning for enrollments, which can be easily anticipated on the basis of the current birthrate, which is seldom used in education planning.

Will You Still Feed Me?

Declining births and increasing longevity (see chapter 4) combine to create an aging U.S. population. With more people retired, and proportionately fewer people working, some policy advisers warn that the United States faces a social security funding crisis. Today more than three workers contribute to the social security fund for every beneficiary; by the year 2030, there will be fewer than two workers for every beneficiary. Former presidential economic adviser Paul Craig Roberts fears that we face the choice of curtailing future benefits or raising taxes to "prohibitive levels." Michael Boskin, chief economic adviser to former President Bush, argues in his book *Too Many Promises: The Uncertain Future of Social Security* that we should begin now to phase out benefits for the well-to-do and place greater reliance on individually financed pension programs.

Other social scientists are much less pessimistic about the ability of tomorrow's workers to support the elderly. No one disputes the unavoidable reality of an increasingly older population, but it is also likely that the pyramid will shrink at the bottom at the same time that it grows at the top. Most demographers also anticipate continued low birthrates so the working population will support a smaller number of young people. The total population dependent on those of working age includes both the elderly *and* children, a fraction that Merton Bernstein, principal consultant to the National Commission on Social Security Reform, estimates to rise to about 72 percent in 2040 from its 1980 level of 63 percent. But this will still be well below the 80 percent dependent proportion that existed in 1960. Based on such evidence, economist Frank Ackerman concludes, "if we could afford to live through the childhood of the baby boom generation, we can afford to live through its retirement."

Those who are more worried about the future of social security respond that *federal* expenditures for children are only about one-sixth the amount currently spent on adults. Thus there will be no easy transfer of funds from one purpose to another, in particular because, as Phillip Longman observes, "we must consider the harsh reality that most parents derive far more satisfaction and reward in spending money on their own children than in paying taxes to support the elderly in general." On the other side, some policy makers favor the use of general federal tax revenues to pay for social security. Such programs now exist in Western Europe to support relatively generous retirement programs for elderly populations already nearly as large on a percentage basis as the United States will experience during the next century.

The debate about the future of social security is complicated because it combines two issues, one demographic and one political. On the one hand, there is a demographic estimate for the future population profile. All researchers agree that the number of elderly will increase dramatically; retirees for the problem years around 2030 are already born. We are uncertain about the future number of young working people and children, but barring a radical change in the birthrate, their numbers will be proportionately less than at present. The second issue is political: how will the smaller-size working population pay for the increased number of retirees during the next century? It is important for researchers not to confuse the two issues. Politicians may prefer to use demographic certainty to defend policies they favor for other reasons. Good social science can ascertain how much demography in fact will constrain future policy, and how much political leeway we have in funding programs such as those for the elderly.

Race and Ethnicity

The fourth question on the 1990 U.S. Census form read:

Fill ONE circle for the race that the person considers himself/herself to be:

__White __Black or Negro __Indian (Amer.)
(Print the name of the enrolled or principle tribe)_____
__Eskimo __Aleut
Asian or Pacific Islander (API)
__Chinese __Japanese __Filipino __Asian Indian __Hawaiian __Samoan
__Korean __Guamanian __Vietnamese __Other API_____
(If Other Asian or Pacific Islander (API) print one group, for example,
Hmong, Fijan, Thai, Tongan, Pakistani, Cambodian, and so on)_____
If Other race, print race_____

Many respondents answered without difficulty; the question is common in student surveys, affirmative action programs, and other questionnaires where policy makers want to assess racial and ethnic populations. But in a debate that is already two centuries old, social scientists remain uncertain how to measure race and ethnicity. As the United States becomes an increasingly multiethnic nation, such classification will be even more difficult. Recent controversy raises three questions: who is black, who is Asian, and who is Hispanic?

Who Is Black?

Enumeration by race dates back to the first U.S. Census in 1790, when black slaves were enumerated separately so that they could be counted as three-fifths of a person in congressional apportionment. For free individuals, tabulation by race presented problems that continue to the present day. The Census Bureau follows the commonplace North American social definition of race by which a person is classified as "black" if one parent is black, or, pushing the definition back one generation, an individual also is black if one grandparent is black, even if three grandparents are white. Responses different from the standard black–white dichotomy, such as mulatto, Creole, African, or Afro-American, are automatically recoded as black. This practice is also used in official U.S. Vital Statistics where instructions read: "When the husband is white and wife is not, the child is assigned the wife's race. When the husband is not white, the child is assigned to the husband's race."

Box 2.2. **Black "Insanity": An Argument for Slavery**

When the 1840 U.S. Census counted the "insane and idiots," they measured an extraordinarily high rate of 1 in 162 for northern free blacks (and 1 in 6.7 in Maine), compared to only 1 in 1,558 in the South. Proslavery advocates cited these census results to argue that "free negroes of the northern states are the most vicious persons on this continent." This curious statistical result was not fully explained until the 1980s when historian Patricia Cohen looked at the original census forms. Apparently many census takers miscoded as black older senile whites, who were considered idiots in common parlance. The mistake was easy to make because the two items were close together on an unwieldy eighty-column form.

Until recently, official U.S. birth statistics followed social convention. Instructions stated that if only one parent is nonwhite, then the child is assigned the race of its nonwhite parent; if both parents are nonwhite, then the child is assigned its father's race. Beginning in 1989, the procedure was simplified to assign the child's race based simply on the mother's race. Even though this new procedure differs from standard social practice in which a child is nonwhite if *either* parent is nonwhite, government statisticians believe it will reduce error and confusion. A study by the U.S. Centers for Disease Control found that the old procedure understated the infant mortality rate for non-whites. Using the new race-of-mother guideline, infant mortality rates were 0.6 percent higher for blacks; 0.9 percent higher for Hispanics, and 3.7 percent higher for Filipinos. The study showed that the "one nonwhite parent" rule caused some infants to be designated nonwhite even though society categorized them as white. Conversely, race at death, often determined by the funeral director based on observation of the body, caused too many individuals to be designated as white. As a result, nonwhite births were overestimated and nonwhite deaths were underestimated, so official statistics understated the already deplorably high infant mortality rate for nonwhites (see chapter 4).

Who Is Asian?

Since 1870, the U.S. Census question about race has included choices of countries of origins for Asian-Americans. Originally only Chinese

---

Box 2.3 **Second Largest "Ethnic" Group: "No Response"**

Students taking the Scholastic Aptitude Test (SAT) are asked to self-iden-
tify their race or ethnicity. But 12 to 14 percent fail to respond, more than
the number of blacks, Asian-Americans, or any other single minority group.
Researcher Howard Wainer at the Educational Testing Service points out
that the no-response group introduces an uncertainty into comparisons of
scores by different ethnic groups that is greater than the measured change
in minority-group test scores over a five-year period. In other words, media
focus on test-score differences, sometimes as little as two or three points
in a single year, may occur entirely because of our uncertainty about racial
identification.

---

or Indian, the choice was expanded by 1930 to include Japanese, Fili-
pino, Hindu, Korean, and "other." When later immigration included
significant numbers from other countries as well, the Census Bureau
intended respondents to use the "other" category. Instead, some Thais
and Cambodians wrote in their background, usually in place of Viet-
namese, causing the computer to misread their forms. In addition,
some respondents used the "other" category to report themselves as
Taiwanese (instead of Chinese, as the census intended) or Greek (instead of white, as the census intended).

To avoid these problems, and to save space in the form, the Census
Bureau proposed that all Asian-Americans write in their background
for the 1990 census. Census officials were eager to abandon the Asian
"race question" because it took so much space in proportion to the
number of respondents affected. Representatives of Asian communities
protested that the procedure would cause a serious undercount because
Asian-Americans with poor English-language skills would be unable
to write in their background. At stake were social programs such as
English education that are sometimes allocated based on census data.
Census officials rejected attempts to reinstate the check-off for Asian
background, compromising only as far as a promise to publish Asian-
American data without the five-year delay that followed the 1980 census.

Who Is Hispanic?

Debate about how to count U.S. residents from Spanish-speaking
countries (except Spain) is now several decades old—but still unre-

solved. The census has changed how it counts Hispanics in nearly every census since 1930, beginning with answers to the race question: "other nonwhite" (1930), "persons of Spanish mother tongue" (1940), "white persons of Spanish surname" (1950 and 1960), "persons of both Spanish surname and Spanish mother tongue" (1970), and finally, differentiation of Hispanics in a separate question (1980 and 1990).

Each of these designations created confusion for respondents. Reinterviews following the 1970 census showed that more than 20 percent of those with Spanish backgrounds changed their answer to the same question, with an approximately equal number shifting themselves from "non-Spanish" to "Spanish" as from "Spanish" to "non-Spanish." And, aside from errors in the original data, researchers do not have a consistently defined population to compare over time.

Dissatisfaction with such uncertain data, coupled with growing political power among Hispanics, resulted in a new question for the 1980 census:

> Is this person of Spanish/Hispanic origin or descent? No (not Spanish/Hispanic); Yes, Mexican, Mexican-Amer., Chicano; Yes, Puerto Rican; Yes, Cuban; Yes, Other Spanish/Hispanic.

Although separation of the race and Hispanic ethnicity questions eliminates one source of ambiguity in the census, other problems remain. Jamaicans and other West Indians are still often confused about how to classify themselves. As non-Hispanics, and nonnative blacks, they often list their background in the "other" category, which, as noted earlier, was intended by the Census Bureau for Asian-Americans only. In addition, West Coast Hispanics, primarily of Mexican background, prefer the term "Latino," which does not appear on the census form.

These uncertainties, coupled with nonresponse to the census by illegal immigrants, leads some researchers to conclude that the Hispanic count in the census is far too low. The Census Bureau admits an undercount as high as 5 million, but some researchers claim there are as many as 16 million uncounted Hispanics, double the official number. At stake are programs to increase Hispanic political representation, as for example in a 1989 court order for the Los Angeles City Council to redraw its districts in order to increase Hispanic representation.

Who Are My Ancestors?

Between 1870 and 1970, the U.S. Census asked about parents' country of birth. Because fewer than 10 percent of respondents reported foreign-born parents in 1970, the question was replaced in 1980 with a space for respondents to write in the "person's ancestry or ethnicity." More than 80 percent of respondents answered the question; 10 percent wrote "American," and a few gave religious backgrounds or other uncodeable responses. Just under one-third listed more than one background. These data provide an enormous resource for researchers. Unlike the census question on race, ancestry responses permit mixed or multiple backgrounds. As a result, the ancestry question counts nearly 5 million American Indians, more than triple the number counted in the race question. Also, because of the census's large size, the likelihood of random sampling error is reduced for small ethnic groups. For example, the sampling error for the approximately 700,000 Ukrainians counted in the 1980 census is less than one-twentieth of the error expected in the Current Population Survey.

Implications

At present, the traditional black–white classification is satisfactory for most research purposes. Modern anthropology demonstrates that the human species is a closely inbred group in which there is little genetic variation between so-called racial groups. This newly accumulated evidence weighs in favor of an argument put forward nearly fifty years ago by anthropologist Ashley Montagu that we abandon race altogether as a meaningful scientific category.

Even if it has no *scientific* basis, self-enumeration by race has legitimate *social* validity. In other words, if people describe themselves as black or white, then for most research it makes sense to classify them in that category. Nonetheless, it is important for researchers to be aware of social changes that may alter our racial and ethnic perceptions. Future censuses are likely to adjust the race and ethnic categories, partly in response to protests from Asian-Americans and Hispanics. Also, new categories are likely to be created to accommodate the increasing number of individuals with mixed race and ethnic backgrounds. Such changes will improve the validity of the census, but they further challenge researchers who want to compare population groups over time.

Box 2.4 **If It's Tuesday, I'm Swedish**

Researchers need to be aware that answers to ethnic ancestry are highly inconsistent; as many as one-half of respondents change their answer from one survey to another. One reason is that the increased number of mixed-ancestry marriages enables individuals to report a variety of ethnic backgrounds. Changing popularity trends for particular ethnic backgrounds cause individuals to report different ethnicity at different times.

Households and Families

The U.S. Census Bureau uses the terms "household" and "family" differently from everyday usage. The household is defined by the housing unit, not by the social or biological relationship of the individuals. Thus, two families sharing a single home are counted as a single household, as are a family and a lodger or a group of individuals sharing a home. Households are subdivided between "family households," groups of two or more persons related by birth, marriage, or adoption, and "nonfamily households," including individuals living alone and unrelated individuals residing together (see Table 2.1).

As recently as 1950, nearly 80 percent of all households were married-couple families. By 1992, only 55 percent of households fell in the traditional family household, largely because of an increase in the number of individuals living alone (see Box 2.5).

Unfortunately, many research projects are limited only to family households, thereby leaving out a significant proportion of the population. Sociologist Christopher Jencks points out that even the Census Bureau is guilty of this bias in its annual report on income (see chapter 8), which understates the well-being of U.S. households by looking only at family incomes, leaving out the growing number of young, affluent individuals who live on their own.

Even less likely to be included in research projects are individuals who not do not live in households as defined by the Census Bureau. For example, the Current Population Survey, the source for many data on housing, education, income, and employment (see chapters 3, 5, 8, and 9), leaves out most of those who live in group-quarter populations

Table 2.1

Types of Households (1992)

	Percentage of total persons in household type
Family households	86
Married-couple family	68
With own children under 18	41
Without own children under 18	27
Male householder, no spouse present	4
Female householder, no spouse present	15
Nonfamily household	14
Living alone	10

Source: Statistical Abstract of the United States (Washington, D.C.: U.S. Government Printing Office, 1993), p. 59.

such as military barracks, prisons, hospitals, and nursing homes (college dormitory residents are counted with the parents' families).

"Oh No, I Forgot to Get Married!"

"Too Late for Prince Charming?" was the provocative title to *Newsweek*'s cover story for June 2, 1986, including statistics suggesting that college-educated women who were still single at the age of 35 had only a 5 percent chance of ever getting married and that a 40-year-old's chances were so low she was "more likely to be killed by a terrorist." This and similar articles were fueled by a single research paper by social scientists Neil Bennett, David Bloom, and Patricia Craig. In addition to frightening well-educated women about their marriage prospects, the research prompted alarm from writers such as Bryce J. Christensen, who predicted that the "flight from marriage" would cause higher health-care costs (because single people are more often ill) and would decrease the future tax base to pay for old-age benefits (because these unmarried women will bear fewer children).

By contrast, a U.S. Census Bureau study only one year later directly contradicted the Bennett–Bloom–Craig conclusions, estimating that

---

Box 2.5. **Head of Household**

Until 1980, the "head of household" was automatically assigned to a man —even if a woman respondent coded herself as the household head. The procedure was abandoned, in part because it perpetuated sexist stereotyping, but also because the increasing number of nontraditional family arrangements made it difficult to identify the head of the household. Now, one individual of either sex can be designated the "householder"; over 1,600,000 married women out of about 52,000,000 married couples identified themselves as householder in 1980.

---

college-educated women over 35 years old actually had a 32 percent chance of marrying. These data generated relatively little interest, and no news magazine cover stories. The lack of attention to the Census Bureau study is especially remarkable because the Bennett–Bloom–Craig findings were only tentative results, read to a newspaper reporter who wanted a Valentine's Day story. When Bennett–Bloom–Craig officially published their research in 1989, the disputed findings about marriage were omitted.

Why did Bennett–Bloom–Craig and the Census Bureau reach such different conclusions? Although both groups used past marriage rates to predict future marriage rates, they differed in the assumptions about how those marriage rates would be distributed across the lifetimes of today's unmarried female population. The Bennett–Bloom–Craig model, used successfully by researchers to fill in missing historical data, assumed that today's women would marry over a similar range of years as their mothers. In other words, the marriage rate would peak at age 25 and decline quickly thereafter. In contrast, the census model assumed that women would spread marriage over a broader range of years so that postponing marriage would not mean foregoing marriage.

Data collected since 1980 weigh against the Bennett–Bloom–Craig position. By 1985, the proportion of ever-married women in the age group 35 to 39 years had *already* increased above the level predicted in 1980 by Bennett–Bloom–Craig for these women during their *entire lifetimes*. But, like the Census Bureau report, such corrections to *Newsweek*'s "Too Late for Prince Charming?" have received relatively little publicity.

Box 2.6. **Individuals Living Alone**

Since 1940, the fastest-growing household type was the single individual, increasing from under 8 percent of all households to over 20 percent of households in 1980. Then, abruptly during the mid-1980s, the trend came to a halt. Demographers identified two sources for the change, each adopted as statistical evidence for divergent political viewpoints. Conservatives acclaimed the decline in single-person households as a return to traditional marriage. Liberals pointed to the number of young adults returning to living with their parents because of adverse economic prospects. Both factors probably play a role in the decline of single-person households.

Divorce

Data on divorce are less accurate than most other family statistics, for several reasons. The usually comprehensive Vital Statistics are incomplete for divorce, leaving out several states, including California, where one-eighth of all divorces occur. To make matters worse, statistics from reporting states lack data on race in more than 25 percent of all divorce reports and on age in over 10 percent of divorce reports. Alternative data from the U.S. Census Bureau are unsatisfactory because respondents do not accurately report their marital history: men report more than 10 percent fewer divorces than women (although the number should be nearly precisely equal). Even the more accurate women's answers measure a divorce rate substantially less than must have occurred based on legal records counted in U.S. Vital Statistics.

Despite these problems in divorce statistics, the trend in the U.S. divorce rate is unmistakable: it more than doubled during the 1960s and 1970s, and declined slightly during the 1980s. The recent trend away from divorce prompted speculation by the popular media about the return to traditional values, and rejection of divorce as a solution to marital problems. Pollster Louis Harris reported in 1987 that "the prophets of doom could not be any more wrong. The American family is surviving." But demographers Teresa Castro Martin and Larry L. Bumpass argue that "it would be foolish" to jump to the conclusion that marital life has become more stable (Figure 2.1).

Figure 2.1. **U.S. Divorce Rate per 1,000 Population.**

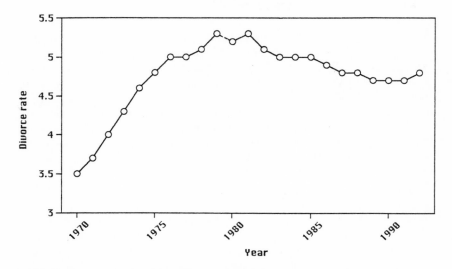

Source: U.S. Bureau of the Census, *Statistical Abstract of the United States, 1994* (Washington, D.C.: U.S. Government Printing Office, 1994), p. 75.

These contrasting assessments occur because no one knows for certain what the future holds. Harris anticipates continued decline in the divorce rate on the basis of survey results showing 89 percent of married respondents satisfied with their relationship. Martin and Bumpass estimate that two-thirds of all current marriages will fail, including marriages ended by separation without divorce, a category not included in official statistics.

Census Bureau researchers Arthur J. Norton and Jeanne E. Moorman take a middle position. They concur that recent marriages appear to have a lower divorce rate—but only slightly. The projected rate of divorce for women 25 to 29 years old in 1985 was 53.6 percent, only 2 percent lower than the projected 55.5 percent total divorce rate for women 35 to 39 years old, and far greater than the 36.4 rate for women 45 to 49 years old. These data suggest to Norton and Moorman that the divorce rate is highest for baby boomers (women 35 to 39 years old in 1985), but the general rate of divorce will remain high for those born afterward.

Few social science studies cause such furor as estimates for the trends in marriage and divorce. Questions about family appear to raise doubts about both our individual futures and our society's well-being. On the individual level, it is important to apply overall statistics with caution. The chance of marriage and divorce depends as much on individual circumstances as on social averages. For example, the divorce rate for couples who marry late in life is far lower than for those who marry young. On the societal level, we should remember that estimates for future marriage and divorce rates depend critically on what assumptions we make. Already the low marriage rates for older women estimated in 1986 appear to be inaccurate. Predictions about the divorce rate vary tremendously; we must wait to see what actually will occur.

Summary

The demographic controversies described in this chapter serve as an introduction to problems researchers find in all social science statistics.

First, we never have complete data. Even when our source attempts universal sampling, as in the U.S. Census and Vital Statistics, some of the population will be missed. There is no secret to this lack of completeness. Census Bureau researchers are at the forefront in identifying the extent of the undercount and developing methods to correct it. Similarly, shortcomings in the Vital Statistics, primarily nonreporting states, are a matter of public record. Responsibility lies with researchers to recognize explicitly the possible implications of less-than-complete data.

Second, all studies are limited by the categories in which the data are classified. This chapter summarizes U.S. experience in racial and ethnic categories. Classification that seemed "natural" in the past is today considered hopelessly naive. Researchers need to remember that today's categories, based on today's social biases, will change with new developments in race and ethnic relations. Official use of the terms "household" and "family" also demonstrate the importance of careful attention to classification. In this case, not only are official definitions different from everyday usage, but the changing characteristics of U.S. living situations mean that research on traditional "family households" will leave out increasing numbers of individuals.

Third, studies of marriage, divorce, and social security demonstrate the hazard of predicting the future. Even when our knowledge about past trends is relatively accurate, estimates for the future must involve debatable assumptions. We do not know if past trends will continue or new trends will arise, as indeed occurred in recent marriage and divorce rates. Although such uncertainties plague all predictive social science research, popular media coverage rarely warns readers about the problem. Moreover, in the case of marriage predictions for older women, the media were selective in emphasizing the projection of large numbers of presumably unhappy unmarried older women, but not the rejoinder from the Census Bureau that found far more flexibility in the choices for older women. Predicting the future of social security was more complicated because it involved not only assumptions about the future but also dispute about which statistic is most relevant. Again, the popular media emphasized only frightening prospects—too many retirees—without reporting the possibly countervailing trend of fewer children.

The overall lesson is one of cautious activism. We have much to learn from demography. It would be a mistake to throw up our hands and reject all research using demographic statistics just because no data are perfect. Instead, the controversies imply a constant struggle to understand the world. By learning about limitations in the data and biases on the part of data users, we can better evaluate the policy implications of current research.

Case Study Questions

1. In a survey using Census Bureau race and ethnic categories, 20 percent of California college students left the question blank. How might these omissions affect research projects on enrollment, financial aid, or graduation rates?

2. About one-half of all Americans who married during the 1980s lived with someone of the opposite sex before their first marriage, four times the percentage a decade earlier. How does cohabitation affect the marriage rate? The divorce rate?

3. There are conflicting measures of the U.S. divorce rate. In the U.S. Census, men report 10 percent fewer divorces than women. Vital Statistics measure more divorces than reported by women or men to the census. Explain these discrepancies.

4. Space for questions in the 3.5 square feet of the Census Bureau's long form is extremely limited. Lobby groups campaign hard for the addition of new questions. In 1990, the successful contenders included questions about access to different forms of transportation and the presence of stepchildren in the household. Losers included questions about home heating and the number of pets. What arguments would you make in favor of or against each of these questions?

5. The 1924 National Origins Act severely restricted immigration based on the proportion of national backgrounds already in the current population. Estimates of ethnicity were derived from surveys of family names in which Mueller might indicate German background, O'Leary might indicate Irish background, and Miller or Leary might represent English background. German and Irish lobbyists challenged the numbers, and gained an increase in their quotas. Why?

6. The U.S. Census counts 20 percent more black men marrying non-Hispanic white women than the U.S. Vital Statistics. Many factors probably are involved, including racial self-identification, incomplete coverage in the Vital Statistics, previous marriages not counted in the census, and cohabitation reported as marriage. Why did each of these factors lead to a discrepancy between the census and Vital Statistics?

7. In Brazil and most Caribbean islands, race is a graduated category, with approximately twenty subtle classifications depending on skin tone and physical features, not necessarily correlated with the racial designation assigned to one's parents. Nonetheless, researchers document discrimination in the social status and pay levels of white versus dark-skinned workers. How would you design a survey form to measure "race?" in these countries? How would it differ from the U.S. Census classification described in this chapter?

Chapter 3

Housing

Housing is the largest single component of U.S. household budgets, comprising more than 40 percent of expenditures as measured by the Bureau of Labor Statistics (see chapter 9). In national income accounts, residential construction is the largest component of investment, averaging about $200 billion per year. Thus, housing statistics warrant separate and detailed attention.

This chapter first looks at two major U.S. housing statistical debates: Have housing standards improved? And is housing less affordable? These two factors are the source of most controversy about the role of government housing programs and the efficacy of private-sector housing. Next, this chapter reviews debate about the number of homeless, an interesting case study of problems that occur when policy makers focus on a single difficult-to-measure statistic. The final section of this chapter looks at geographic divisions used in social science research, most of which are based on place of residence. Researchers need to know how changes in geographic units affect the definition of urban, metropolitan, and rural areas. Two studies based on geographic divisions are summarized: the trend in racial segregation, and comparison of the desirability of different urban areas.

Data Sources

U.S. Census

Although the U.S. Census is best known as a population count, it is officially a "Census of Population *and Housing*." Impetus for a na-

Where the Numbers Come From

Organizations	Data sources	Key publications
Bureau of the Census, U.S. Department of Commerce	U.S. Census	*U.S. Census of Housing*
U.S. Department of Housing and Urban Development Bureau of the Census, U.S. Department of Commerce	American Housing Survey; Census of Construction	*Current Housing Reports; Current Construction Reports*
Bureau of Labor Statistics, U.S. Department of Labor	Consumer Expenditure Survey	*Monthly Labor Review*
F.W. Dodge/ McGraw-Hill Inc.	Private survey	*Dodge Construction Potentials Bulletin*

tional housing survey came during the Great Depression of the 1930s in order to determine the degree of inadequate housing and assess how new housing construction would stimulate the economy. When these surveys proved successful, the U.S. Census added housing to its 1940 population count. By 1990, the housing section of the census had grown to six out of fourteen questions on the short form (administered to all households) and nineteen out of fifty-nine questions on the long form (completed by a sample of nearly 20 million households). Census housing data provide the most comprehensive statistics. The major drawback to the census is timeliness; the mobile-home data cited below were published in September 1993, more than three years after the census.

> *Data Sample:* The 1990 Census of Housing counted 21,266 owner-occupied mobile homes in Nebraska, for which the median monthly cost for those with a mortgage was $411.

American Housing Survey

The American Housing Survey (AHS), called the Annual Housing Survey until 1984, provides data on a speedier and more frequent basis

---

Box 3.1. **U.S. Census versus American Housing Survey**

One might expect that the U.S. Census and American Housing Survey (AHS) would yield similar results. But in 1980 about 200,000 more units were counted in the census; homeownership was approximately one percentage point less; multiple units were 3 percent more common; and 3 percent more houses had been built in the last decade than were counted in the AHS. Several factors are thought to account for these differences:

• Sampling error—as a survey, the AHS is subject to uncertainty because of the random choice of respondents. This error can be calculated precisely and is published in AHS reports.

• Coverage error—both programs have identified weaknesses: the AHS tended to miss new buildings because recent permits were not added to the sample; the census was not effective in finding conversion units.

---

than the census. Conducted by the Census Bureau for the Department of Housing and Urban Development every year since 1973, the AHS samples households across the country on a staggered basis, providing data on the size and quality of housing, neighborhood characteristics, home financing, and recently moved households.

Data Sample: In 1991, the Housing Survey estimated 523,000 households in Houston, Texas, had dishwashers, while 49,700 had signs of rats in the past three months.

Census Bureau economic surveys provide data on the housing industry. Most closely watched are "housing starts," a key measure of the economy's overall health and one component of the Index of Leading Economic Indicators. The Census Bureau collects residential and nonresidential data from local permit-issuing offices. More detailed data are available commercially from F.W. Dodge, based on correspondent reports gathered directly the construction industry.

Data Sample: In *Characteristics of New Housing* we learn that 63 percent of new 1992 houses had fireplaces, up from 50 percent in 1982.

Price Data

The U.S. Census Bureau economic surveys include extensive local data on vacancies, mortgages, and rents, often used by the housing industry for planning purposes. The U.S. Department of Labor's Bureau of Labor Statistics monitors housing costs in the Shelter Index, a part of the Consumer Price Index (see chapter 11). The Shelter Index provides a single statistic for the cost of rents, new home prices, mortgage rates, and home upkeep for the United States and selected geographic areas. Widely reported statistics on new and existing home prices, including the "affordability index" described below, are assembled by the National Association of Realtors based on a combination of census data and their own surveys.

Controversies

Housing Quality

Is there a crisis in U.S. housing standards? Housing experts disagree. In one view, the quality of U.S. housing has improved dramatically since World War II, testimony to the success of the private-sector housing market. Another view argues that serious problems in housing quality remain, requiring an expanded public role in housing markets. These opposite conclusions occur in part because data in the U.S. Census tell a quite different story from data in the American Housing Survey.

By traditional U.S. Census housing statistics, housing-quality problems have almost disappeared. Severe overcrowding, more than 1.5 persons per room, at one time associated with health problems such as tuberculosis, fell from 9 percent of housing units in 1940 to only 1 percent in 1980. Similarly, a second key statistic, lack of complete plumbing, dropped from 45 percent of housing in 1940 to about 2 percent in 1980. The Census Bureau's overall indication of dilapidation declined from 18 percent of all housing units in 1940 to only 3.7 percent of housing in 1970. (This measure was dropped after 1970 because subjective judgments about what constituted "dilapidation" varied so greatly from one census enumerator to another.) Such remarkable improvements in U.S. housing quality are hailed by some policy advisers as evidence that the United States has solved housing problems better than many people realize.

Other researchers maintain that census data focus on limited, out-dated indicators of housing quality. Since 1973, far greater detail has been available in the American Housing Survey, which covers more than twenty-five deficiencies, including leaky roofs, rat infestations, and neighborhood problems such as crime. For rental units, these three deficiencies worsened during the first eight years of the AHS. (There was a slight improvement for owner-occupied housing.) On this basis, some policy makers argue in favor of activist government housing programs, most importantly to assist low-income renters.

Those opposed to new government housing programs complain that a "moving target" is being applied to the housing problem. In other words, when housing was no longer overcrowded or dilapidated, government program supporters changed the definition of decent housing to the much broader criteria in the AHS. In this view, the housing crisis can never be solved if we keep changing our goals to ever-higher standards, when in fact existing housing policy, relying on the private market, has solved the major housing problems.

Implications

For researchers, expanded data in the AHS are clearly an improvement over U.S. Census housing statistics, if only because the housing-quality problems measured by the census now apply to so few houses. Nevertheless, the wide scope of the AHS requires researchers to make decisions about which quality issues are relevant. Because some quality measures usually improve in any given year, while others decline, the overall trend depends on which factors are selected. Researchers should consider using widely accepted indexes of housing quality that combine different variables in the American Housing Survey. Such indexes are available from the U.S. Department of Housing and Urban Development, the Congressional Budget Office, and the U.S. Office of Management and Budget.

Is There an Affordability Crisis?

Beginning in the late 1970s, the most contentious housing policy debates shifted away from the issue of substandard housing toward the problem of reasonably priced housing regardless of quality.

Proportion Spent on Housing

According to most household budget experts, housing costs should constitute no more than 25 percent of household income. But in recent years a majority of renters broke the 25 percent rule; 34 percent paid 35 percent or more of their income for housing. For homeowners with mortgages, 31 percent broke the 25 percent rule, and 21 percent paid 35 percent or more. (Those with paid-off mortgages, primarily the elderly, have much lower housing costs.) These data are cited frequently as evidence for a housing crisis. In fact, given the reality of housing costs, some consumer experts have shifted to 33 percent as a more realistic expectation for housing costs as a proportion of income.

Other experts question this pessimistic view of housing affordability on the grounds that homeowners have chosen improved housing quality in return for higher costs. Not surprisingly, better housing absorbs a greater proportion of household budgets. But the measurement of quality is tricky. The Census Bureau estimates a "new housing price index," taking into account quality changes. By this statistic, over one-half of price increases during the early 1980s resulted from larger houses with more amenities. But new houses are only a small part of the housing market, in particular for low-income families. The U.S. Labor Department's Bureau of Labor Statistics estimates costs for all homeowners (adjusted for quality changes) in its Shelter Index. On this basis, housing costs increased significantly faster than the overall cost of living. (See chapter 11 on controversy about the Shelter Index in the overall inflation rate.)

Proportion Able to Afford the Median-priced Home

The National Association of Realtors calculates a housing "affordability index" based on the income needed to qualify for the median-priced resale home, assuming mortgages should constitute no more than 25 percent of income. In May 1982, the index reached a low of 65.2 percent, meaning the typical, "median" family had less than two-thirds the income necessary to purchase the typical home. As interest rates declined, this affordability index improved steadily, reaching 129.6 in the final quarter of 1992, so, in theory, the median family could afford the median house. (See Figure 3.1.)

Does a low affordability index mean that the middle class cannot

Figure 3.1. **Housing Affordability.** Median family income/qualifying income for a typical house.

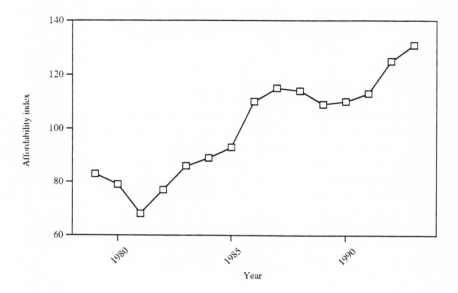

Source: National Association of Realtors, *Home Sales* (Washington, D.C., various issues).

buy a home? Economist Ed Rubenstein points out that the affordability index is misleading because it fails to take into account improvements in housing size and quality. Between 1980 and 1988, when new housing prices rose by 15.9 percent, the average new house contained 13.5 percent more square footage, as well as additional amenities such as air conditioning and multiple bathrooms. He concludes that instead of a housing crisis, "U.S. homebuyers are demanding and getting bigger and better homes than their parents ever dreamed of."

A second problem with the affordability index is that the recent improved homebuying circumstances combine falling home prices in some areas with skyrocketing home prices in precisely those areas where the job market has attracted new residents. Thus, low median 1993 prices in Oklahoma City ($67,200) and Corpus Christi, Texas ($69,600), are no solace to someone with a job in a fast-growing area with high median housing prices, such as New Haven, Connecticut

($142,600), or Orange County, California ($209,490). In addition, housing availability is not evenly distributed across price ranges. Sociologist James D. Wright measures a "housing squeeze" in which the number of low-income households increased faster than the number of low-priced housing units, in his view a critical factor in the recent rise in homelessness (see below).

Implications

The debate about housing costs illustrates the pitfalls of looking at only a single statistic. By itself, national housing data may misrepresent changing housing quality as well as differences in the housing market faced by households in varying regions and income groups. Similarly, a single time period can mislead, as for example the late 1970s when home prices increased, or the early 1990s, when prices moderated. To appreciate the housing market fully, researchers need to look at a variety of statistics.

Government in the Housing Market?

Should governments become involved in housing, either with rent controls or public housing projects? Or should housing be left to unregulated private industry? Those researchers who measure problems in housing quality and affordability tend to argue in favor of government programs, while those who measure improved housing quality and less of an affordability problem argue for the private market. A second difference between these two groups is their assessment of past government programs, in particular rent control and public housing.

Rent Control

No housing policy is more heatedly debated than rent control, especially in view of its relatively minor importance in U.S. housing markets. The most frequently cited example of rent control is an actual freeze on rents imposed in New York City after World War II, even though such restrictions have been enforced practically nowhere else. And, after 1970 in New York City, as well as in the few other cities with rent control, landlords were allowed to increase most rents in line with rising operating and maintenance costs. Despite rent control's limited coverage, housing experts have engaged in an extended debate about its impact.

The argument against rent control is straightforward: low rents cause landlords to abandon housing as a profitable investment, in terms of both maintaining existing structures and building new ones. Not surprisingly, much evidence for this view comes from New York City, where indeed low-cost private-sector housing declined dramatically after World War II. Data also have been collected elsewhere, for example in New Jersey cities, where apartment construction fell by over 50 percent after rent control was introduced.

Defenders of rent control argue that the decline of low-cost housing is a complicated process that cannot be blamed on a single policy. As evidence they point to New Jersey cities *without* rent control where there was an even faster drop in construction than in the rent-control cities. Federal housing surveys document housing abandonment not only in rent-controlled New York City but also in Cleveland, St. Louis, Oakland, and other major cities where there was no rent control.

An additional argument against rent control is that it does not benefit those in need. For example, Hudson Institute researcher B. Bruce-Briggs cites Census Bureau data showing a sizable proportion of New York City rent-control households paying less than 20 percent of their income in rent. (Briggs also points out that Census Bureau data leave out 30 percent of tenants for whom there are no income or rent data, so perhaps even more allegedly undeserving tenants benefit from rent control.) Once again, however, New York City's now-defunct rent freeze is the target; according to rent-control advocates, nationwide there are large numbers of low- and moderate-income households who would benefit from rent control.

Public Housing or Trickle Down?

Direct government provision of public housing is a second major policy controversy that is out of proportion to its actual importance. Again, the argument is about the effect of government programs on the private housing market. Opponents of public housing point to studies measuring little improvement in the housing market in cities with public housing. To the critics this is evidence that public housing simply substitutes for private housing that would have been built in any event.

As an alternative to public housing, these housing experts argue for letting the private market provide all new housing—even if housing is built for the well-to-do. In this view, new high-income housing causes *all* families to move up the housing ladder, eventually benefiting the poor by lifting them out of the worst housing.

Those in favor of government assistance argue that existing public housing, which constitutes only 11 percent of the total U.S. rental housing market, far less than in many Western European countries, is insufficient to affect the overall housing market, particularly in cities with massive economic problems. Moreover, the alleged advantages of the private sector have been difficult to prove because there are no large-scale data on the same housing stock over a long period of time. Indirect evidence from data comparing differences in housing between cities shows modest evidence of the trickle-down benefits of high-cost housing. But supporters of public housing point to rising housing costs for low-income groups as better evidence that increased high-income housing displaces the poor instead of improving the quality and quantity of housing available to them.

Implications

The debate about how to create low-income housing demonstrates an imbalance in the availability of data. Data are relatively abundant on government programs such as rent control and public housing, the effectiveness of which is the source of ongoing debate. In contrast, the impact of high-income housing on the overall housing market is not as well analyzed. Housing experts believe this is a fertile area for research; even though fewer data are available, we have much to learn about the housing process with existing data in the U.S. Census and American Housing Survey.

The Homeless

During the 1980s, the issue of homelessness suddenly emerged as a matter of national concern. Although everyone agreed there had always been homeless people in the United States, the general impression was that the problem had recently become worse. Media reports, however, suggested that social scientists were hopelessly in disagreement about the number of homeless, with estimates ranging from

250,000 to 3 million. This more-than-tenfold range proved unhelpful in determining the appropriate policy response, but it is illustrative of how media coverage rarely asks *why* statistics appear so inaccurate. In this case, the specific count of homeless was less informative than careful research about the origins of less-than-adequate housing.

250,000?

The low estimate of 250,000 homeless derives from a 1984 report by the U.S. Department of Housing and Urban Development (HUD), *Report to the Secretary on the Homeless and Emergency Shelters.* Although the number was reported as an official government statistic, officials responsible for the estimate recognized likely errors in their count, an aspect seldom mentioned in the media. The HUD estimate actually was a range from 192,000 to 586,000, of which 250,000 was determined to be the "most reliable" lower limit. But debate focused instead on the assertion that the HUD report was slanted in an effort by the Reagan administration to downplay the housing issue, an interpretation so widely accepted that in 1985 the Federal Emergency Management Agency refused to use the disputed HUD findings in its disbursement of federal funds for the homeless.

3 Million?

The high estimate of 3 million homeless has been traced to an off-the-cuff remark by homeless activist Mitch Snyder, who told a congressional committee: "How many nationally [are homeless]? Millions. Of that we are certain. Precisely how many? Who knows?" In subsequent written testimony for the committee, Snyder's group, Communities for Creative Non-Violence, conducted a telephone survey, suggesting 2.2 million homeless, a figure that was later rounded up to 3 million and widely quoted in newspaper and magazine reports.

What Do We Mean by Homeless?

In actual fact the HUD report and Communities for Creative Non-Violence agreed far more than was commonly recognized. With the exception of Chicago, a single anomaly in the Communities' data later revised downward by a factor of ten, the city-by-city count was nearly identical. Thus, the overall count in both studies was about 250,000. Martha Burt, author of *Over the Edge: The Growth of Homelessness in the 1980s*, estimates the homeless at 500,000; using the same 1987 survey, Christopher Jencks argues in his book *The Homeless* that the correct number is between 300,000 and 400,000.

According to many housing experts, the effort to pin down a specific number for the homeless deflected attention from underlying housing problems. In this view, the homeless are only the most visible of the inadequately housed. Traditional homeless statistics overlook the fact that most people who leave their homes do not move permanently to the street or shelters, so estimates of homelessness on a single night greatly understate the overall problem. A Rand Corporation study estimated the number who were homeless during any part of one year was as much as four times higher than the traditional statistic of homelessness on a single night. Using different data, Jencks reaches a similar figure, 1.2 million adults homeless at some point during each year of the 1980s. The trend over time is more complicated. The only data available are for Chicago, where demographer Donald Bogue surveyed skid row during the winter of 1958 and counted about 1,400 homeless with an additional 8,000 living in five-foot by seven-foot windowless hotel cubicles. Peter Rossi surveyed the city again in 1985, finding nearly 3,000 homeless, but only 400 living in cubicles. Jencks concludes that today's homeless are more visible because people are more likely to sleep in public places, whereas thirty years ago inexpensive hotels served poor men who otherwise would have been homeless.

Eventually many of the homeless find shelter with relatives or friends, causing "doubling up," which was found among 10 percent of low-income families in a 1983 New York City survey. If the research goal is to measure the shortfall of adequate housing, then these displaced people should be included. A 1987 study by the Neighborhood Reinvestment Corporation, a nonprofit group funded by Congress, projects a shortfall of more than 18 million low-rent housing units by the year 2003. Although these individuals may not be homeless, displacement is a reasonable measure of housing needs and the basis for policy debate about increasing the number of low-cost homes.

This case study demonstrates the shortcomings of media attention on the single "correct" number of homeless. A "ballpark" estimate, approximating the number of individuals who live in temporary shelters or on the street, certainly is useful. And for such purposes, the range 250,000 to 500,000 encompasses most reasonable estimates. Far more helpful for public policy is careful attention to the overall state of the housing market, of which homelessness is only one severe consequence.

Geographic Units

Housing location is used to designate geographic area, a common research variable. Although seemingly easy to define, geographic designation often presents research headaches and, in some cases, requires intervention by the president's Office of Management and Budget.

The smallest geographic classifications are census blocks. For the 1990 census, the United States was divided into about 7.5 million of these units, corresponding in urban areas to city blocks. They were subdivisions of 49,000 census tracts, the statistical unit for many research projects, such as the studies of segregation described below.

What is a city? What is a rural area? These are obviously subjective questions, complicated by the growth of neither-urban-nor-rural suburbia. Not surprisingly, the division between city and country involves arbitrary classification and categories that change over time. Beginning in 1910, the census defined any incorporated place with more than 2,500 residents as urban. The standard shifted slowly so that by 1980, urban areas required a population of 50,000 and "built-up" characteristics. This changing definition caused the measured urban population to rise slightly during the 1970s to 73.7 percent, although under the old definition the urban population actually declined slightly.

Since 1949, the Bureau of the Budget (now the Office of Management and Budget, or OMB) has attempted to create useful boundaries for urban areas called Metropolitan Statistical Areas (MSAs). Approximately 300 MSAs are now used in most U.S. government data, including the U.S. Census and American Housing Survey. Nonetheless, problems remain for researchers when MSAs are eliminated and others are newly created. For example, in 1980, Rapid City, South Dakota, lost its metropolitan status because of population loss, while thirty-five new areas were established in 1981 based on the previous year's census.

The boundaries of MSAs also can present research problems. Some MSAs include entire counties (or cities in New England) that have close social and economic relationships with the central urban area. Because some western counties are so large, the resulting MSA is geographically huge, stretching over fifty miles into the Cascade Mountains in the case of Seattle, Washington, while Los Angeles County extends twenty-five miles into the Mojave desert. In both cases the outer reaches of the MSA are entirely unpopulated. Nationwide in 1980, more than 15 percent of MSA housing units were in rural areas. Widespread urban areas encompassing different political boundaries create special problems for defining MSAs. For example, Nassau and Suffolk counties of New York's Long Island are designated a separate MSA, even though both counties are closely tied to the New York MSA, which includes New York City and counties to the north.

When federal financing is at stake, political leaders suddenly pay attention to OMB's decisions about MSAs. During the 1980s, the population of Buffalo, New York, fell below 1 million, the threshold for certain Medicaid funding. Pressure by congressional representatives caused 220,000 residents of neighboring Niagara Falls to be added so that the new MSA met the Medicaid guidelines.

What can researchers do about these problems? First, consult the data source. Government publications typically comment in detail about geographic issues, including any changes in the definition of urban areas and MSAs. If a researcher needs continuity of geographic units, a second set of statistics may be available based on older boundaries. Or, alternative statistics may be appropriate, such as the new Standard *Consolidated* Statistical Areas combining data for adjacent MSAs. Finally, U.S. Census Bureau data are available on computer tape with which researchers can create their own geographic units.

Segregation

In 1968 the National Advisory Commission on Civil Disorders warned: "Our Nation is moving toward two societies, one black, one white— separate and unequal." Has this prediction come true? Data on segregation were considered so sensitive by the Nixon administration that studies by the Census Bureau were blocked during the 1970s out of fear that evidence of continued segregation would be politically explosive. Many more studies were conducted during the 1980s, sometimes with contradictory findings because of the difficulties in measuring segregation.

The first problem confronting researchers is the relevant geographic scale. On the level of MSAs, the United States became more integrated during past decades in the sense that many cities had more diverse populations. But segregation is still present because, within those cities, racial groups live in separate neighborhoods. Consequently, most research on segregation looks at census tracts, for which total counts by racial group are available in each census. (See chapter 2 on problems in defining racial groups.) But even on this small-scale level there are different types of segregation indexes, about which there is a vast literature and, at times, seemingly contradictory trends. For example, between 1970 and 1980, black–white segregation appeared to decline based on one index that measured whether blacks were evenly distributed among communities, while another index measured greater segregation based on the proportion of blacks in individual communities. These opposite conclusions occurred because of black migration from inner cities to traditionally black suburbs, thus causing a more even distribution of the black population but an increased proportion of blacks in segregated suburban communities.

Recognizing such problems with segregation measures, sociologists Douglas Massey and Nancy Denton surveyed nineteen different ways to measure segregation in their important 1987 study of residential segregation for blacks, Hispanics, and Asians during the 1970s. Some sociologists had anticipated a decline in segregation because of fair housing legislation, more tolerant attitudes by whites, and a growing black middle class. Instead, Massey and Denton found that "most blacks continue to reside in predominantly black neighborhoods . . . race continues to be a fundamental cleavage in American society." Moreover, segregation is as high for blacks with incomes over $50,000 and graduate degrees as it is for blacks with low incomes and a fourth-grade education.

On a positive note, Massey and Denton point out that there was a slight lessening of segregation in small and mid-size cities that included relatively few blacks at the time. Thus the long-term trend is not yet determined, and further study of racial segregation is in order. In addition, investigators of the issue would like to know more about trends in segregation for groups other than blacks and whites. But because of changing categories used by the census, compatible historical data are not yet available (see chapter 2).

Is Seattle the Best Place to Live?

What is the overall desirability of a city or, more technically, an MSA? Obviously, such a statistic must combine a great variety of data. Two contrasting methods for making MSA comparisons illustrate the relative advantages of different summary statistics, one quite simple, the other complex.

Ratings

In 1989, newspapers lauded Seattle, Washington, as the best place to live based on *Places Rated Almanac*, a compendium of living costs, climate, crime, and other attributes of 333 U.S. cities (Pine Bluff, Arkansas, was the worst). Despite widespread reporting on this study, its results should be interpreted with caution because a simple, but potentially misleading, method was used to capture the effect of many variables.

The problem is one of "weighting," that is, how much importance each variable should be given. Should the crime rate count as much as the number of jobs? The *Almanac* simply added up each city's ranking in attributes ranging from climate to recreation. Researchers at AT&T's Bell Laboratories reanalyzed the *Placed Rated* data to show that with an alternative weighting scheme, *134 cities* could claim the number-one spot, or by reversing the process, 150 different cities could be ranked last (see Table 3.1). For example, with a large weight on crime, safe Beaver County, Pennsylvania, reaches number one, but a large weight on its economic outlook pushes Beaver County to the bottom of the list.

Table 3.1 shows how an unscrupulous user can manipulate ratings outcomes, as was true in the case of a Chicago publicist who asked the Bell researchers for a way to make Chicago come out first. Indeed weighting on transportation and recreation lifts Chicago to the number-one spot. In fairness to the authors of the *Almanac* we should note that they caution against use of the overall ratings altogether. Even though press reports focused on precisely this aspect of their study, a short list of "winners" appears late in the book, on page 392, and the losers are not highlighted at all.

Hedonic Index

A more sophisticated estimate for the quality of life measures how willing individuals are to accept higher housing costs and lower wages in exchange for amenities such as good weather and good schools.

Table 3.1

The First Shall Be Last

Depending on the weighting of attributes in the *Places Rated Almanac*, the same city can be rated first (#1) or last (#329).

City	Attributes weighted highly to cause #1 ranking	Attributes weighted highly to cause #329 ranking
Atlantic City, NJ	Economy, recreation	Housing, crime
Beaver County, PA	Crime	Economy
Detroit, MI	Health care	Crime, economy
Duluth, MN	Housing, crime	Climate, economy
Fort Myers, FL	Recreation, economy	Climate, housing, art
Honolulu, HI	Crime, climate, recreation	Housing, education
Minneapolis, MN	Art, health care	Climate
New York, NY	Health care, art	Crime, housing
Salem, OR	Climate, education	Economy, housing
Salt Lake City, UT	Recreation	Education, housing
Washington, DC	Education, transporation	Housing, crime

Using this method, called *hedonic pricing,* economists Glenn C. Blomquist, Mark C. Berger, and John P. Hoehn estimated that residents of Pueblo, Colorado, "traded" $3,289 in higher costs to live in this highest-ranked city, while residents of St. Louis, Missouri, enjoyed $1,857 compensation for their lowest-ranked city. Although this technique avoids the subjective judgments of the *Almanac*, it assumes there is a fluid marketplace for housing. If some desirable cities are inaccessible because of job and family ties, then the hedonic method will not accurately measure a city's "value."

For many social science topics there are relatively simple statistics such as the *Places Rated Almanac*, as well as complex statistics such as the hedonic index. Comparison of the two methods for rating cities illustrates drawbacks for each approach. Simple indexes are arbitrary in the sense that another researcher might attach different importance to each variable, for example, counting rain as a greater disadvantage for Seattle. And the hedonic index and many similar measurements assume a well-functioning economic market in which individuals freely make informed judgments. Because of the complexity of statistics such as the hedonic index, users may not be aware of the underlying assumptions it requires. Researchers can learn from both approaches, borrowing the easy-to-use characteristics of *Places Rated,* with the more subtle insights of the hedonic index.

Summary

The issues reviewed in this chapter underscore the ambiguity of social statistics. Attempts to measure housing cost and quality suggested contradictory trends: housing quality improved and deteriorated; housing affordability rose and fell; the homeless are fewer than 200,000 or over 3 million—or cannot be meaningfully counted. Such discrepancies were the source of media debates. Less often reported was what researchers actually know about housing. For example, on an overall basis, there is evidence of improvement in U.S. housing quality and affordability based on Census Bureau surveys and data on housing costs as a proportion of income. Nevertheless, analysis of specific housing problems such as rat infestation, or specific markets, such as low-income rentals, or local data on affordability reveals considerable problems in housing markets. The lesson for researchers is to specify carefully the research goal before choosing between the nationwide or more specific data.

The debate about the number of homeless illustrates a situation where considerable effort was spent attempting to measure a social problem that could not be summarized in a single number. Statistics on displacement and the effect of high-cost housing on the overall housing market are more likely to give insight into underlying housing problems, as well as the need for government programs such as rent control and public housing. Unfortunately, such statistics are lacking, although some experts believe they can be constructed from existing data.

The choice of geographic units is a common step in research projects. Although the federal government attempts carefully to standardize its data along common geographic boundaries, the definition of urban versus rural areas and the designation of Standard Metropolitan Areas can pose problems for some research projects. For example, analysis of racial segregation requires attention to population shifts within neighborhoods as well as within larger-scale units such as MSAs. Finally, on a less serious level, the "places rated" debate reinforces the lesson that the underlying method for combining disparate data into a single, usable statistic can predetermine the outcome.

Case Study Questions

1. Between 1974 and 1981, the Annual Housing Survey measured the numbers of dwellings with deficiencies, as shown in the following table.

During this time period, the number of occupied structures increased by about 17 percent. How might these data on deficiencies be used to measure improved, stable, and declining housing quality?

Condition present in neighborhood	1974	1981
Crime	12,115,000	18,371,000
Streets in need of repair	13,741,000	14,399,000
Odors	7,240,000	6,640,000

2. Just as there is an underground economy (see chapter 7), there are unreported and often illegal housing units. In particular, illegal conversions are estimated to account for the largest proportion of new housing units for some locales, but they are often missed in the census and the AHS. How might these missing housing units affect measurement of housing quality?

3. The number of new-home sales changes dramatically from month to month. For example, in 1992, January sales rose by 11.9 percent, February sales fell by 7 percent, and March sales fell by 14.8 percent. These data are adjusted for seasonal variation—that is, they take into account typical month-by-month changes during past years. What other factors might cause such erratic month-to-month variation?

4. Average down payments for houses rose from 24.1 percent in 1981 to 27.2 percent in 1987. Columnist Warren Brookes cites this statistic as evidence that families were better able to afford houses in 1987. How might this statistic also indicate the difficulty of homebuying?

5. In 1988, median home prices in Orange County, California, were over three times as high as in Louisville, Kentucky. Nonetheless, housing experts believe this statistic underestimates the actual difference in home prices between the two locations. Why is this likely to be true?

6. From the list below, explain which criteria should be used to define homelessness: visible at 2:00 A.M. on street location known to be used as a sleeping location*; residents of emergency shelters*; hotel residents using social service agency vouchers*; residents of shelters for abused women and runaway youth*; individuals in jail who claim no residence; residents of sober living homes; families doubled up with friends? (Asterisk categories were included in the 1990 U.S. Census homeless count.)

Chapter 4

Health

Health statistics involve the expertise of many disciplines ranging from economics to medicine. This chapter reviews controversies about a cross-section of these statistics, including infant mortality, life expectancy, cancer, and traffic fatalities. These examples are chosen because in each instance there are apparently conflicting statistics, measuring both an improvement and a decline in health. A final section examines benefit—cost analysis, a commonly used technique for evaluating public health policies that also yields contradictory results. As with other social science statistics, careful examination of the underlying data helps resolve the apparent statistical quandaries. The task is made especially difficult by the varied sources used in health research, but an understanding of the data is a necessary first step for successful evaluation of health-care issues.

Data Sources

Some U.S. health statistics are based on complete counts of all relevant individuals. For example, U.S. Vital Statistics attempt to count all births and deaths (see chapter 2), and the U.S. Centers for Disease Control collects as complete a count as possible of many diseases and causes of death. But because it is infeasible to take a complete count for most other health statistics, survey data are used instead. Extensive surveys are compiled by the National Center for Health Statistics in the Vital and Health Statistics publications, known as the "rainbow series" because of the vibrant colors used for each subject. These surveys are

Where the Numbers Come From

Organizations	Data sources	Key publications
National Center for Health Statistics, U.S. Department of Health and Human Services	U.S. Vital Statistics; National Survey of Family Growth	*Monthly Vital Statistics Report; Vital Statistics of the United States; Vital and Health Statistics*
Bureau of the Census, U.S. Department of Commerce	Current Population Survey	*Current Population Reports* (P–20)
Centers for Disease Control, U.S. Department of Health and Human Services	Reports of notifiable diseases	*Morbidity and Mortality Weekly Report*
National Cancer Institute, U.S. Department of Health and Human Services	Surveillance, epidemiology, and end results	*Annual Cancer Statistics Review*
World Health Organization	Individual country reporting	*World Health Statistics Quarterly; World Health Statistics Annual*
Metropolitan Life Insurance	Private survey	*Statistical Bulletin*

For summary information, see *Statistical Abstract of the United States.*

extraordinarily specific, covering such detail as "Percent of persons 18 years of age and over who ate breakfast every day."

Other U.S. government surveys covering health-related topics include the U.S. Census Bureau's Current Population Survey (see chapter 9), specialized data collected by the Social Security Administration, the Bureau of Indian Affairs, the National Highway Traffic and Safety Administration, and the Food and Drug Administration. Private-sector organizations also assemble health statistics, including health-care associations for physicians, nurses, and hospital administrators, voluntary organizations such as the American Heart Association, the American Cancer Association, and the Cystic Fibrosis Foundation, and the insurance industry, most notably the Metropolitan Life Insurance Company surveys of health and medical costs. Because so much health survey data are available, librarians advise researchers to begin with guides to data such as *Facts at Your Fingertips*, the *American Statistics Index*, or *Index Medicus*.

> *Data Sample:* In *Facts at Your Fingertips,* under the subject "Headaches," the recommended references include Health Statistics Series 10–125, a survey on headaches, and the American Association for the Study of Headaches and its publication, *Headache.* Also listed is the name and telephone number for the contact person at the National Center for Health Statistics (NCHS) responsible for the study of headaches.

For worldwide health statistics, research will likely begin with World Health Organization (WHO) publications, complete and detailed vital statistics, and comparative data on infectious diseases and health-care usage. Researchers should be cautious in making comparisons between countries because reporting systems and standards vary widely. The WHO information service will assist researchers in assessing the comparability of data between countries.

> *Data Sample:* In the *World Health Statistics Annual* we learn that in El Salvador there were 65 deaths from meningitis in 1991 and 39 deaths from tetanus in 1990.

Controversies

Infant Mortality

The infant mortality rate is a key health status indicator. Because it is easy to collect data on infant mortality, at least in countries where hospital births prevail, this statistic provides an accurate comparison of health care in different places and at different times. In addition, the infant mortality rate responds quickly to improvements—or failures—in health care. For example, one of the first signals of problems in Soviet Union health programs was an increase in infant mortality dur-

Box 4.1. **Abortion**

Abortion statistics are unusual in that the best data are available from a nongovernmental source. Based on a survey of clinics, hospitals, and doctors' offices, the Alan Guttmacher Institute, a private foundation, provides the most detailed information on U.S. abortions. (Since 1970, abortion data also have been collected by the Centers for Disease Control from state health departments, but the data are incomplete, averaging about one-sixth less than the Guttmacher estimate.) According to Guttmacher data, the number of abortions in the United States more than doubled between 1973 (when abortion was legalized nationwide) and 1980, but since then has remained at about 1.5 million per year, declining slightly as a percentage of pregnancies from about 30 percent in 1980 to 27.5 percent in 1992. By contrast, U.S. government surveys, the National Survey of Family Growth, and the National Longitudinal Survey of Work Experience of Youth typically measure less than one-half as many abortions. According to researchers at the Guttmacher Institute, the accuracy of these surveys declined during the 1980s because women were increasingly unwilling to disclose their abortion experience to government survey takers.

ing the 1970s. Controversy about the U.S. infant mortality rate focuses on an apparent slowdown in its improvement during the 1980s and the continued failure of the United States to reduce infant mortality to levels already achieved in other countries (see Figure 4.1).

Infant mortality traditionally is measured in deaths per 1,000 live births. A 1912 Federal Children's Bureau survey estimated this death rate at more than 100 of every 1,000. Since then there has been nearly constant improvement, and by 1990 the death rate was 9.2 per 1,000. Infant mortality in the United States exceeds that of many other countries, including such relatively poor nations as Spain, Ireland, Singapore, and Hong Kong. Japan and Taiwan have the lowest infant morality of all, less than 6 per 1,000, about 35 percent better than the United States. In one study, the *worst* infant mortality of any Swedish province was lower than infant mortality in Utah, which had the lowest infant death rate of any U.S. state. Differences in the way infant mortality is defined affect these international comparisons. For example, in Japan cultural custom favors recording infant deaths as stillbirths that

Figure 4.1. **Infant Mortality Rate.** Deaths per 1,000 live births.

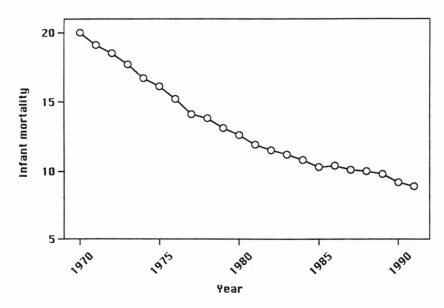

Source: U.S. Bureau of the Census, *Statistical Abstract of the United States, 1994* (Washington, D.C.: U.S. Government Printing Office, 1994), p. 91.

are not counted as infant mortality. Adjusting for stillbirths in Japan drops its ranking slightly to number three behind Finland and Sweden, while this change causes the U.S. ranking to rise to number fifteen from number eighteen.

Medical researcher Harry Schwartz objects to comparisons of infant mortality in the United States with infant mortality in ethnically homogeneous countries such as Sweden and Japan. Indeed, infant mortality for U.S. blacks is nearly twice as high as the rate for whites. Moreover, during the 1980s white infant mortality declined at a faster rate than black infant mortality. Research at the National Center for Health Statistics and Stanford University has suggested that high infant mortality persists even for blacks with favorable economic circumstances and access to prepaid health care. But these results may be social in origin, perhaps caused by transportation and child-care problems, inflexible employment schedules, or lower satisfaction with health-care providers. In one study, prenatal care alone reduced low birth weight for blacks, a major cause of infant mortality, at almost double the improvement measured for whites. As a result of such findings, many policy makers question whether the United States should accept high infant mortality rates because of a heterogeneous population. In this view, endorsed by the *Journal of the American Medical Association*, the United States can achieve the low infant mortality already achieved elsewhere. For example, if black infant mortality had been reduced to the rate for U.S. whites, more than 5,000 infants would have been saved in 1980.

Infant mortality is an example of a social statistic in which the same numbers are interpreted differently by policy analysts. The level of U.S. infant mortality is alternatively a measure of success and failure, and the higher rate for some groups is either an explanation of the relatively high overall infant mortality or an illustration of the failure of U.S. health care. Whichever interpretation one accepts, it is necessary for researchers to be aware of alternative viewpoints.

Are We Living Longer?

It is difficult not to feel a little cheered when one reads about increases in average life expectancy. For example, in 1987, overall U.S. average life expectancy at birth reached 75 years for the first time. But few readers understand the limitations of this statistic.

Blacks' Life Expectancy

Life expectancy is not the same for all groups. There is a troublesome divergence between life expectancy for whites in the United States, which reached 76.5 years in 1992, and for blacks, who experienced declining life expectancy during the late 1980s and then a slight increase to 69.8 years in 1992. Homicide, accident rates, and AIDS are likely the cause of higher death rates among blacks and may indicate a more severe decline in economic conditions for some blacks than is measured by traditional economic variables (see chapter 8).

The Very Elderly

Life expectancy data may also be unreliable for the very elderly because many individuals do not truthfully report their ages in the U.S. Census. Those under 21 years tend to exaggerate their age, and adults

21 through 70 report their ages relatively accurately, while the largest misreporting occurs for the extremely elderly, who tend to exaggerate their age, which results in a tendency for life expectancy for the elderly also to be exaggerated. The reason is that age at death is more likely to be accurately reported on death certificates. Thus there are too many people claiming to be of advanced age in the census, but fewer who actually die at those ages, causing an exaggerated survival rate. According to researchers at the University of Pennsylvania in 1980, this problem caused significant underestimation of the death rate for non-whites and misrepresentation of the trend in the cancer death rate for all persons over 85 years of age.

Mean and Median Life Expectancy

A third problem with longevity statistics is confusion about the meaning of mean and median life expectancy. In 1982, noted paleontologist Stephen Jay Gould was diagnosed with mesothelioma, a serious cancer, for which he learned the *median* life expectancy is only eight months after discovery. Gould recounts how his knowledge of statistics gave him hope, a sense of optimism he credits with helping him overcome the disease (and remain in sound health as of 1994). What Gould knew was that life expectancy for mesothelioma was pulled down by a large number of patients who die soon after the cancer is discovered—that is, one-half are dead within eight months, but an equal number of individuals survive longer, many far longer. Consequently, the *mean*, or average, life expectancy is much greater than the median. Thus, those who survive beyond eight months need not expect to die momentarily, having already lived longer than most who have the cancer. Some individuals will live for years, increasing the value of the mean, but leaving the median at eight months. Being young and receiving the best treatment, Gould thought he would fall in this longer-lived group, an outlook that itself may have helped him fight the disease.

The difference between the mean and the median applies to life expectancy for the population as a whole. For example, the 1990 U.S. mean life expectancy for men ranked tenth in the world at 72 years. Because high infant mortality and young male homicides cause so many early deaths, more than one-half of the population will survive longer, that is, the median life expectancy is greater than the mean life expectancy. At age 65, U.S. men have such better life expectancy that they rank fourth in the world in years of life remaining. For health researchers, mean life expectancy provides a reasonable measure of longevity that takes into accounts death that may occur throughout a lifetime. For individuals who want to know a typical life span, how- ever, leaving out the possibility of tragic early death, the higher median life expectancy is the most representative statistic.

Can We Predict Future Longevity?

Although few individuals can resist the temptation to calculate their own expected lifetimes based on life expectancy statistics, in fact ac- tual longevity may be quite different. The reason is that today's life expectancy calculations assume that today's death rates will continue into the future. In fact, it is not unreasonable to assume that most age groups will have lower death rates in the future and that life expectan- cies will rise slightly, as they have in past years. By projecting past improvements into the future, the journal *American Demographics* es- timates that men will live to nearly 100 by the year 2100. One oddity in this technique is that it anticipates women will average only 93 years. Although women currently live longer than men, the extrapola- tion method predicts shorter women's lifetimes because the current *rate* of improvement in women's life expectancy is lower than for men.

It is possible that there will be extraordinary scientific breakthroughs, extending life expectancy at a faster rate than in the past. Physician– writer Roy Walford suggests that genetic engineering will increase lifetimes to more than 140 years for both men and women. Neverthe- less, the likelihood of life-extending medical benefits is by no means certain; in fact, unexpected effects of war or environmental destruction could turn death rates sharply upward. More serious scientific inquiry attempts to understand why longevity increased in the past.

Why Are We Living Longer?

Is modern medicine responsible for longer lives? Historians and epide- miologists give a mixed diagnosis. The best long-term data come from Great Britain, where health statistics cover several centuries. Historian Talbot Griffith concludes that the increased use of drugs, inoculations, midwives, and hospitals significantly reduced British mortality after

---

Box 4.2. **The Oldest Person on Earth**

Although the number of aged is growing, reports of extreme ages often prove to be false. Reports of yogurt-eating Russian Caucasus villagers living to mid-100 years old lack documentation. Even cases with written records sometimes prove inaccurate, as in the celebrated example of American Charlie Smith, who claimed to be 137 years old based on records of his sale into slavery in 1854. A subsequently discovered marriage certificate showed he was a hearty but much younger 104 when he died. Similarly, another American claiming to be 130 was proved to have used his father's documents to avoid army service in World War I. The oldest U.S. resident with fully acceptable credentials was Californian Fanny Thomas, who died in 1980 at age 113. The oldest human with a verified age in 1994 was Madame Jeanne Calment of Arles, France, who turned 120 in 1995.

---

the eighteenth century. But physician T. McKeown responds in his 1976 book, *The Role of Medicine: Dream, Mirage or Nemesis*, that nutrition, not medical care, was the single most important reason for longer lives. For the period prior to 1900, McKeown makes the strong claim that "therapy made no contributions," and "the effect of immunization was restricted to smallpox which accounted for only about one-twentieth of the reduction of the death rate." For the twentieth century, McKeown allows that immunization has had a greater effect, but one that is far less easily demonstrated and less important than nutrition and hygiene, to which he attributes about two-thirds of the mortality decline.

In summary, life expectancies have strict definitions that are slightly different from everyday usage. They are useful research tools for appraising the overall health of a population, but they can be misleading when used as estimates for individual longevity. Projections of future life expectancy are even more problematic, dependent on the unknown effect of medical and environmental change.

Cancer

On December 23, 1971, President Richard Nixon signed the National Cancer Act, calling for a war on cancer of the "same kind of concentrated effort that split the atom and took man to the moon." Initially, hopes were raised that massive funding could find a cure for cancer by the 1976 bicentennial. Over two decades and hundreds of billions of dollars later, critics point out that cancer death rates have increased. Are we losing the war on cancer?

Recent statistical debate about cancer pitted the National Cancer Institute (NCI), the conduit for National Cancer Act funding, against outside epidemiologists. Representatives of NCI conceded that no cure for cancer appears close at hand. Instead, the institute targets halving the U.S. cancer mortality rate by the year 2000. Critics admitted that cancer research has produced some important life-extending treatments for a few kinds of cancer. But overall, more people were getting cancer, and, in total, cancer patient life expectancy had not increased.

Advocates of the effectiveness of the war on cancer pointed to improvements in cancer survival rates. Although this statistic received much publicity, epidemiologists question its validity. Better record keeping in recent years means that more cancer survivors are retained in the data files, thereby pushing up the measured survival rate. Also, because cancer now is detected earlier, cancer patients appear to live longer. A second statistic used to defend the war on cancer is a decline in the cancer death rate—at least the cancer death rate for the young and for cancers excluding lung cancer. The cancer death rate for those under 55 years old fell, in part because of remarkable progress in treating childhood leukemia. But critics point out that those under 55 years old account for less than 25 percent of all cancers. Because cancer death rates are increasing for those over 55 years old, the overall cancer death rate is up.

Almost all increased cancer mortality since 1950 is attributable to lung cancer. Thus, not surprisingly, the cancer death rate falls if lung cancer deaths are excluded, a statistic used by some NCI officials to argue that the war on cancer has been successful. In this view, increased lung cancer deaths (caused by cigarette smoking) could not be prevented by medical research. Epidemiologist and NCI critic John Bailar III argues that the same logic could be used to exclude stomach cancers, for which early detection, rather than NCI-sponsored research, reduced the death rate. Excluding both lung and stomach cancers removes the apparent progress against cancer.

Few epidemiologists expect medical research to achieve the war on cancer goal of halving cancer mortality by the year 2000. The policy

---

Box 4.3. **Likelihood of Breast Cancer**

U.S. Department of Health and Human Services Secretary Margaret M. Heckler asserted in 1985 that "1 out of every 11 women in this country will develop breast cancer." Although often cited, this statistic does not actually measure the average likelihood for breast cancer among women, but is based on an error similar to misinterpretation of "your chance of marrying after age 35" (see chapter 2). The 1-out-of-every-11 cancer likelihood is derived from the sum of current age-specific rates for ages 1 to 85. Because most women will not live to age 85, and because future cancer incidence rates may change, this figure does not measure the actual likelihood of cancer (although the statistic is useful for epidemiologists in assessing various cancer risks). Physician Richard Love calculates that the actual risk of breast cancer is about 1 in 30 during the fifth and sixth decades of life, the time when breast cancer is most worrisome, and a time period most women can expect to survive.

---

question is whether to continue funding cancer treatment in an effort to raise the survival rate, a goal already partially met, according to NCI officials. Critics, including John Bailar, advocate reallocation of resources toward cancer prevention as a more effective means of reducing cancer deaths. But, in part because of emphasis on survival rate statistics, of a recent $1.5 billion National Cancer Institute budget, only $74 million was allocated for prevention and control.

Cancer Incidence

In addition to the cancer death rate, researchers would like to know the prevalence of cancer among the living, or what epidemiologists call the incidence rate. The problem is that this statistic measures not only changes in the number of people who have cancer but also changing rates of cancer detection. For example, there was an unprecedented increase in reported breast cancer in 1974 when public disclosure of the disease by the wives of the U.S. president and vice-president prompted more women to have their breasts examined. As a result, more borderline lesions were discovered and reported to the NCI, although the cancer mortality rate was not affected in subsequent years.

Similarly, the male prostate cancer rate varies, depending on the level of examination. Prostate surgery and autopsy uncovers prostate cancer in as many as 25 percent of the men examined. But since the overall incidence for prostate cancer is no more than 1 percent, even for the most susceptible elderly, it appears that lesions discovered incidentally during surgery or autopsy are not malignant or grow so slowly that they do not qualify according to traditional definitions of cancer. A similar problem exists for skin cancer and *in situ* cervical cancer, both relatively frequent cancers in need of treatment, but uncommonly fatal. The inclusion of such cancers in incidence reports would cause the cancer rate to vary with the detection rate of these common but less severe cancers.

Because of these problems, the overall cancer incidence rate often excludes superficial skin cancers. Most researchers, however, prefer to look at the incidence rates for specific cancer sites, taking into account possible changes in cancer detection rates.

AIDS

Accurate data on AIDS or its cause, HIV infection, are critical for policy making. Is the epidemic worsening? Who has contracted the disease? And what policies will prevent its spread? Although the Centers for Disease Control attempts to gain a complete record of AIDS cases (6,531 new AIDS cases in January 1994, 3 in South Dakota and 2,025 in New York State), some AIDS cases are not reported. The undercount is particularly high for intravenous drug abusers, who enter the health-care system only when they are near death and there is no need to perform an AIDS test.

Even more difficult to estimate is the rate of HIV infection. The first U.S. nationwide HIV survey conducted between 1988 and 1991 by the National Center for Health Statistics included blood tests and interviews with 7,792 randomly selected individuals 18 to 59 years old. Of this group, 29 people were HIV-infected, leading to an estimate of at least 550,000 infected nationwide. The study's chief author considered the figure an underestimate because the response rate from young men was low and the survey excluded the homeless and those living in institutions. Worldwide, the numbers of HIV infection and AIDS cases are even more uncertain. In Asia and Africa, the death rate from AIDS is not as high as would be expected from the estimated high rate of

HIV infection, a paradox not understood as of 1994. Because of these data uncertainties, we cannot tell how many people AIDS will strike, and thus what level of medical resources will be needed or the degree to which public health measures have been effective in reducing the spread of the disease.

Is Slower Safer?

Speed limits are a health policy issue because traffic fatalities are the number-one cause of death for many age groups. Recent controversy has focused on an unintended consequence of a 1974 government regulation to conserve fuel by lowering the nationwide speed limit to 55 miles per hour. Afterward there was an abrupt 15 percent drop in highway fatalities. When Congress agreed to raise the speed limit on rural interstate highways to 65 miles per hour in 1987, some safety experts feared that there would be an increase in fatalities. Specifically, the National Research Council estimated that the higher speed limit would result in an increase of 500 highway deaths per year. But the effect of this change has been difficult to measure, leading to considerable controversy about the relationship between speed limits and highway safety.

The problem is that highway fatality data have not followed an easy-to-understand pattern. Data collected by the U.S. Transportation Department show that highway fatalities continued to drop long after the lower speed limit was introduced, even though average speeds increased well above the legal 55-miles-per-hour limit. When the 65-miles-per-hour speed limit was introduced there was a noticeable jump in the death rate, seemingly confirming the National Research Council prediction. But in defense of the higher speed limit Transportation Secretary Jim Burnley pointed out that there was an even greater increase in deaths on interstates maintaining the 55-miles-per-hour limit. Critics answered that tolerance of high speeds on these highways, well over the ostensible 55-miles-per-hour speed limit, caused the fatality increase. In this view, the Transportation Department could have enforced the 55-miles-per-hour speed limit by denying funds to states that did not reduce their average highway speeds.

Traffic experts are still trying to sort out the effect of speed limits. One intriguing possibility put forward by economist Charles A. Lave points to variance in speeds as the critical factor. In other words, different speeds on the same highway may contribute to serious accidents. But other researchers disagree, maintaining that speed is still the critical variable; in one study, variation in speed *upward*, that is, higher speeds, caused fatalities, whereas *lower* speeds did not. Better data, examining individual roads, are needed to explain fully the relationship between speed limits and fatalities.

The speed-limit debate is a good example of how public policy making desperately needs good statistics, but often must make do with ambiguous results. It seems likely that the 65-miles-per-hour speed limit will be extended, providing additional data, although if the critics are correct, at the expense of lost lives.

Benefit–Cost Analysis

Is government regulation necessary to protect the nation's health? In answering this question, policy makers often use benefit–cost analysis, a method developed by economists to measure the relative advantages (benefits) and disadvantages (costs) of a proposed program. Although seemingly straightforward common sense, benefit–cost analysis is controversial because of problems in putting a dollar value on all benefits and costs.

Value of Human Life

Full accounting within the benefit–cost framework requires putting a dollar value on human lives. Although the idea often shocks the general public, valuing human life is a well-established practice among economists, who maintain that tradeoffs between money and human life are implicit in everyday life. In this view, whenever we buy a less than perfectly safe car, accept a dangerous job, or even cross the street, we trade a risk of death—albeit slight—in return for measurable financial gain. The proportion between these risks and the gain (see Box 4.4) is called the "willingness to pay" by an individual for his or her own life.

A major problem with the willingness-to-pay technique is that it yields widely varying estimates for the value of life. Risky jobs such as mining and elephant keeping imply values as low as $300,000 per life, whereas surveys about the willingness to pay for environmental safeguards measure values at more than $8 million per life. As an alterna-

---

Box 4.4. **Cost of Tamper-proof Closures**

Mathematically, the value of human life is calculated by dividing the financial gain by the likelihood of death. For example, Paul MacAvoy, a member
of President Reagan's Council of Economic Advisers, calculated that tamper-proof closures, introduced after the 1982 Tylenol poisonings, implied
the value of human life equal to $2 million: $.02 (the cost of the closures)
divided by 1 in 100,000,000 (the chance of a single bottle containing
poison based on historical record). MacAvoy opposed the tamper-proof
closures on the grounds that $2 million per human life was greater than the
"actual" value of a human life measured in willingness-to-pay studies. Neither drug companies nor government regulators followed MacAvoy's advice.

---

tive method, some researchers advocate the use of estimates of lost
earnings. The advantage to this method is that it yields relatively consistent estimates, but it suffers from the shortcoming of severe inequity.
For example, in one study an 85-year-old black woman was "valued"
at $128, an unacceptable measure for most analysis. The variation in
values for human lives makes it difficult to derive policy advice from
benefit–cost analysis. Projects judged wasteful with one measure may
be quite worthwhile if human lives are more highly valued. For example, in opposing a safety standard for construction workers who handle
concrete, the U.S. Office of Management and Budget advocated valuing these workers at $1 million per life rather than the $3.5 million
proposed by the Occupational Safety and Health Administration.

One technique that avoids the problems of valuing human life is
"cost effectiveness." For example, in evaluating different methods of
reducing infant mortality, researchers measure the cost per infant life,
then compare which technique saves the most lives without putting a
dollar value on the lives saved. In a similar manner, Ralph Nader's
associate, Mark Green, advocates separate accounts for human lives
and dollar benefits. By this method, Green calculates that many health
and safety programs cut by the Reagan administration had been value
effective in terms of decreased medical care, lost work time, and other
benefits measurable in money—even without placing a dollar value on
human life.

Risk Assessment

A second controversial assumption in benefit–cost analysis is the measurement of the probability of unlikely events, a calculation called risk assessment. Some policy makers argue that these risks are far less than is commonly assumed. In this view, the public consistently overestimates the risk associated with nuclear power plants, acid rain, and other environmental hazards targeted by proregulation activists. For example, in a series of advertisements, the Mobil Oil Corporation observed that most people accept the potential risks of lawn mowers, vacuum cleaners, bathtubs, stairs, and other everyday necessities that are responsible for over a million yearly accidents because benefits outweigh the risks. Mobil would like the same logic applied to the risks of oil exploration compared to the benefits derived from the use of oil. Nuclear power plants are defended on similar grounds because the worst accident to date, at Chernobyl in 1985, is expected to cause at most about 17,000 additional cancer deaths worldwide. Based on this kind of risk assessment, rational public policy would pay more attention to the 500 *million* cancer deaths from other causes than to the alleged dangers of nuclear power.

Critics of risk assessment agree that why people worry about certain risks more than others is an interesting puzzle, but such apparent confusion about risk may not be irrational. Sociologist William R. Freudenberg points out that the experts are often wrong, as demonstrated by the explosion of the space shuttle *Challenger*. NASA rejected its own studies indicating a failure rate as frequent as 1 in 70 space shuttle boosters, in favor of a study measuring only a 1 in 100,000 risk. The historical track record suggested a 1 in 25 failure rate, which proved sadly but coincidentally correct when the shuttle exploded on its twenty-fifth launch. The "uninformed" consensus of the public, evaluating the risk of new technologies such as nuclear power and off-shore oil drilling, may be more accurate than expert estimates, which have traditionally proved too optimistic.

Implications

Measurement problems for the value of human life and risk assessment seriously undermine the usefulness of benefit–cost accounting for policy-making purposes. As illustrated by the space shuttle tragedy, erro-

neous assumptions can produce seemingly precise but wildly erroneous results. Similarly, different values for human life can cause completely different evaluations of public policies. At a minimum, it is
good research practice to use "sensitivity analysis" for all assumptions,
that is, the use of different values for human life and risk assessment to
see how such substitution alters the results. By demonstrating that
results do not depend on arbitrary assumptions in any of these controversial measures, researchers can broaden the influence of their findings beyond the already convinced.

Alternatively, researchers should consider whether benefit–cost analysis or risk assessment are the most appropriate techniques. As described
earlier, cost-effectiveness measurement may provide useful policy advice
without encumbering the analysis with unwarranted assumptions about
the value of life. In the case of risk assessment, policy adviser Langdon
Winner warns that traditional technique biases the analysis in favor of
the status quo by imposing an unnecessary burden of proof on those
who would like to see alternatives to unsafe technology. For example,
in evaluating genetic engineering, Winner believes that risk assessment
is nearly impossible and that attempts to make this tricky estimate have
caused policy makers to sidestep the more critical moral debate about
direct control of human evolution. In such instances, discussion of a
wider scope may provide better guidance, even if it does not appear as
mathematically precise as the calculations in benefit–cost analysis.

Summary

Each of the controversies reviewed in this chapter occurs because of
statistical ambiguities. There is uncertainty about the trend in infant
mortality and the reason for its remarkably high level in the United
States. There is disagreement about the reason for the increase in life
expectancy as well as about its future trend. Experts debate vigorously
about the success of the war on cancer. And there are conflicting
interpretations of the effect of the 55-miles-per-hour speed limit. Even
attempts to state explicitly the costs and benefits of government policies are controversial because of assumptions about the value of life
and risk assessment.

Nevertheless, most especially in the area of health policy, there is
little opportunity for social scientists to take a wait-and-see attitude.
Decisions must be made about the allocation of health-care resources,

even if the statistics or decision-making techniques are less than perfect. But at least these decisions can be made based on understanding the data's limitations. For example, in the debate about the war on cancer, critics have been able to warn us that statistics emphasized by the National Cancer Institute overstate the success of existing health policies. Similarly, careful analysis of life expectancy statistics provided insights about the uncertain effect of modern medicine and potential shortcomings in health care for black Americans. The analysis of benefit–cost analysis and risk assessment shows that researchers must look critically at official studies that "prove" the efficacy or failure of government regulations. Overall, these examples prove the usefulness of health statistics——but only with careful attention to their limitations.

Case Study Questions

1. Between 1950 and 1967, NCHS data show a 32 percent *increase* in the number of low-weight births among blacks, greater than the low-weight increase measured for war-ravaged Holland and Leningrad during the food shortages of World War II. At the same time, the percentage of out-of-hospital births declined for nonwhites from 42 percent in 1950 to 7 percent in 1967. How might the decline in out-of-hospital births explain the unusual—but likely overestimated—increase in low-weight births?

2. Fertility rates are a critical issue in developing countries. A 12 percent decline in Pakistani fertility between 1960 and 1975 was quite noteworthy. But follow-up research by demographers from Pakistan and the East–West Population Institute claimed that Pakistani fertility actually *increased* for this period from just below seven children per woman to above seven children per woman. According to these researchers, survey respondents often rounded up the ages of children under 6 years of age. For example, a 9-month-old infant would be reported as 1 year old and a 3 1/2-year-old would be reported as a 4-year-old. How did this simple bias cause a major error in estimating the Pakistani fertility rate?

3. Life expectancy for whites increased during the 1980s to a new high of over 76 years in 1991. At the same time, life expectancy for

blacks remained at 69 years. Why do many social scientists consider this statistic a more accurate—and worrisome—measure of black economic problems than traditional economic variables such as unemployment or income?

4. The state of Utah has an extremely low death rate from heart disease, a benefit sometimes ascribed to Mormon abstinence from tea, coffee, alcohol, and cigarettes. But, based on *age-adjusted* death rates —that is, taking into account the relatively young age of Utah's population—Utah's heart disease death rate is higher than its neighboring mountain states. On the other hand, Utah's liver cirrhosis and lung cancer rates are lower, even in the age-adjusted data. What implications can you infer about the benefits of lifestyles prevalent in Utah?

5. During the late 1980s, the Federal Aviation Administration (FAA) used benefit–cost analysis to analyze the need for safety seats on airlines for children under 2 years old. Because young children usually ride in their parents' laps, the primary cost of providing such safety is the additional regular airline seats, estimated to cost $56 million per year. On average, five infants die per year in U.S. commercial airline accidents. The Federal Aviation Authority valued infant lives at $500,000 each. Based on benefit–cost analysis, what did the FAA decide? How would you evaluate this decision-making method?

Chapter 5

Education

Education is widely perceived as a critical issue for the United States. In order to develop sound education policies, we need a wide variety of data about schools, students, and educational outcomes. Indeed, many data are collected, but according to many experts, existing education data are poor, especially in comparison to the extensive statistical programs for other social science statistics. This shortcoming is the first controversy discussed here. In addition, this chapter summarizes debates about such educational issues as dropout rates, illiteracy, black educational progress, school desegregation, international test scores, and SAT scores. Although newspapers and magazines cover these issues extensively, there has been little assessment of the weaknesses and strengths in the underlying education data.

Data Sources

National Center for Education Statistics

The U.S. Department of Education's National Center for Education Statistics (NCES) is the conduit for most U.S. education data. State and local agencies report to NCES data on enrollment, number of teachers, expenditures, and characteristics of public elementary and secondary schools. In addition, the NCES conducts its own surveys for data on private schools and higher education.

> *Data Sample:* NCES survey data show that the number of students studying Latin in high school fell to 164,000 in 1990 from an estimated 655,000 in 1960.

Where the Numbers Come From

Organizations	Data sources	Key publications
National Center for Education Statistics, U.S. Department of Education	Common Core of Data; High School and Beyond; National Assessment of Educational Progress; surveys of private schools, colleges, and universities, and recent college graduates	*Digest of Education Statistics; The Condition of Education*
Office of Civil Rights, U.S. Department of Education	Reporting in compliance with Civil Rights Act	"Civil Rights Survey of Elementary and Secondary Schools"
Bureau of the Census, U.S. Department of Commerce	Current Population Survey	*Current Population Reports* (Series P–20)
National Education Association	Private survey	*Estimates of School Statistics*

U.S. Census Bureau

Data on school enrollment and educational attainment are correlated with other individual characteristics every ten years in the U.S. Census (see chapter 2), annually in the Current Population Survey (see chapter 9), and occasionally in the Survey of Income and Program Participation (see chapter 8).

> *Data Sample:* In the 1990 U.S. Census, 7,148 15-year-olds were reported as enrolled in college.

Other Surveys

Much debate about school desegregation is based on data collected by the Office of Civil Rights in the U.S. Education Department. In the private sector, the National Education Association, an organization of teachers and school administrators, conducts its own survey of state education data, often published in advance of NCES data. Finally, there are sources of longitudinal data, that is, studies of individual students over periods of time. Such data have been collected by the U.S. Education Department in a survey following 1980 high school sophomores called High School and Beyond, as well as the National Longitudinal Survey and several university-sponsored surveys.

> *Data Sample:* In the 1988 National Longitudinal Survey, 15.2 percent of tenth graders reported that they "cut classes at least sometimes."

Controversies

Poor Data

Although the U.S. government has collected educational data since 1869, their quality has lagged far behind comparable statistics for other areas of study. Before the 1950s, each state reported information to the federal government as it saw fit, and sometimes not at all. The Office of Education's handbooks, first published in 1954, attempted to remedy some of these obvious flaws, but truly national data were not collected until the 1977–78 school year in what is called the Common Core of Data. Originally the Common Core was an ambitious project in which educational statistics would be gathered in a speedy and comprehensive manner, similar to the National Center for Health Statistics or the Bureau of Labor Statistics. But lack of funding and resistance by state officials and other federal agencies to relinquish their power over educational data resulted in a much-scaled-back project focusing on enrollment, attendance, revenues, and expenditures.

During the 1980s, the National Center for Education Statistics suffered reductions in budgets more than triple the cutbacks for other federal statistical agencies. Forty percent of the items not dealing with funding were eliminated from the federal data base between 1981 and 1983, including questions about critical policy issues such as school busing and the gender mix of teachers. Researchers identify three overall problems with NCES data: delay, nonstandardization, and irrelevance.

The NCES data often are published so long after collection that they cannot be used for policy making. In order to maintain a reasonably current public record, the U.S. Education Department's chief statistics publication, *Digest of Education Statistics,* relies on data collected by private organizations such as the National Educational Association because their data are available before the department's own official figures.

Unlike the Uniform Crime Survey (see chapter 6), there has not been a successful federal effort to create uniform reporting procedures for educational statistics. As a result, it is difficult for researchers to compare data between states. For example, variations in how states adjust for absent students make it difficult to compare public school enrollment.

According to its critics, the Common Core of Data too often focuses on easily measured items such as numbers of students and dollar expenditures, avoiding sensitive and timely issues such as inequality and student performance. As a result, even the Department of Education itself cannot rely on Common Core data; their own publication, for example, *A Nation at Risk: The Imperative for Educational Reform,* cited other data sources for all but one educational risk indicator.

With resurgent interest in education and the 1990 State Governors' "National Educational Goals," it is likely that efforts will be made to improve the quality of educational statistics. Nonetheless, the stinginess of previous decades will hamper research efforts because there will be no long-standing data base for making historical comparisons.

High School Dropouts

One example of an educational statistic that is poorly measured is the high school dropout rate. It has been particularly contentious in New York City, where according to critics more than one-half of all youths fail to finish high school. In 1993, however, New York City schools chancellor Joseph A. Fernandez reported a 16.2 percent dropout rate, the lowest in seven years of record keeping and lower than other large urban school systems. The extraordinarily low dropout rate occurred because of a new enrollment system that encouraged students to stay for a fifth, sixth, or seventh year, or even kept phantom students on the roster to collect more state aid. The percentage of students obtaining a diploma or equivalent remained constant at about 57 percent.

For the United States, the dropout rate has been estimated as high as

Box 5.1. **Schools Are Only as Bad as We Think They Are**

Currently, the top problems in U.S. schools are drug abuse, alcohol abuse, pregnancy, suicide, and rape. In the 1940s, the top five offenses were talking, chewing gum, making noise, running in the halls, and getting out of turn in line. Between 1985 and 1993, these lists were cited by *Newsweek, Harper's,* CBS News, former Secretary of Education William Bennett, Ross Perot, Senator John Glenn, and columnists Carl Rowan and Anna Quindlen—even though both lists were complete fabrications!

Because so many reputable sources used the lists, often referencing one another, it took detective work by Yale professor Barry O'Neill to track down the origin of the comparison. O'Neill found its creator, T. Cullen Davis, a fundamentalist Christian fighting against sex education and teaching creationism in Texas schools. Davis admitted he made up the list. "How did I know what the offenses in schools were in the 1940s? I was there. How do I know what they are now? I read the newspapers."

The unscientific origins of the list are less upsetting than its repetition as fact by so many reputable sources, none of whom bothered to check it for accuracy. O'Neill traced 250 versions of the list, noting how it changed to suit public concern. For example, Davis placed rape as the number-one problem, inadvertently remembering rape as the most serious, but not necessarily the most common crime on a standard reporting form. The California Department of Education reproduced the list, copied from *Harper's,* but putting drugs at the top of the list, probably to confirm public perception that drugs were a problem. The lesson for researchers is that experts quoting experts can lead to national folklore based more on our fears than on factual research.

30 percent by the U.S. Department of Education based on the proportion of an entering high school class not graduating four years later. Although often cited, this figure does not accurately measure the rate at which individuals fail to complete high school because as many as 40 percent of dropouts in one study earn a high school diploma later on, often through equivalency examinations.

Based on the 1993 Current Population Survey (see chapter 9) the percentage not receiving a diploma, including equivalencies, was about 14 percent of those over 21 years old, down from 18 percent in 1972. Because the survey sample is small for population subgroups, statisticians warn against looking at single-year estimates. For example, the rate for black women jumped by two percentage points twice during the 1970s, only to fall back again the following year. Until we have better data, we can use dropout rates as an indication that there is continued failure in our school systems—about 500,000 students dropping out per year according to Census Bureau researcher Robert Kominski. Nevertheless, the statistics are not precise enough to measure changes over time for subgroups of the population.

Illiteracy

Educational experts agree there is no single measure of illiteracy; it is a relative concept, dependent on how we define *literacy*. Not surprisingly, there is a wide range of measured illiteracy rates, from 0.5 percent based on U.S. Census data for the number of adults who claim not to have finished sixth grade, up to 33 percent based on a functional definition estimating the proportion of U.S. adults who could not read simple instructions such as the antidote on a lye bottle.

In the 1980s, such varying definitions helped fuel a debate about the severity of illiteracy. At that time, U.S. Education Secretary William Bennett defined illiteracy as only 5 percent, those who could only demonstrate the equivalent of a fourth-grade education. On this basis, Bennett concluded that "the United States is not awash in illiteracy," and federal illiteracy programs were cut to less than $100 million per year during the mid-1980s. Advocates of literacy programs argued at least a $5 billion effort was needed.

A 1982 survey by the U.S. Census Bureau for the Education Department measuring about 13 percent illiteracy received a good deal of publicity when it was released in 1986. But critics charged that the survey gave the misleading impression of accurately measuring illiteracy at its estimated range of 17 to 21 million illiterates. Some argued that illiteracy is actually much higher because 20 percent of those surveyed refused to be tested. Others maintained that the Census Bureau measured a peculiar sort of "bureaucratese" literacy because test takers had to decipher language encountered in government offices, such as "you may request a review of the decision made on the application for recertification for assistance and may request a fair hearing concerning any action affecting receipt or termination of assistance." A better-received study by the private Educational Testing Service measured literacy for a variety of tasks. Almost no one failed to find the time of a meeting in a memorandum, but 80 percent could not read a bus schedule accurately, and more than 90 percent could not interpret a four-line poem. This kind of functional illiteracy was emphasized by educator Jonathan Kozol in his 1985 book, *Illiterate America,* where he concluded that 60 million U.S. adults were *functional* illiterates, which is about one-third of the nation.

The lesson for researchers is to be careful in collapsing a complex social issue such as illiteracy into a single variable. The severity of the problem and the amount of government funding needed depend on which type of illiteracy we consider to be relevant.

Black Educational Progress

During the past fifty years, black educational attainment changed dramatically. School enrollment rates, once much lower for black youth, by 1980 were indistinguishable from whites, at about 93 percent. Similarly, the median number of years of schooling completed by blacks more than doubled between 1940 and 1980 to twelve years, near the white figure of 12.5 years of schooling.

But such a positive view of black educational progress is challenged on two grounds. First, as sociologists Reynolds Farley and Walter R. Allen point out in their book, *The Color Line,* schooling received by blacks, while equal in number of years, is likely to be inferior in quality. For example, whites are twice as likely as blacks to attend private schools. Economists Bennett Harrison and Lucy Gorham measure vastly different outcomes from a college education for blacks and whites. In 1987, one in three black college-educated men earned less than $12,000 (the poverty line for a family of four), while only one in six white college-educated men earned under that amount. Worse still, nearly one-half of college-educated black women had incomes below this poverty line.

A second objection to the optimistic view of black educational progress is an apparent reversal beginning in the mid-1970s, especially for black male college enrollment. This trend was noted in an American Council on Education report, *Minorities in Higher Education,* prompting a *New York Times* headline, "Ranks of Black Men Shrink on U.S. Campuses." Although there is indeed a failure to continue earlier black educational progress, the actual data are more complicated than they appear in such headlines. For example, researchers are uncertain about the precise college enrollment for blacks and other minority groups. In theory, the best data should come directly from institutions reporting to the NCES in the Integrated Postsecondary Education Data System. But as University of Wisconsin sociologist Robert Hauser points out, "the NCES has a history of inaccurate and untimely reporting, largely owing to inadequate staff and budget." Moreover, NCES enrollment data conflict with a second source, the U.S. Census Bureau's Current Population Survey (CPS). For example, in some years the two surveys differ by nearly 100,000 for the number of black men enrolled in college. In Hauser's view, the CPS is a "well designed" survey, but it covers a sample of the U.S. population, so only about 180 recent black high school graduates are interviewed each time. Because of random sampling error, the estimated enrollment for population subgroups such as black men is subject to considerable uncertainty.

Education researchers point out that total enrollment is not as important as the enrollment *rate*, for which NCES and CPS data also present a complex picture. Usually enrollment rates are measured as a percentage of 18- to 24-year-olds who attend college, although education experts point out that nearly 40 percent of all college students are above age 24. For black men—and black women and white men, but not white women—the percentage of 18- to 24-year-olds in college was similar in the late 1980s to the level in the mid-1970s. The percentage of black high school *graduates* who went to college had fallen, however, a troubling statistic especially in view of the demonstrable increase in achievement by black high school graduates as measured in college entrance exams (see below.) Thus we should expect increases in the percentage of black high schoolers attending college; Hauser attributes the decline to decreasing financial and social support for blacks in college.

Once again, important educational policy issues are clouded by poor or absent data. The best available data are a snapshot of the population at one point in time. In order to understand the trends in higher education fully, researchers need longitudinal studies tracking the education decisions of young adults. The NCES conducts such large sample longitudinal studies, but only once a decade. The first National Longitudinal Survey followed the high school class of 1972; the High School and Beyond survey follows the class of 1982; and the most recent study began with eighth graders who graduated from high school in 1994. These widely spaced studies force us to wait many years to make comparisons over time and then cannot tell us about the effect of social and economic trends that occur on a time scale shorter than a decade.

School Desegregation: What Has Happened?

Recent debate about attempts to enforce school desegregation during the 1980s illustrates the difficulty faced by social scientists in studying a complex issue in the face of intensive political controversy. At the start of the decade, the U.S. Commission on Civil Rights, a target of civil rights groups for allegedly lax enforcement, initiated a study of the effect of federal programs such as mandatory busing on school desegregation. The effort was plagued by political turmoil from the start. The director, Finis Welch, was challenged when he admitted little experience in studying desegregation. In 1985, a key member of the study, Gary Orfield of the University of Chicago, resigned on the grounds that the project was biased against busing programs and pursued his own separately funded research effort. Finally, in 1987, when the Civil Rights Commission's report was released, three members refused to vote on accepting the study because it allegedly wasted its limited budget repeating already published findings.

To complicate matters further, there were problems with the methods used to analyze desegregation. Finis Welch and his critics debated how to take into account the fact that white enrollment was dropping before desegregation programs were introduced. In other words, it was necessary to estimate whether school attendance patterns would have changed regardless of the desegregation plans. Also, there were debates about the long-run effect on enrollment—did white enrollment stay low?—and on the effect of different desegregation programs. These issues caused additional controversy, although this debate took place in academic journals, rather than in newspapers.

It is not surprising that the Civil Rights Commission and Orfield studies reached opposing policy conclusions. According to Welch, director of the Civil Rights Commission study, the evidence convinced him that "we have spent far too many resources trying to see that our children attend similar schools or some racial balance is attained." In contrast, Orfield and his colleagues opposed efforts by the Reagan administration to curb school integration; they applauded the courts, which had "not followed the election returns." Other research efforts led to similarly conflicting results so that as of the late 1980s there was little consensus about the effectiveness of school desegregation efforts.

Franklin Wilson, a major contributor to research on this issue, argued that much more sophisticated studies were needed in order to assess school integration programs. In particular, he called for long-term studies of strategies used by school districts and studies of the broader question of the effect of school programs on residential segregation. But the existing intense feelings about busing, complicated by ambiguous results, meant that social science research was contributing little to public policy debate.

Testing

Does the United States Rank Last?

A 1992 *Newsweek* headline, "An F in world competition," summarized the standing of U.S. students in a number of recent standardized tests. A sample of these widely reported statistics is listed on page 77. The data come primarily from two sets of international tests, one conducted by the International Association for the Evaluation of Educational Achievement (IEA) for more than thirty years, and a second set from the similarly named International Assessment of Education Progress (IAEP) conducted by the Educational Testing Service in 1988 and 1991 with a third study due for release during the mid-1990s. In addition, independent research has compared student achievement in different countries, most notably a study of schools in China, Japan, and the United States by Harold Stevenson and James W. Stigler published in *The Learning Gap*.

Although the media report these results as a sad commentary on the state of U.S. schools, educational experts are deeply divided about their interpretation. One obvious bias is the failure to mention tests on which U.S. students repeatedly do well, most notably reading and literature. In one international reading study, 9-year-olds from the United States scored second, surpassed only by Finland, and 14-year-olds placed ninth out of thirty-one countries. Stevenson and Stigler, who measured low U.S. math scores, also found U.S. students over-represented among high reading scorers, favorable results that under-

Recent International Tests Scores

Bad news:

The United States ranked last of twelve educational systems in mathematics and ninth of twelve in science. (IAEP)

In twelve math tests, U.S. students scored consistently near the bottom: eleventh of twelve in the thirteen-year old Core math test; fourteenth of fifteen in secondary algebra. (IEA studies)

The highest-scoring American school falls below the lowest-scoring Asian school. (Stevenson and Stigler comparison of fifth graders in Japan, Taiwan, and Minneapolis, ten schools in each city)

Good news:

The United States ranks second out of twenty-seven in reading literacy of 9-year-olds; ninth out of thirty-one in reading literacy of 14-year-olds. (International Association for the Evaluation of Educational Achievement)

cut the subtitle to their book, *Why Our Schools Are Failing,* and were almost never mentioned in media press reports about their study.

A second limitation of international comparisons is that they sometimes compare different populations of students. For example, during the 1960s IEA studies compared U.S. high schoolers with students in countries where as little as 10 percent of the population continue to this level. When the tests applied only to an educational elite, it is not surprising that students scored better than the 70 percent of U.S. students remaining in secondary school.

All the more recent studies cited earlier recognize this bias and limit their comparisons to lower grades, where almost all children are still in school. Taken together, these international comparisons seem to indict the United States, at least in math and science. Diane Ravitch, former assistant secretary of education, summarizes the situation: "We should not cry 'unfair' when we don't like the results of international comparisons. We must be prepared to learn from others." In a rare statement of unanimity, all fifty state governors and President Bush adopted "National Educational Goals" in 1990 that included putting U.S. students "first in the world in science and mathematics achievement."

One problem for researchers is that international comparisons do not tell us *why* some countries do well, so it is difficult to design educational policies that will achieve the governors' lofty goals. Education researcher Richard Jaeger concludes that with the exception of time spent on homework, factors such as class size and amount of time exposed to instruction are poor predictors of variation in test scores between countries. If we are to move beyond the frightening headlines and begin to understand why students perform differently in other countries, we need improved international data, looking at more subjects and educational indicators in addition to standardized tests.

Are Students Learning Less?

A similar dispute examines the *trend* in U.S. education: are schools doing a better or worse job than in the past? The data are more comprehensive than international comparisons and therefore potentially better guideposts to educational reform. Nevertheless, there are competing claims about what the numbers show us.

SAT scores are the most highly publicized. Every year, newspapers report the one- or two-point change in the math and verbal portion of this test taken primarily by high school seniors for admittance to college. In a typically ominous interpretation, President Bush concluded in 1991: "Last week, we learned SAT scores have fallen again. . . . The numbers tell us: Our schools are in trouble." Indeed, over the past thirty years, the trend is clearly downward, especially in the verbal portion, so that by 1992, less than one-third of college-bound seniors could match the average student in 1960. On closer examination, however, the picture is more complicated. Most of the decline occurred before 1975; since then, there has been only a slight fall-off in verbal scores, whereas math scores actually increased (see Figure 5.1).

Moreover, whatever decline has occurred is caused in part by changes in who takes the test. Because the SAT is now required by more nonselective universities, students from poorer backgrounds and with weaker academic skills are taking the SAT. Thus it is not surprising that today's 1 million test takers perform worse than the 11,000, mostly Ivy League–bound students, who first took the SAT in 1941. Nevertheless, even taking the change in the test-taking population into account, researchers still find a decline in SAT scores, especially for

Figure 5.1. **SAT Scores.** Averages for college-bound high school seniors.

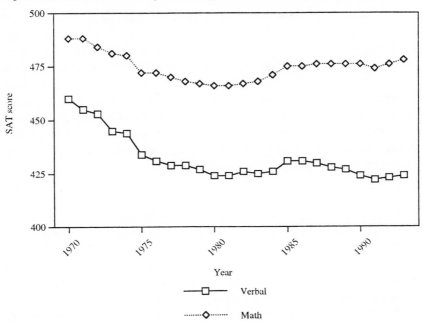

Source: U.S. Department of Education, *Digest of Education Statistics 1993* (Washington, D.C.: U.S. Government Printing Office, 1993), p. 126.

the test's verbal section. It remains unanswered whether this trend is caused by the schools, by changes in families, or by increased television viewing.

Even the overall decline in scores has a bright side: paradoxically, scores *increased* for nearly every subpopulation, most notably a nearly 100-point increase for African-Americans. The decrease in test scores for the entire population occurred because of an increase in the number of test takers who came from lower-scoring, mostly lower-income groups. But *within* these less-well-prepared subgroups, there has been an improvement in academic training. Thus, Richard M. Jaeger concludes that "rather than castigate U.S. schools for the decline in SAT scores, the President should congratulate them for the increases in SAT mean scores that appropriate, disaggregated analyses reveal."

A second source of trend data on student achievement is the National Assessment of Educational Progress (NAEP), a test series begun in 1969 as the only ongoing measurement of achievement for youths in public and private schools in grades 4 through 12. Administered by the Educational Testing Service (the same organization that conducts the SAT) to more than 200,000 students in 1990, the NAEP is recognized by education experts as a relatively accurate evaluation instrument because it involves tight security and relatively little "teaching to the test" by teachers to inflate student scores.

Contrary to public perception, the NAEP does not show a steady decline in performance. High school test scores in reading, math, and science dating back to 1969 are relatively flat, showing a barely significant uptick in reading and a slight downward trend in science. According to NAEP reports, the problem is that even though schools are not doing any worse than in the past, performance levels are still too low. For example, the NAEP notes that "less than half (of high school seniors) appeared to have a firm grasp of seventh-grade content."

Implications

In debates about educational policy, partisans are able to select evidence showing both that U.S. schools are doing well and that they are doing poorly. It is correct neither to be complacent nor to condemn the U.S. educational system. The key question is: are schools failing to such a degree that we need new ways to organize our schools? Unfavorable international comparisons and falling standardized test scores are cited most often by those who favor vouchers that parents could use in public or private schools. In this view, only competition will shake up the dismal failure of public school systems. Many of the same critics also call for national standardized tests to assess which schools are succeeding.

Other scholars maintain that massive school reform and national testing deflects resources from where they are needed. Harold Hodgkinson, director of the Center for Demographic Policy of the Institute for Education Leadership, points out that "we know where the bad schools are—in the middle of our largest cities." In this view, the data show that many, mostly suburban, U.S. schools work well, arguably among the best in the world. Instead of blaming the overall structure of U.S. schools, we should focus attention on inner cities, which need not only better schools but also improved health care, jobs, and safe neighborhoods.

Summary

The fundamental problem with education statistics is poor data. More timely and standardized data will assist researchers, as will increased willingness by the National Center for Education Statistics to tackle controversial issues. In addition, better-quality longitudinal data will provide better information on enrollment rates, dropout rates, and the effect of different schools on students' future careers.

For several of the issues covered in this chapter, including illiteracy, desegregation, SAT scores, and international comparisons of math and science achievement, relatively adequate data exist. Controversies arise because of different interpretation of the numbers. How many adults are illiterate? What are the differences in educational opportunities for blacks and whites? Does desegregation cause lower white enrollment? Do U.S. students perform as well as students in other countries? Is achievement in U.S. schools falling? Media accounts of these disputes rarely explain the origins of the statistical discrepancies, focusing instead on the different policies that researchers recommended. In each case, closer examination of the statistics reveals important information about education. For example, hidden within the debate about the precise illiteracy rate is the more critical issue about what level of literacy is required for functioning in the United States. And, although experts debate whether or not there has been a decline in U.S. student achievement levels, the overriding issue is the unchanged low level of achievement for too many students. Although many educational data remain uncollected, and many research questions remain unanswered, there is still much to be learned from careful attention to the data.

Case Study Questions

1. A higher percentage of U.S. students attend college than in any country in the world. In 1987, over 44 percent of Americans 18 to 24 years old were in higher education, more than double the rate for European nations. What effect do you think this much greater attendance rate has on international comparison of college test scores? On college graduation rates? And on unemployment rates for college graduates?

2. According to a 1988 study of state education departments, *all* claimed their students performed above the national average. This

mathematical impossibility was termed the "Lake Wobegon effect" after Garrison Keillor's mythical Minnesota town where "all the children are above average." Technically, the national average is a median, meaning one-half of tested students score below and one-half score above, but that is not the source of the paradox. The standard was set in the early 1980s. Why were all the children "above average"?

3. In 1990, the Census Bureau changed its question about education attainment from "What is the highest grade (or year) . . . attended?" to the "highest level completed or degree received." Why do you think this change was necessary?

4. In a survey of Illinois high school seniors, 80 percent of respondents reported they had taken a geometry course. Yet high school transcripts showed that 25 percent of students statewide were never enrolled in a geometry class. What might explain this discrepancy?

Chapter 6

Crime

Researchers new to the criminal justice field may be surprised at the amount of data available, including nearly complete records of arrests and crimes reported to police and a survey of crime victims almost as large in sample size as the Current Population Survey (see chapter 9). These data are the source of a number of controversies about crime, each with important public policy consequences. This chapter reviews several debates in criminology, including the accuracy of crime statistics, the chances that an individual will be a crime victim, the age of most criminals, the effect of poverty on crime, the relationship between crime and race, the deterrence effect of capital punishment, and the importance of white-collar crime.

Data Sources

There are two major sources of crime data: the Uniform Crime Reports, a compilation of police reports by the U.S. Justice Department's Federal Bureau of Investigation; and the National Crime Survey of households conducted by the U.S. Census Bureau for the U.S. Department of Justice.

Uniform Crime Reports

When we hear that crime is up or down, the figures usually come from the Uniform Crime Reports (UCR). Since 1930, the Federal Bureau of Investigation (FBI) has collected reports from over 16,000 police de-

---

Where the Numbers Come From

Organizations	Data sources	Key publications
Federal Bureau of Investigation, U.S. Department of Justice	Uniform Crime Reports	*Crime in the United States*
Statistics Division, U.S. Department of Justice	National Crime Survey	*Criminal Victimization in the United States*

---

partments across the country. These data include type of crime; time of occurrence; locality; and age, sex, and race of the offender. Crimes included in the UCR, or "index crimes," are homicide, forcible rape, robbery, aggravated assault (defined as violent crimes); and burglary, larceny over $50, and auto theft (defined as nonviolent crimes). Specifically excluded are petty theft, and so-called victimless crimes such as drug abuse because arrest criteria for these crimes vary from place to place and from year to year.

Data Sample: The 1992 UCR lists 13 violent crimes and 623 property crimes at the University of Georgia.

National Crime Survey

The second major data source on crime in the United States comes from crime victims in the National Crime Survey. These data are published annually by the U.S. Justice Department's Bureau of Justice based on a special Census Bureau survey of more than 50,000 households. The survey includes crimes regardless of whether they were reported to the police, but excludes murder, commercial burglary, and robbery, victimless crimes, prostitution, and white-collar crimes such as fraud and embezzlement (see below).

Data Sample: In the 1990 National Crime Survey individuals in families with income under $7,500 said they reported 38 percent of crimes to police; individuals in households with incomes over $50,000 said they reported 42.5 percent of crimes to police.

Box 6.1. **The Crime Index**

The "Crime Index" is a composite number including the total number of index crimes counted in the UCR during a year, usually calculated per 100,000 inhabitants. As an unweighted index, the Crime Index is dominated by its largest category, property crime, constituting nearly 90 percent of the index, of which more than one-half is larceny-theft. Because the Crime Index is overly responsive to changes in property crimes, it can misrepresent the trend in more serious violent crime. For example, the overall Crime Index showed a 2.2 percent drop between 1982 and 1986, solely on the basis of declines in larceny and burglary. During the same period, violent crime actually rose by over 8 percent. Those who want to emphasize the growing threat of crime typically refer to violent crime, which has increased almost every year since 1977. Those who maintain that crime is under control report the total Crime Index, which has been relatively steady since 1980.

FBI reports feature a "Crime Clock" showing the frequency of index crimes, one every two seconds in the UCR Index for 1992. Critics charge that such presentation unnecessarily provokes public fear of crime and not coincidentally argues for higher law enforcement budgets.

Controversies

Is There a Crime Wave?

Almost every year the headlines tell of an increase in violent crime. These statistics usually come from the Uniform Crime Reports, which have shown a fairly steady increase in crime for many decades. Less often reported are National Crime Survey statistics that show nearly constant or falling crime rates since 1973 (see Figure 6.1). These numbers come from entirely different data sources, each with its own bias and reliability problems.

It is generally acknowledged that far more crimes occur than are reported to the police and thus included in the Uniform Crime Reports. Indeed, set side by side with the UCR, the National Crime Survey counts about three times as much crime, although, as indicated earlier, different definitions about what constitutes crime mean that the two data sources are not strictly comparable. The UCR counts crime perpe-

Figure 6.1. **U.S. Violent Crime Rates.** UCR based on rate per inhabitant; victimization rate based on rate per persons age 12 or older.

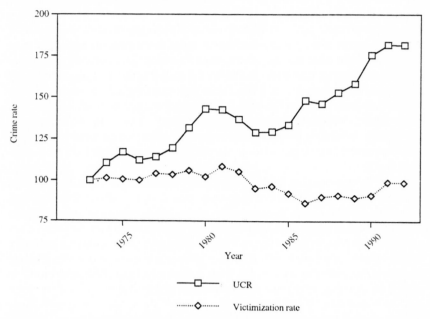

Sources: U.S. Department of Justice, Uniform Crime Reports, 1993; U.S Department of Justice, *Criminal Victimization in the United States, 1992* (Washington, D.C.: U.S. Government Printing Office, 1992), p. 6.

trators, while the survey counts crime victims. Thus, when a group robs one victim, it is overrepresented in the UCR relative to the survey. In contrast, when one criminal robs two people at the same time, there are two victims in the survey, but only one crime in the UCR. Finally, the UCR counts only the most serious crime for each arrest, leaving out other offenses that may have other victims.

Although the National Crime Survey counts more crime, it is not necessarily more accurate for research purposes. As in all household surveys, there are uncertainties about what respondents report. For example, one respondent usually answers for everyone in the household, a practice that leads to underreporting of crimes for other household members, but exaggeration of minor crimes committed against the respondent. To make matters worse, when a person has been the victim of several crimes, he or she tends not to report all the crimes. Apparently, respondents feel they have been cooperative by reporting a

Box 6.2. **Murder in Gotham**

For some crimes, such as murder—obviously reported only in the UCR, not the victimization survey—statistics have remained so accurate over time that criminologists use them as a baseline to compare with other less-reliable crime numbers. But even the murder rate can be deceiving if interpreted too narrowly. A *USA Today* first-page headline reads "Murder Rates Climbing on Main St. USA," and even the usually more sedate *New York Times* reports "Number of Killings Soars." These stories focus on a temporary increases in the murder rate that occurred between 1988 and 1991, omitting the *decline* in the murder rate that preceded it and continued in 1992.

Even the perception that big-city murder rates have increased applies to some cities, but not others; it dropped during the 1980s in Chicago, Los Angeles, and Houston. Overall, the urban murder rate is higher than in suburban or rural areas, a difference that may explain why so many people think the murder rate is increasing. Christopher Jencks speculates that many adults who work in cities mistakenly compare the higher urban murder rate with the lower rate they remember from their childhood in suburbia. Jencks concludes: "When today's children grow up and remember their [suburban] youth, they too will think the world has grown more violent, even if the crime rate remains unchanged."

few crimes and do not want to be bothered to recollect the entire number of crimes. Finally, respondents tend to telescope past events, including in the "past year" crimes experienced more than a year previously. These errors tend to be greater for some social groups, especially those in low-income households who have suffered repeat victimization but report to survey takers only the most serious or most recent crime. In 1989, the Bureau of Justice Statistics announced changes in the survey so that questions encourage victims to report all crimes. Instead of asking, "Have you been the victim of a crime?" the survey asks about crime in the context of the respondent's daily routine with questions such as: "While you were shopping. . . ." Field tests of these changes increased crime incidence reports by 25 percent, clearly an improvement in crime reporting, but also a challenge to researchers who want to compare crime rates before and after the new questions were introduced.

The Uniform Crime Reports also has been improved over time, so much so that some crime rate increases featured in the media represent only greater reliability in the statistics, not an increase in actual crime. At one time, the source of the UCR, individual police department records, was subject to considerable error. There are several documented examples of apparent changes in the crime rate that were later traced to purposeful manipulation by police departments. For many years, researchers omitted New York City crime statistics because they were based on individual precincts, where it was common practice for police to underreport crime in order to protect the reputation of their service neighborhoods. When New York City shifted to a centralized reporting system, burglary reports increased more than fourteenfold in three years. During the 1970s, when President Nixon launched a law-and-order campaign for the District of Columbia, police officials met their quotas for less crime by downgrading the seriousness of crimes so that they would not appear in the UCR. Subsequent investigation by a newspaper reporter revealed that stolen goods often were valued at $49, just under the threshold for grand larceny, the lowest-level crime included in the UCR. A similar strategy to "fight" crime was used in Indianapolis during the mid-1970s, where the police department achieved lower crime rates by tripling the number of crime reports determined to be "without merit" and thus unreported in the UCR. It is difficult to quantify improvements in reporting, but one study by sociologist Christopher Jencks suggests that violent crime doubled between 1960 and 1988, instead of the fourfold increase based on the UCR measure of aggravated assault.

Implications

Although there are drawbacks to both the UCR and the National Crime Survey, no major alternative data source exists. Consequently, the challenge for researchers is to choose the data for which inaccuracies are least likely to affect the issue being studied. For some purposes the choice is readily apparent: the UCR more accurately designates types of crime because it uses standard legal definitions; but the National Crime Survey gives a better estimate of the total number of crimes, including those not reported to police.

For measuring the overall crime rate, the choice between these two crime measures is less clear-cut and unfortunately is sometimes based on political convenience. Criminologists Albert Biderman and James P. Lynch conducted an exhaustive comparison of the UCR and NCS in which they point out numerous reasons why researchers cannot use the two crime measures interchangeably. Different denominators— population in the UCR and households in the NCS—by themselves account for a 13.9 percent divergence in the two series. Moreover, year-to-year variations in the crime rate may occur entirely because of errors in measurement and thus do not reflect any changes in crime policy for which political leaders can take blame or credit. The lesson for researchers is to be aware of both sets of crime statistics, and to wait for longer-term data to determine the upward or downward trend.

Rape

Most social scientists agree that both the UCR and NCS seriously understate the number of rapes. It is a crime often not reported in the victimization survey and even less frequently reported to the police. In a much-quoted survey of 6,159 college students, psychologist Mary P. Koss found that 15 percent of female students reported having been raped. In a rejoinder, social welfare professor Neil Gilbert suggests that the *lifetime* chance of rape is more likely in the range of 3 to 5 percent, and perhaps as low as 1 in 1,000 per year for college students. Gilbert accused Koss and others who found similar results of tilting the numbers to fit preconceived "feminist prescription."

	Rapes reported to police (in UCR)	Rape victims (in NCS)
1976	57,080	145,000
1981	82,500	178,000
1986	91,460	130,000
1991	106,590	173,000

The major point of contention is the definition of rape. One finding emphasized by Koss herself was that three-quarters of the victims did not identify themselves as rape victims; they had reported "sexual intercourse when you didn't want to because a man gave you alcohol or drugs" an experience that Koss defined as rape. Indeed media coverage of Koss's research emphasized the high rape frequency and not her revised definition of rape. Koss defended her work on the basis that

---

Box 6.3. **A Worldwide Problem?**

U.S. political scientist James Q. Wilson argues that rising crime is a relentless, worldwide problem for which there are few social remedies. Critics point out exceptions to the worldwide crime wave, including countries as different as Japan, Switzerland, Cuba, and the Scandinavian nations. Moreover, in countries such as England, where crime increased thirteenfold during this century, it was from such a low base that the English crime rate is still far below the level in the United States. According to critics of Wilson, the United States stands alone with an extraordinarily high rate, especially for serious crimes. To put the matter baldly: the city of Chicago has more burglaries than the entire country of Japan; there are more murders in Detroit than in the more populous and ostensibly violence-plagued Northern Ireland; homicide death rates for U.S. men are more than ten times higher than in Austria, Germany, Sweden, England, or Denmark.

---

many victimized women mistakenly blame themselves instead of reporting a rape or even understanding that a rape had occurred. Similar disputes cloud efforts to measure sexual assault against children, for which victimization rates for women vary from 6 to more than 60 percent, depending on how abuse is measured. The lesson for researchers is that sexual crimes have quite varied definitions, and so no single statistic fully captures its actual frequency.

Will You Be a Crime Victim?

Based on the National Crime Survey, the U.S. Justice Department calculates an individual's chance of becoming a crime victim in his or her lifetime. According to the Justice Department, these statistics are necessary because of a "false sense of security" provided by the apparently low crime rates measured on an annual basis. In this view, the public is misled by statistics measuring only an approximately 5 percent rate for violent crime in a given year, when according to the "lifetime likelihood," it is in fact more than 80 percent. (For blacks, the data are even grimmer: 1 in 30 black men is murdered, compared to 1 out of 133 for all people in the United States.)

One problem with likelihood statistics is that the Bureau of Justice Statistics does not adjust the lifetime likelihood for the fact that crime is concentrated among persons and places. In other words, some unfortunate people will suffer from several crimes, so actually far less than 80 percent of the population will experience any violent crime. Statisticians at the FBI are fully aware of this issue, discussing it at length in the methodological appendix to the technical report. In the NCS about 18 percent of respondents report another crime in the second interview, but there are insufficient data to calculate total repeat lifetime victimization rates. Few media reports mention this limitation, leaving readers with a greatly exaggerated impression of an individual's actual lifetime likelihood of being a crime victim.

A second problem with likelihood statistics is that they assume today's high crime rates will stay constant, which is perhaps an unduly pessimistic view. Most experts agree that the crime rate is likely to fall because there will be fewer young men in the age group most likely to commit crimes. Also, likelihood predictions make the conservative assumption that future social policies will not affect the crime rate, a too-gloomy prognosis according to critics who argue that employment and income programs could substantially reduce crime. Thus, "your likelihood to be a crime victim" is a statistic similar to a "woman's likelihood to marry" (see chapter 2). Both estimates will be accurate only if past experience is a reasonable guide to the future. Although the statistics can be instructive, as in the high murder rates for black men, the estimates are imperfect predictions of the future unless we make the extremely conservative assumption that social relations will be unchanged either for the better or for the worse.

Does Poverty Cause Crime?

It seems obvious that crime is associated with poverty. Basic street sense tells us that poor neighborhoods are more dangerous than wealthy neighborhoods. Superficially, at least, the data support such generalizations. Highland Park, Michigan, a section of inner-city Detroit, suffered twenty-one murders in 1990 according to the UCR. Nearby suburban Grosse Pointe Woods, with a similar population, had no reported murders. Robberies were also disproportionate: 376 in Highland Park; 10 in Grosse Pointe Woods.

Nonetheless, some social scientists are uncertain about how poverty is related to crime. The problem is that grouped data such as the comparison between Highland Park and Grosse Pointe Woods do not necessarily imply individual differences in the propensity to commit crimes by residents in those neighborhoods. In other words, just because crime is correlated with poverty at the group level (crime is high in poor neighborhoods), it does not necessarily follow that crime is correlated with poverty at the individual level (poor individuals commit more crimes).

Sociologist C.S. Tittle and other researchers argue that low-income Highland Park residents are no more likely to be criminals than high-income residents of Grosse Pointe Woods. Tittle rejects grouped data studies for perpetuating the "myth of social class and criminality" and the "prejudice that lower class people are characterized by pejorative traits such as immorality, inferiority and criminality." In place of grouped data, Tittle suggests we look at self-report studies in which sociologists ask *individuals* about their criminal past. According to Tittle, self-report studies show practically no association between social class and criminal activity.

If economic circumstances are not responsible for crime, then income or job programs are unlikely to lower the crime rate. But those who support these economic solutions to crime take issue with Tittle's reliance on self-report studies. Surprisingly, the rebuttal does not focus on the obvious drawback of obtaining accurate self-incriminating data. Instead, self-report studies are criticized for failing to take into account the seriousness of crimes. It is only by including very minor thefts as crimes that middle-class and upper-class youths have as high a crime rate as lower-class youths. Or, as sociologist Elliott Currie mocks the result, we learned that "American youths of all backgrounds sometimes acted up."

To support the view that the self-report studies overemphasize minor crimes and therefore disguise the relationship between poverty and serious crime, Currie points to 1983 research by the Colorado Behavioral Research Institute showing that the seriousness and frequency of criminal behavior are strongly correlated with social class. Based on such studies, Currie and other criminologists contend that there is sufficient correlation between poverty and crime on an individual level to override the potential pitfall of drawing conclusions from grouped data. Nevertheless, researchers should keep in mind that there are situations where group data can be misleading.

Why Is the Black Crime Rate So High?

The Uniform Crime Reports tabulate criminal offenders by sex, age, and race. The most obvious observation is that men make up the largest percentage, nearly 90 percent for violent crimes. Second, about one-half of all offenders are under the age of 20. Third, and most controversial, blacks constitute about 50 percent of those arrested for violent crimes. It is the disproportionate number of young black men in the criminal justice system that has provoked heated research debate. Part of the difference in crime rates between racial groups depends on what we define as crime. Whites are arrested more frequently for white-collar offenses, a type of crime larger in dollar amount than other crimes (see below) but not included in the UCR. Also, for one of the most common crimes of all, drunk driving, which is also not in the UCR, the arrest rate for blacks is lower than for whites.

Overall, however, blacks constitute 45 percent of those in prison, many times the percentage of blacks in the U.S. population. Sociologist Andrew Hacker ascribes part of this difference to the discriminatory access to crime; that is, black offenders often resort to street robberies, which almost always result in arrest, whereas white offenders are able to operate freely in better-off neighborhoods where they can commit burglaries, a far more profitable and less hazardous occupation. New York State Supreme Court Judge Bruce Wright adds that police discrimination causes blacks to be arrested more frequently, and discrimination by the judicial system causes blacks to receive more frequent and longer prison sentences.

Criminologist Elliott Currie responds that outright bias explains only a small part of the difference in crime rates for blacks and for whites. As evidence, Currie cites homicide data available from the Public Health Service showing that black men from age 25 to 44 are eight times as likely to be murdered as their white age-mates. Because other studies show that most murders are intraracial (black against black), it seems likely that the higher homicide rate for blacks is real and not a result of police or judicial bias. Currie maintains that the eagerness by some researchers to dismiss race as an important factor in crime has distracted policy makers from the task of accounting for what Currie calls the "genuine social disaster wrought by extremes of economic inequality we have tolerated in the United States."

The issue of race and crime has a long, controversial history. Statistics from the Justice Department's Bureau of Justice Statistics show a grisly past in which, for example, blacks have constituted about one-half of those executed by the legal system, including many for crimes other than murder. Researchers need to be aware of the issues raised by Hacker and Wright that cause bias in official statistics, as well as of the complex social factors that Currie urges us to address in understanding the relationship between race and crime.

Does Prison Pay?

It costs about $25,000 per year to keep a prisoner behind bars. Does society save an equal amount in crimes not committed? National Institute of Justice economist Edwin Zedlewski says yes: the typical offender commits 187 crimes a year, costing $2,300 per crime, for a total of $430,000 in benefits by keeping the criminal in prison. His study was widely quoted by advocates of more prisons, for example, in the *Reader's Digest* article "Why Don't We Have the Prisons We Need?" which concluded that "to pen every serious offender will cost billions, but it's money well spent."

Penologists Franklin E. Zimring and Gordon Hawkins disagree with Zedlewski's findings. Most criminals are arrested for only a small proportion of their crimes, so Zedlewski estimated the number of crimes per offender based on self-reports by prison inmates. According to Zimring and Hawkins, the actual number of crimes per inmate is far lower and the cost of each crime is much less than the estimate used by Zedlewski. Thieves and burglars commit a large number of less serious crimes so that the *average* number of crimes per inmate is high. But one-half of those imprisoned committed fewer than fifteen crimes, albeit perhaps more serious crimes. Using this *median* number of crimes reduces the apparent savings of imprisonment from over $400,000 to about $10,000 per year.

Princeton University researchers John J. DiIulio and Anne Morrison Piehl take a middle position based on estimates for the cost of different crimes ranging from fraud, forgery, and petty theft at only $110 per incident to robbery at $12,060 per incident. In their view, imprisonment saves society $46,000 for the typical prisoner, although less than $2,000 for the 10 percent of prisoners who committed the fewest and pettiest crimes and nearly $2 million for one exceptional individual who committed 151 robberies.

In addition to the number of crimes, other assumptions in these cost estimates affect the disputed savings from imprisonment. The social cost of each crime is based on jury awards, providing only a crude estimate of the cost of victims' pain and suffering. And most estimates omit drug sales as "victimless crimes" that are nearly impossible to value but that cause researchers to leave out about 90 percent of crimes reported by prisoners. Because of the varying estimates, partisans can find statistics to support both cost effectiveness or alternatively the wastefulness of imprisonment. Careful users will be alert to the underlying data problems that complicate measurement of this important social issue.

Does Capital Punishment Deter Murder?

Much recent criminology research focuses on punishment as a determent to crime. At the center of the debate is the efficacy of the death penalty. According to a 1975 study by economist Isaac Ehrlich, approximately eight murders are deterred by every legal execution. In a 1976 brief to the Supreme Court, the U.S. solicitor general quoted Ehrlich's results as "sophisticated" evidence that "execution actually deterred a significant number of murders."

Anti–capital-punishment forces take issue with this view. In competing testimony to the Supreme Court, researchers pointed out that Ehrlich's analysis depends crucially on several arbitrary assumptions. Any one of the following changes reduces the deterrence effect measured by Ehrlich: if Vital Statistics replace Ehrlich's FBI crime data, if raw numbers are substituted for the logarithms used by Ehrlich, if the years 1963 through 1969 are removed, and if states that never had a penalty are studied separately. Each of these limitations indicates that Ehrlich's results are not robust—that is, he can reach his conclusion only under narrow specifications. Research should ideally be immune to slight changes in the analysis. If changing the data source, the use of logarithms, the years studied, or the states included causes the effect of the death penalty to disappear, then it is likely that the original conclusion about the effect of the death penalty was the result of statistical happenstance.

Ehrlich answered his critics with a second study in 1977, comparing murder rates in different states. Again, Ehrlich found a deterrence effect; in this case, more than twenty murders were prevented by each

---

Box 6.4. **Missing Children—How Serious a Problem?**

"Missing children" became a national obsession during the 1980s, when their pictures appeared on milk cartons, buses, and national television. Fifty million households watched a fictionalized account of Etan Patz's disappearance in New York City, following by President Reagan's appeal to find missing children whose pictures were shown to viewers. Soon afterward, Child Find, an organization devoted to the plight of missing children, estimated that 50,000 children were abducted annually, of whom 5,000 were killed and 40,000 cases remained unsolved. In 1986, *Denver Post* reporters won the Pulitzer Prize for demonstrating that most missing children were runaways or involved in custody disputes. Jay Howell, director of the National Center for Missing and Exploited Children, points out that "the most dangerous place for a child in this country is his or her own home."

According to official FBI statistics, kidnapping is an extremely rare crime. At any one time, fewer than 100 children are listed as kidnapped by strangers, and the crime is so infrequent that it is not included in the National Crime Survey because it would show up in the 60,000-household sample an average of once every fifteen years. Using data from the National Center for Missing and Exploited Children, Joel Best estimates that just over 500 children were kidnapped in 1984, far more than reported to the FBI, but many times less than the discredited Child Find statistics.

---

execution. But, as with his 1975 study, other researchers challenged Ehrlich's method on the grounds that small changes in the research method would cause the deterrence effect to disappear. In this instance, critics argued that the murder rate increased because of factors not considered by Ehrlich, perhaps differences between states in the likelihood of conviction, differences between states in cultural attitudes, or differences between states in the availability of handguns.

Even if we cannot rule out a deterrent effect to the death penalty, the difficulty in proving that deterrence exists suggests that the deterrence effect is quite small compared with other factors affecting the crime rate. Other social policies, especially programs to provide jobs and income, have been demonstrated to affect the crime rate strongly. But such social policies are less well studied; as economist Richard McGahey points out, there are exhaustive studies of the death penalty, but no corresponding "spate of articles on . . . 'Murder and Poverty,' or 'The Preventative Effect of Higher Incomes.'"

What about White-Collar Crime?

In 1939, Edwin H. Sutherland used the occasion of his American Sociological Society presidential address to urge study of what he termed "white-collar crime." Sutherland suggested that criminologists previously ignored "upper-world" crime committed in the course of an occupation, offenses he claimed were as important as traditionally defined crime. But measuring the amount of white-collar crime has not been easy.

A few white-collar crimes are counted in national statistics. FBI records counted 5,000 convictions for fraud in 1985 and a lesser number for embezzlement, counterfeiting, and regulatory offenses. As federal crimes, they are not included in the UCR, although in any event they would be swamped by the 13 million crimes recorded in 1985. The National Crime Survey also omits white-collar crime because many victims are not aware of the crime.

Many researchers, including Sutherland, have argued for a definition of white-collar crime that would be far broader than the offenses recorded by the FBI. In this view, most white-collar crime is committed by high-status individuals in the course of their work without any arrests, or even a record of a crime. By such a definition, white-collar crime includes violations of antitrust law, safety rules, and environmental standards. As examples the critics often cite egregious cases such as the promotion of Chloromycetin by Parke-Davis pharmaceutical company and the exploding gas tank in Ford Pinto automobiles. The cost of these crimes can only be estimated; according to Mark Green, former aide to Ralph Nader, price fixing and safety lapses alone caused several hundred billion dollars harm to society.

At stake in the definition of white-collar crime is the allocation of crime-prevention resources. Criminologists Harold Pepinsky and Paul Jesilow argue that even the lowest estimates for the value of white-collar crime are still about ten times as high as the total property loss in traditionally defined crime. But crime prevention funds are allocated in just the reverse proportions, with most money spent dealing with non–white-collar criminals. Philosopher David Reiman argues that rational allocation would increase policing of operating rooms and dangerous

workplaces where four times more people are killed than in traditionally defined murders.

Most research projects have little choice but to work with existing
official definitions of crime; certainly the approach makes sense if one
wants to study those who actually are arrested. But if the goal is to
study total lawbreaking or the cost of crime to society, then researchers
need to consider a broader approach, taking white-collar crime into
account. The problem, of course, is how to measure white-collar crime
when few available statistics do so. As a minimal corrective, researchers can acknowledge this shortcoming in the data base.

Summary

Research on crime enjoys relatively complete statistics published in a
timely way. Nonetheless, this chapter has illustrated several major
problems in the use of crime statistics.

First, crime statistics are unusual in that the same organizations—individual police departments and the FBI—are responsible for carrying
out public policy as well as collecting and publishing the most important source of crime data, the Uniform Crime Reports. This conflict of
interest sometimes causes inaccuracies in the data, as in the case of
police department misrepresentations to the UCR. In addition, critics
charge that some statistics, such as the Crime Index and the Likelihood
of Being a Crime Victim, are constructed in a manner that helps the
criminal justice system justify budgets rather than increase our understanding of crime. A different sort of survey error affects the National
Crime Survey in which respondents are not necessarily forthcoming
with accurate answers about their experience with crime. Overreporting of crime occurs when respondents exaggerate their own experiences or telescope distant events into the past year being surveyed.
Underreporting appears to be the more serious problem, including a
severe undercount of the number of rapes, as well as underreporting
for other crimes caused by noncooperation or lack of knowledge about
crimes involving other household members. All of these measurement
problems are well studied. Even if there is no method to "correct" the
underlying data for under- or overreporting, the criminal justice literature provides ample evidence of the direction in which survey errors
are likely to lie.

Second, there is disagreement in the study of crime about the fundamental question, "What is crime?" The most commonly used crime data, the UCR, include only crimes reported to police, a number that most certainly is much less than the number of crimes committed. A more complete count of crime is available in the National Crime Survey, but it omits categories such as victimless crime and white-collar crime. This last category is most controversial of all. There is no standard definition for what constitutes white-collar crime, and there are only imprecise estimates about its dollar value. Similarly, the crime of rape is subject to varying definitions, which has led to a bitter dispute about the prevalence of rape victimization. Because alternative definitions are, by necessity, somewhat arbitrary, most research projects rely on the "official" crime definitions. Nonetheless, careful researchers will note these measurement issues and speculate about the effect they may have on the study of crime. For example, conclusions about the cost of crime and the relationship between race and crime depend critically on how crime is defined.

Third, as with other social statistics, crime statistics are only as meaningful as the skill of the researcher who uses them. Misinterpretation of official numbers was documented for single-year trends in the crime rate that are too erratic to measure the impact of crime policies, and for the Crime Index, which does not distinguish between different types of crime. In these cases, there are simple corrective guidelines to be followed, involving the use of longer-term data and indexes that take into account different types of crimes. More problematic is the use of crime statistics in a selective manner. The issue arose in two critical matters of social policy: the relationship between race and crime, and the impact of the death penalty. In both cases, critics charged that much standard crime analysis focuses too narrowly on the issues of race and the death penalty in isolation, ignoring other social and economic variables that are more important for understanding crime. The choice of variables for analysis crosses over into theoretical issues of criminology that are beyond the scope of this book. At a minimum, however, researchers can be clear about how they have made such choices, making sure their selection of variables has a sound theoretical basis.

Case Study Questions

1. The total number of offenses in the Crime Index rose to 14,438,200 in 1992 from 13,923,100 in 1988. Yet the Crime Index rate fell to 5,660.2 from 5,664.2. Explain.

2. Mr. Smith, who profits from "inside" knowledge about the stock market, is robbed by three youths. How many crimes have been committed according to the Uniform Crime Reports? According to the National Crime Survey?

3. In the National Health Survey, a group of individuals known to have visited the doctor within the previous two weeks were asked if they had done so. About 30 percent denied having been to the doctor during that time. Some researchers think this study has implications for the National Crime Survey. What are they?

4. Comparison of National Crime Survey with police data on nonfatal gunshot injuries suggests that the survey undercounts these injuries by a factor of three. Why might this occur?

5. In 1981, the following headlines appeared in national magazines: "The Curse of Violent Crime" (*Time*), "The Epidemic of Violent Crime" (*Newsweek*), and "Our Losing Battle against Crime" (*U.S. News*). The indexes of violent crime are listed below.

Based on these data, write a more accurate headline and short article on the trend in crime.

	National Crime Survey (100,000 persons 12 years of age and older)	UCR (100,000 inhabitants)
1977	3,390	475.9
1978	3,370	497.8
1979	3,450	548.9
1980	3,330	596.6
1981	3,530	594.3

Chapter 7

The National Economy

This chapter looks at statistical controversies for national economic statistics including gross domestic product, productivity measures, savings rates, imports and exports, and interdomestic investments. These statistics are very much in the news, but often in contradictory terms, portraying at the same time both the good and the bad health of the economy. In some instances, these discrepancies have occurred because of problems with the underlying data; for example, information on imports and exports was collected so haphazardly that some researchers question official trade statistics. More often, U.S. national economic data are considered a model of survey technique, refined over several decades of collection with well-understood limitations. In these cases, contradictory statistics arise because of different methods for interpreting the data. Such examples provide constructive case studies of the intersection between economic theory and the construction of economic statistics.

Data Sources

U.S. Commerce Department

National Income and Product Accounts

The U.S. Commerce Department's Bureau of Economic Analysis is the single most important agency for statistics on the entire U.S. economy. It is the conduit for data collected throughout the government, consolidated in National Income and Product Accounts, better known

Where the Numbers Come From

Organizations	Data sources	Key publications
Bureau of Economic Analysis, U.S. Department of Commerce	National income and product accounts	*Survey of Current Business*
Bureau of the Census, U.S. Department of Commerce	Economic censuses	*Census of Manufactures* (and other sectors); *Survey of Current Business; U.S. Exports; U.S. Imports*
Bureau of Labor Statistics, U.S. Department of Labor	Productivity computations	*Monthly Labor Review*
Board of Governors, U.S. Federal Reserve Board	Flow of funds	*Federal Reserve Bulletin*
U.S. Small Business Administration	Small Business Data Source	*State of Small Business; Handbook of Small Business Data*

by its most comprehensive statistic, gross domestic product, or GDP.*
These data were first collected systematically during the 1930s under
the leadership of economist Simon Kuznets, who later won the Nobel
Prize in economics for his efforts. At that time, new categories were
created that gained worldwide acceptance for the measurement of
national economic activity.

---

*Prior to 1992, the Department of Commerce reported GNP, or gross *national*
product, including the profits earned by U.S. firms on production overseas, but not
the profits earned by foreigners on production in the United States. For the United
States the difference between GDP and GNP is slight.

Box 7.1. **The People behind the Numbers**

Take a moment to consider who is responsible for the data we use. For example, U.S. Census Bureau statistics on shoe production are part of the responsibility of six statisticians, assisted by two clerks, who make up the section "Food, tobacco, textiles, apparel, and leather goods." These men and women design the survey forms, tabulate the returns, and review the tables subsequently published in the *Annual Survey of Manufactures* and the *Census of Manufactures*. Multiplied many times in government and private industry, similar groups work largely unrecognized—but willing to talk with interested researchers—to assemble the data we depend on for our research. Thus we learn that U.S.-produced women's dress shoes declined to 46 million pairs in 1982 from 50 million pairs in 1977, data of vital importance to those in the industry, and a stepping-stone toward understanding why U.S. manufacturing employment fell by 900,000 and why the overall economy grew by only 7 percent during these five years.

In brief, total economic transactions are added up twice. On one side of the ledger, total incomes, including wages, salaries, rents, profits, interest, and taxes are computed from data collected by the Internal Revenue Service, Bureau of Labor Statistics, Social Security Administration, and other government agencies. On the other side of the ledger, total expenditures are computed based primarily on Census Bureau economic surveys.

Data Sample: Gross domestic product reached $1,000 billion in 1970, $2,000 billion in 1978, $3,000 billion in 1981, $4,000 billion in 1985, $5,000 billion in 1989, and $6,000 billion in 1992.

Industry Statistics

Frequently researchers require statistics on parts of the economy, for example on a single industry or a particular geographic area. Such data are available in U.S. Census Bureau surveys, most notably the economic censuses taken every five years. The *Census of Manufactures* alone generates eighty-two separate reports on data for groups of industries, as well as geographic and summary data for the entire manufacturing sector. Similar surveys are conducted for retail trade, government, and construction. A useful source of local information is the annual County Business Patterns, with data on employment, payroll, and type of business, for every U.S. state and county.

> *Data Sample:* The 1987 *Census of Manufactures* estimated $104 million receipts in the category "standardized tests including both test and answer sheets," an increase from $45.4 million in 1982.

Trade Statistics

The U.S. Commerce Department's Bureau of Economic Analysis publishes many international statistics, based on data collected by other government agencies. Imports and exports are measured from Customs data; military sales are derived from Defense Department reports; foreign investment income comes from Treasury Department data; and travel expenditures are estimated from postcards distributed during one week every three months to travelers at airports and other border crossings.

> *Data Sample:* Trade statistics reports are extraordinary in detail, reporting, for example, $673,000 in pignolia nuts (shelled, blanched, or otherwise prepared) imported from Portugal in 1987.

U.S. Labor Department

Productivity

U.S. Commerce Department data on production are used by the U.S. Labor Department's Bureau of Labor Statistics to calculate productivity, that is, the relationship between national output and inputs such as labor or capital. Most often, productivity is measured in terms of hours of labor, although the Bureau of Labor Statistics has other productivity measures, including a new multifactor productivity statistic that attempts to take into account changes in both labor and capital inputs.

> *Data Sample:* According to the Bureau of Labor Statistics, U.S. gasoline service-station productivity increased by 29 percent from 1980 to 1985, but only 3 percent from 1985 to 1990.

U.S. Federal Reserve Board

The nation's central government bank, the Federal Reserve, tracks the economy in its own statistical series. Most important for researchers are flow-of-funds data, a quarterly report on the flow of money through the economy. This is a fundamental source on banking, credit, investments, and international capital transactions. In addition, the Federal Reserve Board compiles statistics on industrial production, including the frequently consulted index of capacity utilization, a measure of how different sectors of the economy are using their existing resources. These data are used for Federal Reserve monetary policy decisions. For example, during the Vietnam war, when the Department of Defense underestimated the war's cost to President Johnson's economic advisers, the Federal Reserve took corrective action because of its own data-collection capability.

> *Data Sample:* In August 1993, the Federal Reserve Board of Governors reported consumer installment credit on gasoline company credit cards was $4,728,000,000.

Private Sector

Private credit-reporting and investment-grading firms also gather economywide data. Among the most often used of these statistics are those from Dun and Bradstreet Corporation on business startups and business failures. Dun and Bradstreet data are also used by the U.S. Small Business Administration as the basis for the Small Business Data Base on the characteristics of different size firms.

> *Data Sample:* Based on Dun and Bradstreet data, the U.S. Small Business Administration reported 793 new liquor store businesses in 1986.

Controversies

Which GDP?

Because national economic accounts are so important for policy making, the Commerce Department estimates GDP statistics with as little delay as possible. The first available data are called "advance GDP," published one month after the end of the quarter-year being measured. (A "flash" estimate, published fifteen days before the end of the quarter, was abandoned because it proved too inaccurate.) The day before the GDP data are published, they are calculated on a stand-alone com-

---

Box 7.2. **Forecasting**

The business "cycle" is irregular, so a major task of economic researchers is to forecast future GDP. The most well known predictor, called the Index of Leading Economic Indicators, is published by the U.S. Department of Commerce. Other indexes and economic forecasts are calculated by business magazines and university research centers, including McGraw-Hill publishers, the National Industrial Conference Board, and computer models at the Wharton School of Business, Chase Econometrics, Data Resources, and Townsend-Greenspan.

None of these methods for predicting the future are perfect, nor do they appear to be improving. A study by Geoffrey H. Moore of Columbia University's Center for International Business Cycle Research measured an error rate of 1.8 percent for private forecasters during the mid-1980s, less than the 2.9 percent error rate for government projections but still more than double the previous decade's error rate. In recognition of this issue, the National Bureau for Economic Research and the U.S. Federal Reserve Board calculate the *likelihood* of a recession, predicting, for example, a 6 percent chance of a recession in the six months following December 1989 according to the National Bureau, and 20 percent according to the Federal Reserve. As indicated by differences in these two estimates, this method is also not without uncertainty.

---

puter to which only a select few officials have access. Such secrecy is necessary because an unexpected rise or fall in GDP can affect stocks and other financial markets, creating the possibility of personal profit by those who knew GDP data before the general public. In 1985, two government employees were dismissed for such activity; since then, security has been improved.

Advance GDP estimates are almost always revised as more data become available. Experts recommend that researchers wait for final revisions a year later, or even more preferably, look at annual rates of change rather than the volatile and potentially misleading quarterly reports. Often researchers cannot afford to wait for revised GDP estimates. Such haste can cause erroneous economic policy, as occurred in 1965, when the original GDP growth estimates were almost 3 percent too low and therefore failed to warn President Johnson's economic advisers that the Vietnam war had overheated the economy. More

Table 7.1

GDP Revisions (real GDP growth for April–June 1992)

Advance estimate (July 1992)	1.4%
Preliminary estimate (August 1992)	1.4%
Final estimate (September 1992)	1.5%
Annual revision (August 1993)	2.8%
Annual revision (July 1994)	2.4%

Source: U.S. Department of Commerce, *Survey of Current Business* (Washington, D.C.: U.S. Government Printing Office).

recently, GDP growth was overstated at an annual rate by more than 3 percent in the final quarter of 1984, causing the Federal Reserve Board to take steps that slowed an economy they mistakenly thought was growing too fast. Finally, a major revision introduced during the late 1980s to take into account the improved quality of computers caused a nearly $100 billion increase in the measured 1988 GDP, raising the estimated growth between 1982 and 1988 from 3.8 to 4.1 percent. (See Table 7.1.)

These changing estimates underscore the tentative nature of GDP accounts. Because national income and product statistics rely on survey data, adjusted to take into account new trends such as improved quality of computers, there will never be a final "correct" statistic. For researchers, the revisions can be an inconvenience, as for example when results must be recalculated because of newly released data. Fortunately, national income account data are compiled frequently in the Commerce Department publication *Survey of Current Business*, along with comprehensive discussion of revisions to the original numbers.

Problems with GDP

Gross domestic product statistics, both preliminary numbers and subsequent revisions, are estimated according to a set of accounting rules developed by the Commerce Department in consultation with the economics profession. But the standard accounting method is not universally accepted. In recent years several potential problems have led researchers to propose alternative statistics to those officially published.

In designing the original GDP accounts, Simon Kuznets deliberately chose to include all production regardless of moral or aesthetic considerations. Thus it was considered better to add together all production, including cigarettes and the health costs they incur, rather than create different GDP accounts based on the subjective values assigned by each economist. Increased environmental awareness during the 1960s prompted many economists to reassess GDP as a measure of actual well-being. E.J. Mishan, Kenneth Boulding, and others questioned whether *any* GDP growth was desirable if it polluted the environment and depleted scarce resources.

Noted economists William Nordhaus and James Tobin attempted to correct GDP for measurable "economic bads" in a 1972 study, "Is Growth Obsolete?" Their Measure of Economic Welfare computed 35 percent less economic growth between 1925 and 1965 than was measured by traditional GDP. According to Nordhaus and Tobin, this new statistic was a "challenge to economists to produce relevant welfare-oriented measures." But two decades later, their call is largely unheeded; although the Measure of Economic Welfare is mentioned in most economics textbooks, it has not been incorporated into mainstream economic research.

Closely related to the problem of environmental destruction is the issue of resource depletion, which also may accompany an increase in GDP. Robert Repetto, director of the Program in Economics and Institutions at the World Resources Institute, points out that it is possible for a country to increase its income by exploiting its resource base, resulting in short-term gains in income at the expense of permanent loss in wealth. Just as a business keeps track of its assets, Repetto believes National Income Accounts should keep track of its resources. In a 1989 study of Indonesia, Repetto calculated that production rose only about 4 percent per year between 1971 and 1984, far less than the officially reported 7.1 percent. According to Repetto, sufficient data on fuels, timber, minerals, and water resources are available for many countries in order to calculate resource depletion as a part of national income accounts. In 1993, the Bureau of Economic Analysis at the U.S. Department of Commerce agreed to experiment with a "Green GDP." The first account published in 1994 showed an increase in the value of underground resources such as oil, gas, coal and some minerals because of advances in mining and extraction capabilities. Thus, the United States is not in imminent danger of running out of resources, as are countries such as Papua New Guinea, Ethiopia, and Mali. Nonetheless, Repetto warns that a true Green GDP also will include the effects of environmental pollution, obviously a large deduction in U.S. accounts.

Underground Economy

Some economic transactions are not reported to the government, either because the activity is illegal or because those involved want to avoid taxation. Together these transactions constitute the underground economy, a difficult-to-measure entity that may cause underestimation of total economic activity and, according to some economists, overestimation of the poverty rate (see chapter 8) and the unemployment rate (see chapter 9). One of the most frequently cited researchers on the subject, economist Peter Gutmann, estimated the underground economy at about 10 percent of GDP in 1977 based on increased circulation of cash used primarily for illegal or tax-avoiding transactions. But economist Edgar Feige estimated an underground economy of over one-quarter of GDP, although U.S. Commerce Department officials maintained that a much smaller amount goes uncounted in GDP.

Given all the problems in measuring what people want to conceal, it is unlikely that we will ever know the precise size of the underground economy. For researchers, however, the important question is not the actual size of unreported transactions, but their effect on key research variables. For example, the U.S. Commerce Department's main criticism of Gutmann's studies is that he mistakenly assumed all unmeasured activity would be counted in GDP. In fact, many underground transactions are simply transfers of money that do not involve production and thus would not be counted in GDP. (Transactions such as theft may not be voluntary, but they are transfers nonetheless.) For this reason, economist Edward Denison argues that official measures of economic growth are accurate and are not underestimated as Gutmann claims.

A final problem with traditional GDP accounting is that it focuses narrowly on production that can be readily measured. For example, almost all housework is left out of GDP, even though the market value of child care and home maintenance is estimated at about one-third of

GDP, or more than $1,700 billion in 1990. As with the Nordhaus-Tobin Measure of Economic Welfare, however, these necessarily imprecise adjustments to GDP are little used in policy making or research.

Implications

Although professional economists recognize each of these problems in GDP accounting, few corrections are ever made in actual research practice. The major difficulty is that even if adjustments can be justified on logical grounds, the alternative data require many poorly understood assumptions. Researchers do not want their results to depend on data that are not widely credible. Nonetheless, researchers and other users of national economic statistics should be alert to situations where traditional data can be misleading, for example, in comparing the national economies of different countries.

Intercountry Comparisons

Gross domestic product is the most common variable for comparing the economic size of nations. The absolute level of GDP measures a country's overall economic size, while GDP per capita (per person) measures a country's production level, corrected for population size. Technically, most research purposes require the use of *real* GDP, taking into account the effect of inflation (see chapter 11). On the basis of these numbers, countries often are designated "low income" or "less developed." For example, the World Bank classifies forty-one economies as "low income," with 1991 per capita GNP below $635, ranging from Mozambique at $80 and Tanzania at $100 to Indonesia at $610. (Per capita GNP could not be measured for Afghanistan, Burma, Guinea, Kampuchea, and Vietnam.) But these statistics can be misleading for several of the same reasons that cause error in U.S. statistics.

Unreported transactions are especially significant in Third World countries, including the underground activity described earlier, and nonmarket production such as home-grown food, family help in medical care, and community construction of homes. These activities, largely unreported in GDP accounts, make it possible for a resident of Ethiopia to live on $120 per year, an income on which survival would be impossible in the United States. To complicate matters further, some countries' GDP measures are subject to revisions even greater than the multibillion-dollar revisions noted earlier for the United States. In countries without sophisticated data networks, new products or services may go unrecognized for years, requiring substantial changes in existing statistics. Major revisions of this sort have taken place for national economic data of Malaysia, Bangladesh, and Egypt.

Uncounted items may cause a bias in highly developed countries as well. For example, residents of many Western European countries enjoy superior vacation and holiday benefits (nearly seven weeks total per year in Sweden). Such benefits contribute in a major way to well-being, but they are not accounted for in traditional GDP accounting. In summary, although there are few alternatives to GDP for comparisons between countries, researchers need to be aware of the many factors that cause GDP to be an imperfect measure of economic development.

Measuring Productivity

For the United States, recent economic controversy has focused on changes in GDP, most especially a measured downward trend in U.S. economic growth since about 1970. One of the most frequently cited indications of this slowdown is the decline in productivity as estimated by the U.S. Labor Department's Bureau of Labor Statistics. Technically, productivity can be measured in many ways, but the most common statistic, and the one regarded as most reliable, is labor productivity measured as output per hour of labor. There appears to be a definite downward trend in this statistic during recent decades, which has prompted many newspaper and magazines stories about the "U.S. productivity crisis." But there are such severe problems in measuring productivity that economists disagree about whether this crisis is waning or even whether it ever existed.

At one extreme, economist Harry Magdoff argues that productivity data are unable to "tell us anything fundamental about the nature of the economy itself." In his view, productivity problems are a myth, generally accepted "by constant repetition and widespread publicity." Other economists accept the measured productivity collapse since the 1970s as a real economic event, but maintain it was a transient setback, probably caused by the energy crises of the 1970s. And, of course, many economists believe there is an ongoing productivity crisis. Why is productivity so difficult to understand? At least three measurement problems confront researchers.

Figure 7.1. **Year-to-Year Productivity Changes.** Business-sector output per hour.

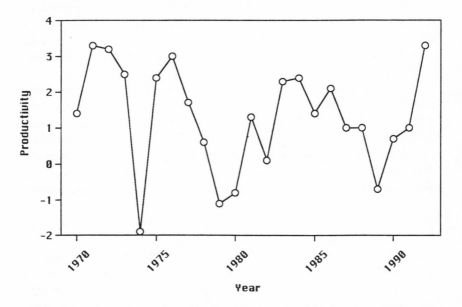

Source: U.S. Department of Commerce, *Economic Report of the President 1994* (Washington, D.C.: U.S. Government Printing Office, 1994), p. 323.

Which Years?

The first problem is identifying the trend in productivity. As shown in Figure 7.1, annual productivity statistics jump from year to year in an apparently erratic manner. Selective choice of years can lead to a misleading picture of productivity, as for example in a widely distributed U.S. Chamber of Commerce program supporting President Reagan's economic policies that used productivity data for 1966, 1973, 1978, and 1979, conveniently selected to show a steady decline in productivity. Other years—1969, 1973, 1976, 1983, for example—would have indicated *increasing* productivity.

These erratic year-to-year productivity changes are caused by fluctuations in the business cycle, that is, alternating periods of growth and stagnation in the economy. When sales begin to falter, employers cut back on output, thereby causing measured productivity to fall until workers are laid off. Conversely, when the economy starts to pick up after a recession, output at first increases faster than new hiring, causing an apparent increase in productivity. Accurate use of productivity data requires correction for the business cycle, for example, looking at productivity changes between peak growth years. On this basis, a definite productivity decline appears to have occurred since 1973, but this interpretation is clouded by two less easily resolved measurement problems.

Changing Products

One major problem for productivity statistics is that today's output includes items that once did not exist. Thus it is difficult to measure productivity for the manufacture of VCRs and microwave ovens. In addition, other products changed very quickly in quality: a typical home computer purchased in 1990 is entirely obsolete and is no longer manufactured in 1995. The U.S. Commerce Department attempts to measure these changes in GDP accounts, but substantial gaps remain. For example, according to one study, *all* construction-sector productivity improvements between 1948 and 1986 were overlooked because of problems in measuring the value of buildings. Other researchers charge that despite new procedures introduced during the late 1980s, major errors remained in the measurement of computer productivity, causing a likely underestimation in productivity.

Services

The most vexing challenge is measuring the productivity of services not associated with a physical product. In the goods-producing sector, productivity is based on the number of items produced. Although this task is complicated by the changing quality of goods (see above), at least government statisticians have data, for example, on the number of cars, computers, and shirts produced. But what is the productivity of a physician, a schoolteacher, or a police officer? Is the physician more productive for seeing twice as many patients in an hour, or the teacher more productive with a larger class size, or the police officer more productive for giving more tickets? Ironically, the issue is illustrated at the Bureau of Labor Statistics itself, where we would wonder if productivity increased when statisticians attempted to measure productivity in forty service-sector industries in 1992, an increase from fifteen service industries in 1982, despite no increase in staff. One staff member explained, "I guess you could say we're becoming more productive, or perhaps it would be more accurate to say we don't have enough people to do a job that in any event is just about impossible."

Because of these difficulties, the Bureau of Labor Statistics attempts to measure productivity for only 30 percent of the service industry, leaving out health care, real estate, stockbrokers, and insurance. Moreover, the productivity data that are available may be highly inaccurate. For example, banking and retail sales show stagnant productivity despite evidence that recently introduced computers speeded up operations in both industries. The large gaps and likely measurement error in service-sector data cause many economists to be uncertain about the effect of the service sector on the overall economy. In particular, it may be premature to attribute the overall decline in U.S. productivity to the service sector.

Implications

The problem of year-to-year changes in productivity caused by the business cycle can be resolved with the adjustment suggested above. But the problem of changing products and services is a dilemma that requires far more caution in the use of productivity statistics than is commonly found in media reports or even some research projects. Ongoing cooperation between the Commerce Department and its critics may result in better productivity data, especially for fast-changing sectors such as the computer industry. But problems in measuring service-sector productivity are so fundamental that they will not be easily overcome. At issue are policy decisions in areas such as government services and health care where it is alleged that costs have increased without comparable improvements in output. Researchers should interpret these numbers with extreme caution, realizing that some overall productivity statistics, such as "private business productivity," include questionable productivity inferences for the service sector.

The Savings Rate

In an unusual display of unanimity, both Democrats and Republicans on Congress's Joint Economic Committee declared in a 1989 report that the nation's chief economic problem is a low savings rate. As evidence, policy makers point to the Commerce Department's estimate

Figure 7.2. **U.S. Savings Rates.** Personal savings rate; flow-of-funds household savings; Change in net worth. Personal saving is a percentage of disposable personal income; flow-of-funds household saving is a percentage of GDP; change in net worth is a four-year moving average as a percentage of GDP.

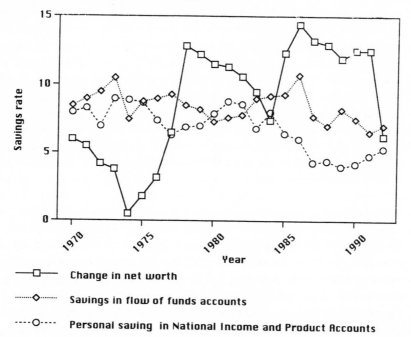

Change in net worth

Savings in flow of funds accounts

Personal saving in National Income and Product Accounts

Sources: U.S. Department of Commerce, *Economic Report of the President 1994* (Washington, D.C.: U.S. Government Printing Office, 1994), p. 260; Dean Baker, "Conceptual and Accounting Issues in the Analysis of Saving, Investment and Macroeconomic Activity," in Robert Pollin, *The Macroeconomics of Finance, Savings, and Investment* (Ann Arbor: University of Michigan Press, 1995).

of personal savings that fell to 4 percent in 1993 from 9 percent in 1973. But according to many economists, this statistic is misleading because there are both problems in measuring the personal savings rate and theoretical questions about its appropriateness for assessing the health of the national economy. (See Figure 7.2.)

Which Savings Rate?

The most commonly used savings rate comes from the U.S. Commerce Department's GDP accounts. It measures a decline in the savings rate that is quite different from estimates by the U.S. Federal Reserve's flow-of-funds accounts, which show household savings falling only slightly since 1973, and the Federal Reserve's *Balance Sheets for the U.S. Economy,* which measure a rising savings rate for most of the 1980s.

Measurement Problems

One reason for the different savings rates is their varying data sources. The Commerce Department's savings rate is based on national income accounts that subtract spending from total income to estimate how much is saved. The Federal Reserve flow of funds tracks money through the financial system, while the balance sheet estimates the savings rate based on changes in asset ownership.

The major conceptual difference between the three savings rates is the way each counts the value of assets such as real estate, stocks, and bonds, which are a form of savings for many households. The flow of funds includes consumer durables not counted in the GDP accounts. The balance-sheet method includes almost all assets, but is complicated because of uncertainties about how to value these assets. For example, what happens to household savings when the stock market rises or falls? Using what is called the "market value" approach, the balance sheet measures dramatically rising and falling savings rates as the stock market went boom and bust during the 1980s and 1990s. If the research goal is to measure consumer behavior, these erratic market values may exaggerate how households perceive their savings.

To complicate matters further, many economists believe that the frequently cited *personal* savings statistics are misleading. Although popular newspaper and magazine articles suggest a link between declining personal savings rates and declining investment, the two trends may not be related because much investment comes from *business* savings. Some economists go further, maintaining that investment is unrelated to savings altogether. In this view, investment depends on the health of financial markets, which are largely unaffected by household or business savings.

Implications

Controversy about the savings rate is instructive in the dangers of trying to oversimplify economic problems to a single statistic. The idea of "spendthrift" U.S. households hurting the U.S. economy carried a moral tone that gained attention in popular accounts. But when analyzed closely, savings are a complex concept, both difficult to measure and tricky to conceptualize in terms of their effect on the economy. Researchers need to take care to assess the accuracy of the numbers they use, as well as the relevance of those statistics to the policy question at hand.

International Statistics

In recent years, the U.S. international economic situation has come under increased scrutiny. Headlines asked: Is the U.S. trade deficit too large? Are foreigners buying too much of the United States? Answers to these questions depend critically on the accuracy of statistics collected by the U.S. Commerce Department and the U.S. Federal Reserve.

Month-to-Month Volatility

Month-to-month changes in U.S. trade typically are reported as important news: "October's trade deficit highest ever," followed confusingly by "November trade deficit falls." These sudden shifts in monthly trade figures do not usually signify a trend. Often a single event unrelated to the economy's health will cause trade figures to change, as for example, in 1986 when the Japanese government bought more than $2 billion worth of gold for medals honoring Emperor Hirohito's sixtieth anniversary. Because the gold was shipped through the United States (it was purchased in Europe), exports temporarily appeared to improve.

Most experts recommend that we look at quarterly or annual data instead of monthly data. Even so, the extent of the U.S. deficit was difficult to measure because of measurement problems.

Poor-Quality Data

One indication that worldwide trade data are inaccurate is the difference between all countries' imports and all countries' exports, which should match because every import is also another country's export. But according to the Organization for Economic Cooperation and Development there has been as much as an $80 billion excess in total imports measured worldwide compared to total exports. Much of this error may occur because of the difficulty in measuring services. According to Harry L. Freeman, vice-president of American Express, for the United States alone, as much as $40 billion in administration, legal advice, consulting, and other services provided in other countries was underreported in 1983.

To make matters worse for U.S. data, because of budget cuts in the early 1980s, the number of Customs agents who gather the basic data on imports was reduced at precisely the time when imports surged. In 1985, more than one-half of the trade entries were behind schedule, so shipments were not recorded in the month they actually occurred. In addition, investigators found significant nonreporting by truckers carrying goods to Canada, the largest trading partner of the United States, and comical miscoding of country origins, such as "not available" data mistakenly ascribed to Namibia, which is also abbreviated "NA."

The Real Deficit?

Finally, some researchers argue that the official statistics misrepresent the actual trade situation by not including production in other countries by U.S.-owned firms. This adjustment causes the U.S. deficit with Japan to disappear entirely because the Japanese spend nearly twice as much on IBM, Coca Cola, Xerox, and other U.S. brand goods manufactured in Japan than U.S. consumers spend on Japanese imports. On this basis, some economists argue that the United States competes well in the international arena, a success masked by the official trade deficit.

In Debt to the World?

According to official U.S. Commerce Department statistics, during the mid-1980s, the U.S. net investment position became negative, that is the value of U.S. investments abroad totaled less than foreign investment in the United States. By 1988, the officially measured gap totaled more than $500 billion. This enormous sum prompted a debate among economists about whether the United States was selling off America and living on the proceeds or whether the country was simply enjoying the benefits of being the most prudent place in the world to invest. But so many economists criticized the official measure of net investment that the U.S. government abandoned it in 1991. The major problem was that it valued investments at their original cost, thus underestimating the current value of U.S. investments abroad, many of them older than foreign investments in the United States. New statistics were introduced that caused the measured 1988 investment gap to fall to somewhere between $38 billion and $184 billion, depending on the method used to update the cost of older investments. By 1991 the net international investment position of the United States had grown to $300 billion using the new method. Economists still debate whether this gap measures failure or success of the U.S. economy, but at least the official numbers more closely reflect the actual value of investments at home and abroad.

Implications

These measurement problems in trade statistics pose different challenges to researchers. The misleading character of month-to-month trade data is widely recognized by economists, if not by newspaper and magazine reporters. Longer-term data are an easy solution. The issue of inaccurate or missing data is less controversial, but one that will have no solution until international trade statistics are improved. The final controversy about the role of foreign debt is a complex theoretical question. Researchers need to contend with disagreement among economists about the impact of the debt, as well as several ways in which the debt can be measured.

Summary

In this chapter we have seen debates about a wide range of national economic issues. One goal was to unravel the source of apparently contradictory findings that appear both to applaud the success of the U.S. economy during the 1980s and to measure apparent continued economic decline. Three major problems contributed to contradictory statistics.

First, the time period of analysis is critical. For productivity, it was necessary to take into account the business cycle that causes swings in the rate of productivity unrelated to the long-term historical trend that researchers want to measure. For GDP and trade statistics, the lesson was to use data covering a long enough time period to smooth out short-term fluctuations unrelated to the overall economic issues of interest. Both of these research precautions are relatively easy to follow with well-documented procedures available in the economics literature.

Second, and less easily resolved, is the problem of unavailable information. Many areas of economic activity are not readily measured because there are no prices attached to products, or because the prices used do not represent actual value. Gross domestic product leaves out entire sectors of production, such as housework, because no prices are attached to those services, a bias that strongly affects comparisons between countries. The same problem also affects comparisons of countries with different levels of vacation benefits because leisure time is not a commodity with a price. Similarly, investment in the form of education and training is not counted as part of the investment category of GDP accounts because the increased value of human "investments" has no easily measured resale price (see case study question 2). Commerce Department statisticians recognize these measurement problems and have commented extensively on them. Nonetheless, it is the responsibility of researchers to make sure that their use of the statistics is not unduly influenced by what is not included in the underlying data.

Third, the service sector is a problem area for economic statistics, complicating the measurement of productivity and international trade. This sector is growing and thus will provide an increasing challenge to researchers. In response to the issue, government researchers have developed new statistics, but whether a service-dominated economy can be measured as accurately as one dominated by the production of tangible goods remains to be seen.

The challenge for researchers is to make discriminating judgments when competing statistics are available: when should a statistic be used and what are its shortcomings? For example, as this chapter demonstrates, there are objections to official GDP accounting methods —and economics textbooks list even more. Yet there are practically no widely accepted alternative statistics, so most researchers have little choice but to use official numbers. At a minimum, researchers can recognize and cite the importance of the assumptions that lie behind the traditional methods.

Competing measures also exist for the savings rate, the trade deficit, and international investment. In these cases, researchers can use economic theory to make informed choices between different statistics.

This link between theory and the use of data should be clearly stated. Failure to do so is a major shortcoming in many research projects. Such lack of theoretical clarity contributes to the confusing state of affairs in which it seems that statistics can be chosen to fit any conclusion, when in fact it is the implicit economic theory that leads researchers to use particular statistics.

Case Study Questions

1. The U.S. Department of Commerce defines U.S. assets as those belonging to residents who have been in the United States twelve months or longer. What should happen to the estimate of U.S. international accounts as new immigrants move to the United States? (This correction is rarely made.)

2. In U.S. national economic statistics, investment includes only physical investments, such as machinery or buildings. But according to economist Robert Eisner, almost one-half of the U.S. stock of productive capital takes the intangible form of investment in people and ideas. How might the traditional measure including only physical investments lead to inefficient policies regarding investment?

3. During the 1980s, the Bureau of Labor Statistics developed measures of productivity for some government services. For which types of government employment would it be possible to measure productivity with reasonable accuracy? Which government services do not lend themselves to easy measurement of productivity?

4. Critics of the World Bank charge that the use of official GDP statistics causes a bias against investment projects that would help women. Why might this occur?

5. Assume the underground economy is 10 percent of GDP, and GDP is about $6,000 billion, and there are about 100 million U.S. households. Based on these data, approximately how much does each household consume in "underground" products? Does this number seem a reasonable estimate? Explain.

Chapter 8

Wealth, Income, and Poverty

Economists differentiate between wealth, a stock of value such as a house or stock, and income, a flow of value over time, such as a salary or interest payment. Data on wealth and income typically come from different sources, each with its own set of problems. There is relatively little information on the distribution of wealth in the United States. One reason for the scarcity is difficulty of measurement. Because many items of wealth have not been sold recently, they do not have a readily identifiable price. A second reason for the lack of data on wealth is its ownership by a relatively small group who are not eager to share information about how much wealth they own. As the controversies below illustrate, this second factor severely restricts how much we know about wealth. Unlike wealth, incomes leave a "paper trail" of readily measured dollar amounts. As a result, income is well documented in a variety of government and private-sector sources. But, as this chapter demonstrates, there is still serious disagreement about fundamental findings, including the trend in well-being for the typical family and the extent of poverty in the United States.

Data Sources

Wealth

Federal Reserve Survey

The most comprehensive survey on wealth holdings is conducted by the U.S. Federal Reserve, a quasi-independent government body that

Where the Numbers Come From

Organizations	Data sources	Key publications
Board of Governors, U.S. Federal Reserve System	Survey of Consumer Finances	*Federal Reserve Bulletin*
Bureau of the Census, U.S. Department of Commerce	Survey of Income and Program Participation; U.S. Census of Population; Current Population Survey	*Census of Population; Current Population Reports* (Series P-60)
Bureau of Labor Statistics, U.S. Department of Labor	Establishment Survey	*Employment and Earnings; Current Wage Developments*
Internal Revenue Service, U.S. Department of the Treasury	Tax returns	*Statistics of Income*

Summary data in *Statistical Abstract of the United States.*

acts as the country's central bank (see chapter 11). At three-year intervals during the 1980s, the Fed conducted its own independent survey of several thousand households, asking 100 pages of questions about each family's financial status.

> *Data Sample:* The 1986 Survey of Consumer Finances found that 19.3 percent of households owned stocks, with a median value of $6,000 and an average value of more than $80,000.

Survey of Income and Program Participation

The second major U.S. wealth survey is conducted by the Census Bureau. These data were collected on a regular basis only between 1850 and 1890 and then not again until 1984 in the Survey of Income and Program Participation (SIPP).

Data Sample: In the 1984 survey, equity in homes constituted 59.7 percent of the wealth of households with incomes less than $10,000, but only 30.1 percent of the wealth of households with incomes over $48,000.

Indirect Estimates from Tax Records

Historical data on wealth distribution are calculated by two major methods. The "estate-multiplier" method pioneered by Robert J. Lampman of the National Bureau for Economic Research uses Internal Revenue Service records for the 1 percent of estates subject to taxes (only holdings greater than $600,000 in 1987). A related method called "income capitalization" works backward from tax reports of rent, dividends, and interest to estimate wealth from which these incomes are derived.

Data Sample: Lampman measured a decline in the share of wealth held by the top 1 percent from 36 percent in 1929 to 26 percent in 1956.

Direct Counts

The extraordinarily rich usually are well-known individuals about whom information can be obtained from public sources. Based on stock-ownership records, media coverage, and independent investigation, *Forbes* and *Fortune* magazines each estimates wealth holdings for a select number of these individuals.

Income

U.S. Census

Every decennial Census of Population since 1940 has included questions about income, providing researchers with a tremendously detailed data source, but one that is available only at ten-year intervals.

Data Sample: In the 1990 U.S. Census, Hunters Creek Village, Texas, reported median household income of $134,961, the highest of any city in the state.

Current Population Survey

By far the most frequently cited source of income data is the Census Bureau's Current Population Survey (CPS). Covering more than 60,000 households, the CPS is the largest survey taken in between census years. (See chapter 9 on the origins of the CPS.)

> *Data Sample:* According to the Current Population Survey, Manchester-Nashua, New Hampshire, had the fastest increasing per capita income between 1979 and 1983 of all U.S. metropolitan areas.

Bureau Labor Statistics' Establishment Survey

Data collected in the BLS Establishment Survey are often quite accurate because the survey is based on employer records rather than on respondent recall. But the Establishment Survey measures earnings for individual jobs, not the total income for a worker, who may have more than one employer, or for a family with several separate sources of income.

> *Data Sample:* In the March 1994 Establishment Survey, the lowest-paying industry was "Women's blouses and shirts," with average hourly earnings of $6.35 for nonsupervisory production workers.

Panel Study of Income Dynamics

For comparisons over time, or longitudinal studies, researchers frequently turn to a private survey, the University of Michigan's Panel Study of Income Dynamics (PSID). Begun with 5,000 households in 1968, PSID followed 7,000 households in 1986, including many of the original sample, as well as those split off when children married or couples separated.

Controversies

Are the Rich Getting Richer?

Are the rich getting richer? The answer is: "We don't know." Attempts during the 1980s to measure wealth distribution generated considerable controversy, but ended in continued uncertainty whether wealth own-

---

Box 8.1. **I've Got a Secret**

In addition to the small sample size and possible coding errors described in the text, data on wealth are subject to outright refusal of respondents to answer questions. The problem is particularly severe for the Census Bureau's Survey of Income and Program Participation. Nearly 90 percent of respondents report the size of their checking accounts, but more than 40 percent refuse to tell the interviewer the value of stocks and mutual funds. The University of Michigan's Survey of Consumer Finances does somewhat better, failing to gather data on stocks for 25 percent of respondents. Research on this type of measurement error suggests that those who do not answer are likely to be either poorer than average or far richer. The latter group introduces a possibly critical error into all wealth data: we are missing precisely those who own the most. Although statisticians who gather the data are aware of its shortcomings, the problem is rarely highlighted in official reports and almost never mentioned in press coverage about the concentration of wealth.

---

ership is becoming more or less concentrated. Nonetheless, this research failure illustrates the problem of surveying wealth or any other variable so unequally distributed that even large surveys are unlikely to include those who own a significant part of the total wealth.

In 1983 the U.S. Federal Reserve changed its usual format for measuring wealth by adding 438 individuals already known to be wealthy. In theory, this commonly used method of "enriching" the data sample should have increased our knowledge about wealth holdings. Indeed, the survey indicated that the share of wealth going to the top 0.5 percent increased to 35 percent in 1983 from 25 percent in 1962. But these startling results were not destined for much public notice. As usual, the Federal Reserve survey was published in the *Federal Reserve Bulletin*, from which the numbers made their way into academic studies and textbooks.

Then, in 1986, the Joint Economic Committee of Congress released its own interpretation of the Federal Reserve's study using catchy labels —"super rich," "very rich," "rich," and "everyone else"—to underscore the vast holdings of the wealthy that apparently had increased since 1962. After a barrage of media reports on these results, the Reagan administration asked the Federal Reserve to reexamine the survey. Suddenly an error appeared: one of the 438 wealthy individuals was not as rich as he or she reported. Removing this individual caused the estimate for the share owned by the super-rich to fall by almost 10 percent, wiping out the apparent increase since 1962.

The accuracy of the one data point is difficult to determine. A 1986 follow-up survey showing this person's wealth to be only $2.3 million led the Fed to conclude that the reported 1983 wealth of $200 million was a coding error. Critics responded that the individual, known to own Texas oil and gas wells, indeed may have suffered a financial setback reported between 1983 and 1986. Whatever the actual circumstances of this one Texas magnate, the dispute shows how difficult it is to measure wealth. A basic research principle is to include a survey sample that is large enough so that errors for a single individual do not affect overall findings. Even the relatively large Federal Reserve survey —fewer than 4,000 households—was still too small to measure changes in wealth holdings accurately because so few individuals owned so much.

What Is Wealth?

For the less-than-extremely wealthy, Federal Reserve Board data are relatively accurate. Overall they measure total average net worth in 1986 at more than $145,000 per household, while the median net worth was nearly $44,000 (see Box 8.2 on the difference between average and median). For black and Hispanic households, median net worth was only $11,000 in 1986, about one-fifth of median net worth for white households.

Most household wealth is in housing, an average value of $80,000 in 1986 for those who owned a home. For some research purposes, it is best to exclude ownership of homes and other consumer durable goods in order to focus on ownership of wealth that is a source of economic power, such as stocks and bonds. This "financial wealth" is even more unequally distributed than total wealth; the top 10 percent of households owned 86 percent of financial wealth in 1983. Some researchers argue that we should move in the other direction, expanding the definition of wealth to include the value of pensions and social security. Although most people do not consider these benefits to be wealth, they are similar to bonds and other arrangements that promise a source of future income. A former chief economic adviser in the Reagan admin-

---

Box 8.2. **Mean, Median, and Mode**

The *median* is the data point for which one-half the observations are above and one-half below; the *mean* is the average, or in this case, total income divided by number in the sample; the *mode* is the data point with the most observations, a statistic rarely used in income analysis. Median income is the most common starting point for research on the "typical" household. A relatively small number of families with very high incomes skews the mean at about 15 percent higher than the median. Thus, mean annual household income in the United States was about $39,000 in 1992, while the median income was $31,000. The major drawback to using the median is that it is unchanged by redistribution of income above and below it. For example, when the poor become poorer and the rich become richer, it is possible for the median to stay the same.

---

istration, Martin Feldstein, advocated such an approach, by which measured inequality in U.S. wealth holdings would be reduced by nearly 30 percent.

Researchers need to choose carefully between these different measures of wealth. For analysis of the distribution of resources, total wealth measures are appropriate, perhaps also including the value of retirement funds. But if the research goal is to understand how wealth affects power, then it might be proper to use a narrower definition that excludes housing and retirement benefits.

Who Is the Richest of Them All?

In 1994, the wealthiest individuals in the *Fortune* and *Forbes* surveys were as follows. Both *Forbes* and *Fortune* openly discuss problems in finding out about wealth; every year an individual will catapult to near the top when it is discovered that he or she is in fact quite wealthy. A previously uncounted Mars Candy Company benefactor, billionaire heiress Jacqueline Mars Vogel, was belatedly "discovered" and added to the *Forbes* list in 1987. Lester Crown, owner of General Dynamics stock inherited from his father, as well as real estate and sports teams, weighed in at $5.7 billion in the 1987 *Fortune* list, but only $2.1 billion according to *Forbes*.

Wealth (in billions)	
Fortune (worldwide)	*Forbes* (U.S. only)
1. Sultan of Brunei $37.0	1. Warren Edward Buffett $8.325
2. Walton Family $24.0	2. William Henry Gates $6.16
3. Taikichiro Mori $14.0	3. John Werner Kluge $5.9

One source of such discrepancies is the lack of information on privately held wealth. The Mars Company, for example, is one of a small number of large firms still owned entirely by a few individuals. Unlike publicly held corporations, there is no stock price to estimate the value of the company (see chapter 10). Similarly, *Forbes* and *Fortune* must estimate the value of property that has not been bought or sold in recent years. Finally, family trusts complicate wealth measurement by dispersing fortunes among various descendants. As a result, *Forbes* publishes a separate wealth list for total family holdings, led by the DuPonts, Gettys, and Rockefellers.

Are We Better Off?

Is the typical American better off than twenty years ago? This simple question has provoked a broad spectrum of answers depending on the data source used. Between 1973 and 1993, Americans were somewhere between 20 percent *worse* off measured by average weekly earnings and almost 30 percent *better* off measured by income per capita. At stake in the interpretation of these data is the direction of U.S. economic policy. (See Figure 8.1.)

Per Capita Income

The rosiest view of economic progress is based on per capita personal income, a statistic from the U.S. Commerce Department national income accounts (see chapter 7). Per capita income is simply the total of all wages, interest, rents, and other incomes divided by the number of people in the country. Because it showed 20 percent growth during the 1980s, per capita income was cited as evidence of success in the Reagan–Bush economic program. Critics charge that the statistic was

Figure 8.1. **Are We Better Off?** Amounts shown are in 1992 dollars.

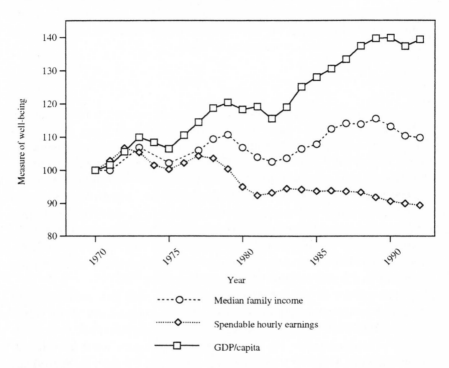

Note:	1970	1992
GDP/capita	$18,799	$23,792
Median family income	$33,519	$36,812
Average hourly spendable earnings	$9.84	$8.80

Sources: U.S. Department of Commerce, *Economic Report of the President, 1994* (Washington, D.C.: U.S. Government Printing Office, 1994), p. 277; U.S. Bureau of the Census, *Statistical Abstract of the United States, 1994* (Washington, D.C.: U.S. Government Printing Office, 1994), p. 469; Thomas E. Weisskopf, "Use of Hourly Earnings Proposed to Revive Spendable Earnings Series," *Monthly Labor Review,* November 1984, p. 40, update courtesy of David M. Gordon, Graduate Faculty, New School for Social Research.

misleading because the number of wage earners has increased relative to the number of dependents. Or, to make the same point with a story: Assume a household of four people in 1980 with one person working outside the home earning $20,000 had a per capita income of $5,000. If, in 1990, the original worker's income falls to $18,000, but a second family member now works outside the home, and earns $10,000, then per capita income increases to $7,000 ([$18,000 + $10,000] ÷ 4). In other words, total income increased, but only because more people were working, each of whom earned less.

Earnings

What is the trend in earnings of the typical worker? This question changes the original question from one of *income* from all sources including rents, interests, and dividends, to one of *earnings*, including only wages and salaries. (Sometimes earnings is defined also to include self-employment income and farm income.) For many years, the Bureau of Labor Statistics Establishment Survey measured "spendable weekly earnings for the typical family of four with one full time worker and three dependents." According to this measure, this statistically "average" family was better off in 1959 than in 1981! In 1982, the Reagan administration suspended publication of the series on the grounds that it was inflammatory and inaccurate.

Even critics of the administration agreed that this measure used outdated assumptions about tax rates and the composition of the workforce. But even though correcting for these deficiencies was a relatively simple matter, no official replacement data were introduced. Consequently, University of Michigan economist Thomas E. Weisskopf attempted to revive the series on his own, using spendable *hourly* earnings data in order to avoid the problems with the discredited *weekly* earnings data. According to Weisskopf, this new statistical series still shows steady deterioration of earnings after 1972, falling by more than 13 percent by 1987. Thus it appears that pay levels for U.S. workers indeed stagnated during the 1970s and 1980s.

Family Income

One way to combine the effect of additional workers with the effect of lower earnings is to look at the trend in income for household units. In fact, the most widely cited statistic on income is featured in the annual Current Population Survey publication, "Money and Income of Households, Families and Persons." According to this source, median family income was nearly constant during most of the 1970s, 1980s, and early 1990s at about $35,000 in 1991 buying power, and improved to only

$35,939 in 1991. This statistic is often quoted, but usually without reference to serious shortcomings in the data.

One problem is that the U.S. Census carefully defines a "family" as two or more related individuals living together, thus leaving out more than 30 million individuals in 1990 who lived in nonfamily households, either as single-person households or with unrelated individuals. Median income for families is more than double the median income for nonfamily individuals, so looking only at families overstates the typical income of U.S. households. On the other hand, in recent years nonfamily household incomes increased faster than the average, so research only on families underestimates improvement in overall well-being.

A second problem with family income data is that they do not take into account the decline in family size from 3.58 in 1970 to 3.16 in 1993. According to one measure of family well-being, these smaller families are 20 percent better off because there are fewer children to support. Other researchers object that these families might have fewer children precisely because of stagnating incomes. In this view, families are worse off because they could not afford as many children as they might have liked.

Because of these problems, researchers need to be careful in using the family income data. Overall, the limited improvement in the median family income level was a worrisome trend during the 1970s and 1980s. But used by itself it does not tell the whole story about changing living standards.

Disappearing Middle Class

Most social scientists agree that top income groups did well during the 1980s, better than middle- and lower-income groups. But how much better? During the 1992 presidential campaign Governor Bill Clinton read MIT economist Paul Krugman's study showing that 60 percent of the gains from economic growth in the 1980s went to the top 1 percent of families. His press secretary reported that Clinton "was reading the paper that morning and went crazy. The story proved a point he had been trying to make for months, so he added the statistic to his repertoire."

The Republican rejoinder was twofold. According to a study by the Bush administration's Treasury Department, only 11.3 percent of income gains went to the top 1 percent, far less than the 60 percent reported by Krugman. One reason for this difference was the definition of the richest 1 percent. In the Treasury Department study, the top group was defined as those who *began* the time period at the top. This approach minimized the gain for the rich because many who started at the top were there only temporarily; during the following years, their incomes fell because of retirement or a return to more normal earnings. Standard statistical practice is to define the top group at the midpoint of the study's time period. As an illustration, Urban Institute economist Isabel V. Sawhill pointed out that for the years 1976 to 1986, defining the rich at the beginning of the time period causes them to appear to lose 11 percent of their income share, whereas if the rich are defined at the end of the ten years, their share rises by 65 percent. Because the Treasury Department refused to test the robustness of their conclusions by using different assumptions, experts discounted their study.

Republicans also study criticized Krugman for beginning his analysis with 1977, including several years before the 1981 inauguration of Republican President Reagan. A study released by Republican Senators Phil Gramm and Pete Domenici showed gains favoring the rich during the 1979–83, "Carter–Reagan" period, but nearly identical gains for the rich and poor between 1983 and 1989, the years they identified as most affected by President Reagan's economic program. The critical period was the severe 1980–82 recession, when we would expect inequality to worsen. Depending on whether these years are defined as "Democrat" or "Republican," the growth in equality can be assigned to either party.

Mobility

Some conservatives maintain that the emphasis on gains for the rich are misplaced because the United States has so much economic mobility. In this view, distribution of income at one point in time does not matter as much as the potential for large numbers of people to reach the upper echelon. Indeed, year-to-year income statistics show considerable "churning," as it is called by statisticians. University of Michigan economist Joel Slemrod found that typically 20 to 25 percent of individuals shift in and out of the top income categories from year to year, largely from transitory negative effects such as illness or one-time positive changes such as earnings from the sale of property.

These temporary transitions suggest that year-to-year data are a poor guide to the actual level of equality. Instead, sociologists typically study mobility between generations: do children fall in the same economic category as their parents? In 1992, two studies using new data sources, the Panel Study of Income Dynamics and the National Longitudinal Survey (see chapter 5), economists Gary Solon and David J. Zimmerman independently challenged traditional ideas about mobility in the United States. Both studies looked at fathers' and sons' income data for a longer period of time and for a larger random sample than had been available previously. Instead of nearly zero correlation between fathers and sons as measured in most earlier research, Solon and Zimmerman found correlations of at least 0.4, where 1.0 would have meant that every son fell in the same category as his father. Solon concludes: "It's not that you inherit the same position, but there's substantial correlation." These findings are controversial. The true extent of economic mobility will remain unresolved until we have better data, including information on women and daughters, for whom income data are especially scant.

Statistics for Every Theory?

At this point it may be tempting to question the usefulness of income statistics that tell such conflicting stories. If policy advisers from every political persuasion can find ample evidence to support any position, what good are income statistics? The answer is that each income statistic measures a slightly different concept; they must be used together, with careful distinction about what is being measured. For example, per capita income provides an indication of well-being, but it tells us nothing about the distribution of that well-being, which must be measured by other statistics. The confusing statistics on earnings and family income showed that major changes were occurring in the labor force and the family in addition to an underlying slowdown in the growth of income. Finally, the disappearing-middle-class debate illustrated what can go wrong when researchers and the popular media reporting the findings do not pay careful attention to the limitations inherent in the data. Research by the U.S. Treasury Department faced considerable criticism when it was shown that alternative assumptions caused a reversal in their findings. The lesson for researchers is that it is necessary to anticipate objections by proving the robustness of results under different assumptions.

What Is Poverty?

Research on poverty typically confronts a perplexing question: how to define poverty? The easy solution is to rely on the official U.S. Census Bureau poverty line, the most commonly used in social science research. But, as demonstrated by its origins, the Census Bureau poverty line is quite arbitrary and is therefore inadequate for some purposes.

The Official Poverty Line

During the early 1960s, Molly Orshansky, a Social Security Administration staff economist, was asked to develop a definition of poverty for the War on Poverty. By her own admission, this "Orshansky" poverty line was a compromise between scientific justification and political expediency. She began with a U.S. Agriculture Department estimate for a nutritionally sound diet and then estimated the total poverty budget based on the proportion of food expenditures in a typical total family budget. Orshansky was unhappy with these assumptions, especially the food budget, which was intended as a stopgap grocery list but required a sophistication of purchasing and food preparation that was not likely to be practiced by poor families. But Orshansky was under pressure from the administration to calculate a poverty line at about $3,000 for a family of four, low enough so that the War on Poverty could reasonably be expected to help all those designated as poor. She had more leeway in defining poverty for other-size families, so she set the poverty line on slightly more favorable terms for smaller-size households and families with more than four people.

Not surprisingly, these highly arbitrary poverty lines have been criticized on many grounds. But researchers disagree whether this measure under- or overestimates the actual rate of poverty.

The Poverty Line Is Too Low

The official U.S. poverty line is an absolute standard, adjusted only for inflation. (In 1990 there was renewed debate about how to adjust for inflation, including a Census Bureau proposal to use a new inflation adjustment that would substantially reduce the official poverty line; see chapter 11.) Over the years since 1965, the standard of living in the United States has increased, so that on a *relative* basis, the poverty line has fallen. In 1965, it was just under one-half the U.S. median income; by 1986 the official poverty line was less than one-third of the median income. If the poverty line measured poverty at a constant *relative* rate, then measured poverty would have increased between 1965 and 1988, instead of falling, as it did in the official absolute standard.

The Poverty Line Is Too High

Others have criticized the Orshansky poverty line for overestimating the poverty line. For example, economist Rose Friedman points out that poor families spend a higher proportion of their income on food than the ratio used by Orshansky. Friedman recalculates Orshansky's poverty level with new ratios, estimating U.S. poverty at one-half its official level.

A second correction that reduces the apparent level of poverty is to include the value of noncash government programs such as food stamps, school meals, housing subsidies, and medical care. One such effort measured government programs at their market value, that is, what it would cost the poor to buy services comparable to those provided by the government. By this estimate, the poverty rate falls by about one-third, which prompted President Reagan's chief economic adviser Martin Anderson to conclude that the War on Poverty had been "won." But many economists question the relevance of market values for adjusting the poverty rate. In particular, medical care is so expensive in the private sector that the market value of Medicare and Medicaid is sufficient by itself to lift—in theory—almost all the elderly poor out of poverty.

Implications

The official Orshansky poverty line has withstood the test of time. It makes sense for many research projects because conclusions can be compared readily with other studies that also use this poverty line. Nonetheless, researchers should be aware of biases in the official number. Most notably, the absolute standard means that poverty today is measured by the same living standards used in 1965 (again, corrected only for inflation). The arbitrary assumptions made by Orshansky may be less of a problem. *Any* poverty line will be arbitrary, and the problems with the official one in part cancel out one another: Friedman's complaint about the food budget ratio is offset by the low food budget originally used, and the failure to include noncash benefits for the poor is offset by tax breaks and other government assistance available to the nonpoor.

One alternative research strategy is to adopt more than one poverty measure, including both absolute and relative standards. By using several poverty lines, it is possible to demonstrate the constancy, or robustness, of results under alternative assumptions. For example, the issue of how to count noncash benefits can be resolved by looking at alternative poverty measures published by the U.S. Census Bureau. Replacing the questionable market valuation for noncash benefits with more realistic assumptions reduces by about one-half the number of the poor who are raised above the poverty line by their noncash benefits.

Do the Poor Stay Poor?

The official poverty rate is based on a snapshot view. If our research interest is to find out if the same households are poor in different years, then we need longitudinal studies, that is, surveys that reinterview respondents over a long period of time. Surprising data from the University of Michigan's Panel Study of Income Dynamics (PSID) and the Census Bureau's Survey of Income and Program Participation (SIPP) show remarkable movement in and out of poverty. The PSID found that only 2.6 percent of the population was poor in eight out of ten years between 1969 and 1978, while over 24 percent were poor for at least one year. Similarly, in SIPP, only 6 percent of the population was poor in *every* month of 1984, but 26 percent were poor for at least one month.

For some conservative policy advisers, these data prove that poverty is less serious than CPS data indicate. In this view, most poor people require little government assistance because their poverty is temporary. Moreover, the small number who stay poor have become dependent on welfare programs and would gain by being forced to find regular employment. In contrast, liberal social scientists often emphasize the surprisingly large proportion of the population experiencing temporary poverty. In this view, the welfare system is a much-needed security

---

Box 8.3. **The Economic Consequences of Divorce**

According to Lenore Weitzman's 1985 book, *The Divorce Revolution*, women suffer a 73 percent loss in economic status after divorce. Criticism published subsequently in the journal *Demography* suggested that this widely cited statistic is quite inaccurate. Weitzman's sample consisted of only 228 men and women who became divorced in Los Angeles County in 1977. Data from the far larger Panel Study of Income Dynamics measured an average of about 30 percent loss in economic status for women in the first year after divorce. The critics conclude that the economic well-being of men and women indeed diverges substantially in the years after divorce, but not nearly to the extent publicized by Weitzman's findings.

---

cushion for many families who are precariously close to the poverty line. Along similar lines, sociologist Mary Jo Bane used longitudinal data to show that most poverty occurred because of income or job changes, not because of family composition changes such as divorce or abandonment. Bane concludes that "the problem of poverty should be addressed by devoting attention to employment, wages and the development of skills necessary for productive participation in the labor force rather than hand-wringing about the decline of the family." This policy recommendation has not been tested, but it shows how one can use dynamic data available in the PSID or SIPP to go beyond the debate about the "actual" low or high rate of poverty.

Summary

Without improved data on wealth, we will not understand its distribution in the United States. At present, however, the barriers to better data appear insurmountable. The uneven distribution of wealth means that even extremely large surveys will tell us nothing about the very wealthy; it is unlikely that any of the *Forbes* 400 will be interviewed in the extremely large sample Current Population Survey, and even more improbable that they will be included in the Federal Reserve survey. For example, the enriched sample of 438 known-to-be-wealthy households in the 1983 Federal Reserve survey included none of the wealthiest Americans identified by business magazines.

Additional data on income also would be helpful, for example, replacing the spendable weekly earnings series and increasing funding to the Survey of Income and Program Participation. But in general, simply increasing the quantity of data will not be sufficient. As economist Isabel Sawhill concludes, "we are swamped with facts about people's incomes and about the number and composition of people who inhabit the lower tail, but we don't know very much about the process that generates these results." In other words, we need more data about income dynamics, that is, when and how income changes over time, and we need data about why incomes differ for different jobs.

Controversies about the distribution of income and the rate of poverty both demonstrate the need to test different assumptions in research projects. This kind of sensitivity analysis can preempt criticism about what may appear to be arbitrary choices, such as years chosen for study, inflation indexes, or poverty lines. Such care can help researchers reach an audience beyond the already convinced.

Finally, despite the apparent existence of contradictory statistics, researchers have been able to reach important conclusions about income distribution and poverty. In other words, although it is possible to "lie with statistics," bending the numbers to agree with one's prejudice, it is also possible to use income statistics correctly if one understands the limitations of the underlying data.

Case Study Questions

1. Even though the Census Bureau spends considerable effort training its survey takers to gather accurate data, respondents may nonetheless misrepresent their income. One study comparing Current Population Survey (CPS) data with tax returns showed that actual self-employment income was 24 percent higher than reported in the survey; actual government transfer programs other than social security were 42 percent higher; and actual property income such as interest, rent, and dividends was 135 percent higher. How might these possible errors affect research on wealth and income distribution?

2. Current Population Survey data on income exclude capital gains, that is, income derived from the profitable sale of homes, stocks and bonds, or other investments. What effect does this exclusion have on studies of the distribution of income?

3. A 1987 *Ebony* magazine article celebrated a more than 50 percent increase between 1980 and 1986 in the number of black families with incomes between $25,000 and $50,000. By contrast, there was only an 18 percent increase in white families within this income bracket. How might these statistics exaggerate the improvement of income for blacks relative to income for whites?

4. Many studies of income focus exclusively on family incomes. What biases are introduced by leaving out nonfamily households when we study the well-being of the "typical" household?

5. The gap between men's and women's pay has received much attention in recent years. Usually the gap was measured by the ratio of women's pay to men's pay, which was approximately 71 percent in 1992. But there are several potential problems with this measure.

a. Most researchers use *weekly* earnings measured in the Current Population Survey. However, *annual* earnings that include second jobs measure a slightly larger pay gap. Why?

b. Most researchers compare pay for only full-time, year-round workers. Why would the pay gap appear larger if all workers were studied? What are the reasons for studying only full-time, year-round workers? What would be the reasons for studying all workers?

c. The measured pay gap between men and women closed by 7 percentage points between 1979 and 1987. But during this period men's median pay fell by more than 7 percent. How does this additional statistic affect assessment of women's progress in achieving equality?

Chapter 9

Labor Statistics

This chapter examines labor statistics, a broad range of data on unemployment, the number of jobs, occupations, union membership, strikes, and workplace safety. Because these statistics directly affect so many lives, they are mainstays of public policy. American macroeconomic policies, government training and education programs, equal rights efforts, and regulation of labor relations and the workplace all depend on labor statistics. In each case, however, there are significant measurement problems that complicate policy choices.

Data Sources

U.S. Bureau of Labor Statistics

A researcher's first stop often will be the U.S. Department of Labor's Bureau of Labor Statistics (BLS), which publishes a wide range of information about the U.S. workforce. The best-known statistics on unemployment are computed by BLS based on survey data from the U.S. Census Bureau. In other cases, BLS simply publishes statistics collected by other U.S. government agencies. These include job injuries counted by the Occupational Safety and Health Administration (OSHA) and union membership estimated by the U.S. Census Bureau. Finally, BLS collects its own statistics, most important of which is the Establishment Survey, a monthly survey covering 200,000 employers for data on the number of jobs and average pay levels.

Where the Numbers Come From

Organizations	Data sources	Key publications
Bureau of Labor Statistics, U.S. Department of Labor	Current Population Survey; Establishment Survey; Occupational Safety and Health statistics; international comparisons	*Employment and Earnings; Monthly Labor Review; Handbook of Labor Statistics; Occupational Injuries and Illnesses; Current Wage Developments*
U.S. Bureau of the Census, U.S. Department of Commerce	U.S. Census of Population; Economic censuses	*U.S. Census of Population; Census of Manufactures* (and other economic sectors)

For summary data, see *Statistical Abstract of the United States.*

Data Sample: For April 1994, the Bureau of Labor Statistics estimated the unemployment rate for married men at 4.0 percent; for widowed, divorced, or separated men at 9.7 percent; and for single, never-married men at 11.5 percent.

U.S. Census Bureau

While the Bureau of Labor Statistics publishes the most current labor data, the data published by the U.S. Census Bureau are the most comprehensive, although they are untimely (see chapter 2). The long form of the census completed by about 20 percent of the population provides labor force data with great accuracy for relatively small geographic areas.

Data Sample: In the 1980 Census of Population, male hotel and lodging executives, administrators, and managers outnumbered females by 96,637 to 66,178, while hotel and lodging room cleaners were predominately female by a 193,482 to 62,053 margin.

At five-year intervals the Census Bureau surveys businesses in the Economic Censuses. These surveys are also quite detailed, providing labor force data by economic sector.

Data Sample: In the 1987 Census of Government, Harlan County, Kentucky, employed 1,356 workers: 823 in education, 37 in the police force, and 24 in firefighting.

Controversies

Unemployment

On the first or second Friday of every month, the U.S. Bureau of Labor Statistics announces the unemployment rate for the previous month. It is a touchstone for U.S. economic policy; changes of a fraction of 1 percent are headline news, enough to bolster or shake confidence in a national administration. But practically unnoticed by the media is uncertainty about the interpretation and accuracy of the measured unemployment rate.

How It Came to Be

The Bureau of Labor Statistics came into prominence because of an embarrassing gap in U.S. social statistics. At the height of the Great Depression of the 1930s, no one knew how many people were out of work. Limited funding prevented the BLS from conducting the kind of nationwide survey necessary to measure unemployment accurately. Instead, the BLS relied on partial surveys of the *employed* by individual states where strong labor lobbies had pressured for comprehensive workplace surveys. These data were misleading as a measure of unemployment; for example, in January 1930 President Hoover declared "the tide of employment has changed" based on an apparent upswing in the job count, although within one year more than 3 million people lost their jobs.

After a 1937 postcard survey yielded worthless returns by leaving out everyone without a permanent residence, the Roosevelt administration finally agreed to a large-scale, house-to-house survey. Ironically, the task was assigned to the Works Progress Administration, itself a government effort to provide jobs. The resulting 15 percent unemployment rate estimate proved that the country still suffered from economic depression. Once it had been demonstrated that a direct sampling of individuals could measure unemployment, the U.S. Census Bureau

---

Box 9.1. **How to Survey the Unemployed**

Old survey: "What were you doing most of last week? . . .
'working' 'keeping house' 'going to school.'"

New survey: "Last week did you do any work for pay?"

In January 1994, the Bureau of Labor Statistics introduced new survey questions intended to remove biases in the older format. Most worrisome was a tendency of survey takers to prejudice the response from a woman by first asking her whether she was "keeping house," whereas a man was more likely asked if he was "working." As a result, too many women were counted outside the labor force and thus technically not unemployed, even though they were actively looking for work at the same time that they maintained a household. Combined with other new questions, the unemployment rate jumped 0.6 percent above what it would have been under the old method. BLS statisticians think the increase would have been even greater if survey takers had not been aware of the reason for the change. Before the new questions were introduced, survey takers may have tried to make their questions less gender biased, thereby raising the measured unemployment rate during the last few months of 1993.

---

took over, initiating the monthly Current Population Survey in 1947. Today it is the largest regularly conducted poll in the world, covering about 60,000 households, and is used to estimate many important social science statistics (see chapters 2, 4, and 5), but its key focus remains the unemployment rate. In the CPS, unemployment has a specific, technical definition: those respondents who are not working (but are not on sick leave) and who actively searched for work during the last four weeks. The unemployment rate is the number of unemployed divided by the labor force, consisting of the employed plus the unemployed. Researchers disagree whether this method causes under- or overestimation of the actual unemployment rate.

Undercount

Two well-documented shortcomings in the official definition of unemployment cause it to underestimate the actual number of people in need of work. First, the official statistic leaves out part-timers who would like full-time work; anyone who works, even as little as one hour per week, is counted as employed. Second, discouraged workers who are not actively seeking a job are left out of the labor force entirely, that is, they are neither employed nor unemployed. Only those who made a specific effort to find work, such as writing letters, canvassing, or reporting to an agency, are counted as unemployed.

The BLS recognizes these potential limitations to the official unemployment rate. Indeed, the BLS introduced new survey questions in January 1994 (See Box 9.1) that partially corrected the undercount of unemployed homemakers. But according to official 1994 BLS statistics, there were still 500,000 discouraged workers and about 4 million part-timers who desired full-time employment. These and other adjustments to the unemployment rate are published by BLS under the labels U-1 through U-7. The news media typically report only the official one, called U-5, but the other rates provide researchers with important —although seldom used—statistics.

Overcount

Two measurement problems can cause overestimation of the official unemployment rate. First, some individuals may misrepresent their work status to CPS surveyors in order to cover up illegal jobs. No one knows the precise size of the unreported workforce (see chapter 7), but underground economy expert Peter Gutmann argues that it causes official unemployment rates to be 30 percent too high.

A second problem arises because the single official unemployment statistic does not take into account *who* is unemployed. When there is an increasing proportion of women and youth in the workforce, the unemployment rate may rise because these inexperienced workers possess fewer skills and are more likely to change jobs frequently. One interpretation of this trend is the existence of a rising "natural rate" of unemployment compatible with nonaccelerating inflation. In this view, attempts by the government to achieve lower unemployment than the natural rate, about 6 percent during the 1980s, would have been inflationary. Other economists dispute these findings on the grounds that the term "natural rate" gives the false impression of immutability, when in fact the natural unemployment rate can be lowered with better investment and training programs.

Table 9.1

Unemployment (August 1994)

Official unemployed (Actively seeking a job)	8,023,000
Not counted as unemployed, but . . .	
Searched during past 12 months and not currently	
looking for a job because . . .	1,726,000
Discouraged over job prospects	489,000
Child care or other commitments	1,237,000
At work part time, want a full-time job because . . .	6,675,000
Slack work or business conditions	3,055,000
Could only find part-time work	3,239,000

Source: U.S. Department of Labor, Bureau of Labor Statistics, "The Employment Situation: August 1994," USDL 94430, Tables A3, A8.

Alternative Measures

In *Out of Work: The First Century of Unemployment in Massachusetts*, historian Alexander Keyssar explores the importance of an alternative measure of unemployment, the proportion out of work at some point during a year. Between 1830 and 1930, this statistic frequently reached as high as 40 percent, indicative of a far greater impact of unemployment than the traditional unemployment rate would suggest. In other words, if we want to measure how many individuals are affected by unemployment, either because they are currently unemployed or have faced unemployment recently, then the statistic used by Keyssar is more accurate.

A more optimistic appraisal of the labor market occurs when researchers use statistics on the number of jobs rather than unemployment. For example, the BLS Establishment Survey provides a frequently updated count of jobs. Because these data are collected directly from employers, there are no problems caused by survey respondents who do not want to admit unemployment. The disadvantage of the Establishment Survey is that it counts all jobs, thereby overstating the employment picture when more individuals have two jobs. President Bush used Establishment Survey data to claim large numbers of jobs created during his administration. Nevertheless, his promise of 17 million new jobs backfired during the 1992 campaign when the jobs were not forthcoming. Also embarrassing to Bush's campaign was the revelation of two errors in the government's job count. In 1992, the Establishment Survey counted 640,000 too many jobs because the survey accidentally relied on the number of paychecks issued by large companies rather than the number of people who were employed. And, in 1992, California's recession job losses were six times as high as previously reported, in this instance because bankrupt businesses were underreported in the Establishment data.

Implications

Debates about labor market statistics teach several lessons about the use of data. First, the existence of data depends on social priorities. Students of the labor market are fortunate that because of its origins, the largest monthly U.S. survey, the CPS, has more questions on unemployment and employment than on any other single subject. The challenge for social scientists is to select from these numerous labor statistics choices that depend on the research purpose. For example, in studying the social consequences of unemployment, or social distress, the official U-5 unemployment rate is inadequate. Researchers may need to use less-often-consulted statistics such as U-7, or to make further adjustments to take into account measurement problems in official statistics (see Table 9.1).

If the research goal is to measure the overall state of the macroeconomy, then the official unemployment rate has the advantage of tradition. But because of changing labor force characteristics, the official unemployment rate may not be a constant measure of how well the macroeconomy is using labor resources. The debate about whether or not to call this effect the "natural rate" of unemployment illustrates the significance of language in social science research. During many recent years, labor force growth has caused both more employment in the Establishment Survey *and* increasing unemployment in the CPS. Consequently, researchers need to keep an eye on both surveys for a complete picture of the labor market.

Better Jobs?

Researchers on occupational change owe much to U.S. Census Bureau statistician Alba Edwards, who between 1910 and 1940 undertook the massive task of classifying jobs into a usable number of occupations. The major categories developed by Edwards are the basis for much research on occupations, including controversial conclusions about the trend in job quality and intergenerational mobility.

Self-fulfilling Scale

Historian Marjorie Conk charges that some of Edwards's assumptions about job status were based on sexist and racist biases. For example, the nurses and midwives occupation was graded "semiskilled" because it included mostly women workers. Similarly, other occupations were labeled low skill because they were dominated by black or foreign-born workers. The system appeared satisfactory to Edwards because it reflected existing notions of "high" and "low" status. Other researchers point out that Edwards overestimated the increase in the skill level of U.S. jobs because of mistaken assumptions in the semiskilled category, which was first introduced in 1910 as a category for work with machinery. On this basis, a large number of workers were promoted out of so-called unskilled occupations based on work with machinery—even if the tasks involved were less complex than the "unskilled" occupations. Later, repetitive task assembly-line jobs also were classified as semiskilled, likely overstating the increase in the average occupational skill level.

White Collars

One of the major uses of the Census Bureau occupational classification is for the study of intergenerational mobility. Based on a special set of questions in the 1962 and 1973 Current Population Survey, a 1967 study by sociologists Peter M. Blau and Otis Dudley Duncan, and updated by David L. Featherman and Robert M. Hauser in 1978, found significant upward mobility when sons of low-status fathers moved into higher-status white-collar jobs. (Data on mothers were not collected. Later studies found the effect of mothers' educational attainment outweighed the effect of fathers' status.)

Critics of the Blau and Duncan approach charge that categories based on the original Edwards classification may be misleading about status levels. In particular, jobs grouped as "white collar" do not necessarily involve more skill than the manual occupations they replace. For example, clerical occupations are white collar even though they include low-status filing and typing jobs with what is today the second-lowest pay of all major census classifications. The white-collar designation is a holdover from the nineteenth century, when clerical workers were a tiny enclave of privileged male workers. On the other hand, the "non-household service worker," a 1950s category introduced to separate service workers employed by corporations and government from personal maids and butlers, still retains the "lower manual" designation, even though these occupations include relatively high-skill jobs such as nursing, firefighting, and police work. Finally, the Census Bureau measured an increase in the number of managers but made no distinction between the head of a major corporation and the person responsible for a fast-food franchise. Thus, although there are more managers, not all possess the status once accorded to this job title.

New Classification

Many anachronisms in the old classification scheme were rectified in the 1980 census when individual job titles were reallocated within the classification hierarchy. These corrections were welcomed by researchers, for example, shifting 240,000 practical nurses from the catchall service category to the more specific—and higher-status—technician occupation. But as a result of the new classification, historical comparison with previous censuses is nearly impossible (although part of the 1970 census was recoded, making it compatible with 1980 data). Moreover, problems remain, such as "managers, not elsewhere classified," the largest detailed classification including over 5 million individuals in 1980. But this catchall classification covered such diverse work settings that it was not useful for many research purposes.

Implications

The pre-1980 Census Bureau occupational classification demonstrates the problem of fitting data into a few usable categories. In the case of

Edwards's scheme, there were obvious initial biases, as well as subsequent changes in many occupational characteristics. Even though "semiskilled" and "white and blue collar" were commonly used groups, they may not have measured what researchers intended. Extensive reclassification in the 1980 census presents another challenge to researchers because of incomparability between recent and past data.

Unions

The U.S. Bureau of Labor Statistics is the main source of national data on labor unions. Recent problems in measuring union membership and strike activity illustrate how researchers must pay careful attention to changes in data-collection methods.

Membership

Prior to 1973, the only data came directly from union reports of their own membership. After 1973, the Current Population Survey added a question on union membership, which, beginning in 1981, replaced the direct count in government publications. Some social scientists charge that anti-union sentiment in the Reagan administration prompted the abandonment of the direct count. Yet even the critics admit that there were problems with the older data source, in particular an upward bias caused by exaggerated union membership reports from unions wanting to present a strong image to employers, as well as a downward bias when local unions failed to report all members to the national union in an effort to avoid dues payment. No one knows the extent of either bias.

By avoiding self-serving membership reports, CPS data may be more accurate. Moreover, CPS unionization data can be correlated with CPS questions on industry of employment, occupation, race, sex, and other variables. But such survey data are only as good as the informants' knowledge. There is evidence that respondents may not know whether they or other household members actually belong to a union. The primary problem is that many unions, most notably teacher and nursing "associations," do not use the title "union." The original 1973 CPS question about union membership was changed in 1976 to include "associations." But it was found that respondents answered yes if they simply belonged to a workplace club or "association." So the question was changed once again in 1979, to read "union or employee association similar to a union."

Researchers need to be aware of changes in the way in which union membership has been measured. Although all statistics show a dramatic decline in U.S. union membership since the 1970s, the extent of this decline and the years in which it occurred depend on which data source is used.

Strikes

The CPS sample is too small to estimate accurately the number of workers on strike. Consequently, the BLS relies on newspaper, magazine, and government reports to assemble data on the number of strikes, number of workers involved, and days idle. These data are comprehensive for strikes involving more than 1,000 workers; however, budget cutbacks in 1981 caused termination of data on smaller strikes (involving at least six workers for one eight-hour shift). According to BLS officials, these data were deleted in order to preserve the quality of such statistics as the Consumer Price Index, which is more important for policy decisions.

Researchers may agree that it was important to maintain the integrity of the Consumer Price Index, but the reduced quality of strike data is a major handicap for labor relations research. It is true that larger strikes account for most strike days lost, but these large strikes were less than 10 percent of the total number of strikes. Thus, a full picture of labor relations requires information that was no longer available.

Is the Workplace Safe?

Concern about occupational safety and health is a long-standing BLS tradition. In 1909, a BLS study documented phosphorus poisoning in the match industry, causing Congress to impose a tax on the dangerous product. In 1910, the BLS began publishing accident statistics based on reports from individual states and insurance companies. Congress refused authorization for a separate division on safety, so in subsequent decades safety data covered only 25 percent of the workforce. Under the 1970 Occupational Safety and Health Administration (OSHA) legislation, BLS coverage was expanded, but still excluded most small farms, the self-employed, and government workers. Critics charged that OSHA data should be comprehensive because, unlike other government surveys, the information is used both for enforcement and for research purposes. In fact, the most common penalty meted out by OSHA was for not reporting accidents.

In 1992, BLS redesigned the survey in two ways. Deaths are counted in a Census of Fatal Occupational Injuries covering almost all workers. Injuries and illnesses are now measured in a sample survey of 250,000 private businesses that includes previously uncollected demographic data on workplace victims as well as better information on the severity and circumstances of the injury or illness. As a result, researchers have a greatly expanded and largely unexplored data set. BLS offers assistance to researchers who want to use the new data as well as help in comparing data from the different BLS survey sources. Adjusting for the change in surveys, the overall injury and illness rate shows a steady decline from 11.0 cases per 100 workers in 1973 to a low of 7.6 cases in 1983 and then an increase slightly to 8.9 cases in 1992. Some researchers believe that the rapid improvement during the 1970s was a result of long-overdue enforcement, so further reductions in injury rates were slower to be realized and disguised by improved reporting. Critics charge that additional injuries resulted from cutbacks in OSHA inspections imposed during the 1980s.

International Labor Statistics

Intercountry comparisons of labor statistics are tricky because similar-sounding statistics—the labor force, unemployment, and employment —may differ in meaning. Researchers would be at a loss if it were not for the help available from statistical agencies. Regularly published BLS bulletins provide comparable data on the labor force, employment, and unemployment in large industrial countries. Additional comparison data are assembled by the International Labor Organization, based in Geneva, Switzerland, and the Organization for Economic Co-operation and Development, based in Paris.

Unemployment

Two sets of problems confound direct comparison of unemployment rates in different countries. The labor force is defined variously to exclude those people under 16 years old (in the United States), those

under 15 years old (in many other countries), full-time students looking for work (Sweden), and those waiting for a job to begin (Japan).
Also, definition of those available for work varies from those who
actively searched for a job during a four-week period in the United
States, to a sixty-day period in Sweden, to an unspecified amount of
time in Japan.

A second problem is variation in the level of distress caused by
unemployment in different countries. Relatively comprehensive social
welfare systems in Western Europe cause unemployment rates to mean
quite different economic circumstances than they would in the United
States. In the Netherlands, for example, it is estimated that reported
unemployment would rise by 3 percent if it were not for relatively
generous benefits that enable otherwise unemployed workers to retire
and thus leave the labor force.

Employment

Which country creates the most jobs? During the 1980s, supporters of
the Reagan and Bush administrations pointed proudly to Establishment
Survey statistics measuring more new jobs in the United States than
similar surveys counted in Western Europe and Japan *combined.* But
data incompatibility clouds interpretation of these intercountry comparisons. The European workforce is older than the U.S. workforce, so
a smaller proportion of the population is in the traditional working-age
group for whom jobs must be created. (The reverse, however, is true in
Japan.) In both Europe and Japan, many fewer teenagers work, again
reducing the need for new jobs, although in Germany, it appears that
many teenagers have left the labor force precisely because work was
unavailable. (Japanese teenagers have never worked in large numbers.)

In summary, international comparisons require careful attention to
how data are collected. Again, this problem is recognized by the U.S.
Bureau of Labor Statistics as well as by the international statistical organizations that provide standardized statistics for most major countries.

Summary

Seemingly small changes in labor statistics can have dramatic human
consequences. Consider the U.S. unemployment rate, where every 1 percent change translates into at least 1 million more jobs. An increase of

1.0 per 100,000 in U.S. job-related fatalities means more than 1,000 additional deaths. But as this chapter demonstrates, there are many problems in measuring labor statistics, ranging from definitional issues for the unemployment rate to changing survey techniques for union membership. The challenge for researchers is to understand the limitations of these numbers without losing sight of their effects on human lives. For example, the official U.S. unemployment rate is an extremely limited and easily criticized single statistic. But it is possible to obtain a fascinating, and relatively complete, picture of the U.S. labor markets—*if* researchers look at all the statistics available, including alternative unemployment statistics, employment counts, and the causes and duration of unemployment. Similarly, there are flaws in the most commonly cited statistics about job quality, union membership, strikes, and workplace safety. International data compound each of these issues, requiring yet more skepticism about comparisons of simple statistics. But, properly interpreted, the vast quantity of data collected has the potential to illuminate our understanding of labor issues.

Case Study Questions

1. The official unemployment rates for teenagers are quite high, over 15 percent in many recent years. But this statistic does not mean 15 percent of all teenagers are out of work. What does it in fact measure?

2. Sometimes the Current Population Survey and the Establishment Survey measure different direction of changes in the number of jobs. During the first eight months of 1994, businesses reported more than 2 million new jobs in the Establishment Survey, whereas households reported only about 1.2 million jobs in the Current Population Survey. Economists believe that the following factors are responsible: multiple job holders, newly created businesses, and undocumented aliens. How does each factor cause a difference in the number of jobs counted in the CPS and the Establishment Survey?

3. The average duration of unemployment depends on the state of the economy. During the economic recession of the early 1980s, unemployment lasting more than six months constituted about one-quarter of all unemployment but only one-eighth of unemployment during

subsequent years of economic recovery. How might this change affect public policy based on the official unemployment rate?

4. Using the CPS employment questions, explain why a high percentage of farm women with children in the North Central farm states are reported as "working." How do these responses affect the measured unemployment rate for women with children?

5. In Japan between 1955 and 1975 there was a twofold increase in the number of women attending college. Also, many women moved from farms, where they had combined farm work with child care, to cities where they had no paid employment. How might these factors explain declining labor force participation for Japanese women, the opposite of the trend in most other countries? (Hint: Few Japanese college students have outside jobs.)

Chapter 10

Business Statistics

Information about business is itself a very profitable business, serving a large market of information-hungry investors. Thus, for research purposes, primary data directly from businesses are plentiful, as are secondary sources interpreting these data. The Data Sources section below reviews this vast field. The Controversies section focuses on one fundamental aspect of business statistics: the many ways to measure business size, including sales, assets, stock market price, and profits. These statistics are important as indicators of the success of individual firms and for public policy, especially the enforcement of antitrust law.

Data Sources

The availability of data depends critically on the type of business being studied. The approximately 17 million U.S. businesses divide into two basic forms of legal organization. Corporations are least in number, about one-sixth of all businesses, but predominate in economic importance, accounting for four-fifths of sales and profits. Corporate data are voluminous and are usually publicly available. In contrast, more than 14 million sole proprietorships and partnerships account for only about one-tenth of business revenues. Data on these mostly smaller businesses are much less accessible.

Public Corporations

SEC Disclosure

The financial distress of the Great Depression, coupled with complaints about corporate misrepresentation, led to the creation of the

Where the Numbers Come From

Organizations	Data sources	Key publications
U.S. Securities and Exchange Commission	Corporate reports	*SEC Monthly Statistical Review; Official Summary of Security Transactions and Holdings*
U.S. Small Business Administration	Small Business Data Base	*State of Small Business; Handbook of Small Business Data*
Federal Trade Commission	Corporate reports to FTC	*Quarterly Financial Reports; Statistical Report on Mergers and Acquisitions; Annual Line of Business Report*
Dun and Bradstreet	Credit reports	*The Failure Record*

Securities and Exchange Commission (SEC) in 1933. In addition to monitoring the stock exchange and other capital markets, the SEC sets strict guidelines for corporate disclosure, that is, what corporations must tell the public about the type of goods or services produced, the names of corporate officers, the names of major stockholders, and most important, a summary of corporate finances. Lists of companies reporting to the SEC—and the data as well—are available directly from the SEC offices or through private firms that employ researchers who will locate and photocopy SEC files for a fee. A few large corporations are privately held, that is, they do not sell stock to the public. Data on these private firms are considered separately below.

Annual Reports

The SEC's financial disclosure requirements for stockholders are fulfilled by the annual report, a publication expanded by most corporations to a multipage glossy magazine that advertises the company's investment potential. The annual report is an easily accessible source of data, available in many public libraries or from the corporation itself. Nevertheless, experts warn users not to rely entirely on annual reports. Additional, possibly more revealing, information is publicly available in SEC reports. Moreover, the text that fills most space in annual reports can be misleading; corporations are under no obligation to discuss unsavory prospects in this written material.

> *Data Sample:* In the 1988 General Motors Annual Report the president and chairman told shareholders: "We are very pleased with GM's performance in 1988. . . . With its accelerating momentum, GM is well positioned to achieve its ultimate objective of strong profitability. . . ." Nowhere do they mention GM's share of the U.S. auto market, which declined to 34.7 percent in 1987 from 38.5 percent the previous year.

Handbooks

For research on a number of corporations, it is most convenient to consult handbooks containing data collected by private companies such as Moody's, Standard and Poor's, Value Line, and Dun and Bradstreet. Each of these handy reference books is updated frequently to include all key data from SEC reports, as well as recent stock prices, debt, capitalization, and usually to add an impartial assessment of each corporation's current financial status. Supplementary handbooks help researchers find corporate addresses, subsidiary ownership, corporate leadership, and product lines.

Business Magazines

Based on the popularity of the *Fortune 500* largest industrial corporations, first introduced in 1955, we now have the *Business Week 1,000*, several *Forbes 400* rankings, and an expanded *Fortune 500* to include nonindustrial corporations as well. These business magazines also publish special issues with comprehensive listings of corporate management, corporate compensation, and data on unusually successful small businesses. Because of deadline pressures, errors appear regularly in these issues. Researchers should look out for anomalous-looking data and should consult subsequent issues for corrections. Nonetheless, these compilations are quite handy for home and office use because they are far less expensive than corporate handbooks.

Privately Held Corporations

Some major U.S. corporations are nearly exempt from public scrutiny because they do not have publicly traded stock. Most are companies owned by only a few shareholders, for example, the Mars Candy Company, which is owned by members of the Mars family. *Forbes* magazine uses outside sources, and in some cases voluntary disclosure, to estimate the size of the 400 largest privately held firms, topped in recent years by Cargill Inc., a Minneapolis grain-trading company with more than $47 billion revenues in 1993. Overall, these 400 private corporations average about 20 percent of the revenue of the 400 largest corporations with stockholders.

For data on privately held companies that are not large enough to be described in the *Forbes 400,* researchers face a substantial challenge. A helpful resource is *A Guide to Information on Closely Held Corporations*, developed by labor relations experts with experience in researching corporations. The *Guide* recommends first checking business magazine and newspaper indexes to see if a reporter has already conducted the research you wish to do. Next look in directories such as Dun and Bradstreet and Thomas Register, which include privately held firms. Finally, additional information can be gained from records of corporate formations filed with state offices, and real estate, litigation, and court judgments in local jurisdictions.

> *Data Sample:* In Dun's Marketing *Million Dollar Directory* we learn that Kut Rate Fashions, Inc., of Columbia, South Carolina, has 85 employees and annual sales of $11 million.

Small Businesses

The great majority of U.S. businesses are small. Defined as employing less than 100 workers, small businesses constitute over 98 percent of all businesses, although these small firms take in less than 40 percent of all business sales. For data on individual small businesses, a researcher may need to do some data digging. Local libraries are a good place to start; librarians often are familiar with sources on local businesses, and reference works on local economies are frequently in their collections. Private data firms, most notably Dun and Bradstreet, collect data on small firms, but access to the data is expensive.

Aggregate Statistics

Many research projects require aggregate statistics, that is, combined data for groups of businesses, perhaps in a single location or in a single line of business. For these numbers, U.S. government statistics are almost certainly a researcher's starting point. The U.S. Commerce Department's economic surveys (see chapter 7) provide a core set of data, detailed by geographic area and product lines. The U.S. Labor Department's Establishment Survey uses similar organization by locale and product, but is limited to data on the workforce.

For aggregate data on small businesses, a recently developed source is now available from the Small Business Administration, an independent federal agency. The Small Business Data Base is unusual in that it follows the record of individual businesses, rather than the typical single-point-in-time "snapshot" view of most aggregate statistics. As a result, the Data Base will answer important questions about which small businesses grow—and which fail. In addition, the Data Base fills a data gap on business startups not always recorded immediately in U.S. Census reports.

> *Data Sample:* The Small Business Data Base analyzes changes in the number of jobs for 1976 to 1984 as follows:
>
> New business startups: 26 million new jobs
> Existing business expansion: 8 million new jobs
> Businesses going defunct: 16 million jobs lost
> Layoffs: 3 million jobs lost
> _____
> Net change: 14 million new jobs.

Controversies

Who Is the Biggest of Them All?

The size of a business can be measured in many ways: by the value of a firm's sales; by the value of a firm's assets; by the value of a firm's profits; or by the number of a firm's employees. As shown in Table 10.1, these measures of size cause different rankings of U.S. companies; General Motors, IBM, and Citicorp can all legitimately claim the

Table 10.1

Big by Any Measure: Corporate Size, 1993 (in billions)

	Sales	Assets	Stock Market Value	Profits
1.	General Motors $138	General Electric $252	General Electric $90	Exxon $5.3
2.	Ford $109	Fannie Mae $217	Exxon $81	General Electric $4.4
3.	Exxon $99	Citicorp $217	AT&T $71	AT&T $4.0
4.	Wal-Mart $67	Ford $199	Wal-Mart $65	Philip Morris $3.6
5.	AT&T $67	General Motors $188	Coca-Cola $55	Ford $2.5

Source: The Business Week 1,000, March 28, 1994, p. 80.

number-one spot. There are advantages and disadvantages to each measure of size, so researchers must consider carefully which to use.

Sales

The oldest and most famous ranking of U.S. corporations, the *Fortune 500*, is based on annual sales. When the list was first published in 1955, economist M.A. Adelman wrote to the magazine to complain that sales data are "almost meaningless" because they include production by the company's suppliers that is passed on in the company's sales. As an example, Adelman pointed to the Du Pont Corporation with $1.7 billion sales, which appeared smaller than meat processor Swift and Co. with $2.5 billion sales. But almost all of Du Pont's sales were based on its own production, whereas 90 percent of Swift's sales came from supplier costs passed on to customers. *Fortune* admitted the data were imperfect, but defended them as the best available.

Because of the problem with incomparability between different industries, the *Fortune 500* initially was limited to only industrial corpo-

---

Box 10.1. **Which Is Larger: GM or Switzerland?**

A frequently cited criticism of the power of large corporations is their size, measured by annual sales, in comparison to the GDP of relatively large countries. In this manner, General Motors, the largest U.S. corporation in sales, ranks ahead of Taiwan, Finland, and Denmark.

GDP or Annual Sales—1991 (billions)

1.	U.S.	$5,686
.		.
.		.
22.	GENERAL MOTORS	$ 124
23.	Taiwan	$ 123
24.	Finland	$ 122
25.	Denmark	$ 122
26.	Ukraine	$ 121
27.	Indonesia	$ 111
28.	ROYAL DUTCH SHELL	$ 107
29.	Saudi Arabia	$ 105
30.	EXXON	$ 103

Technically this list is an invalid comparison of statistical apples and oranges. Gross domestic product measures a country's total production, whereas corporate sales include that corporation's production *plus* production by other firms used as raw materials, machinery, and other inputs. A correct comparison would measure corporate production by what economists call "value added," the concept used in GDP accounts to avoid the double counting that arises in corporate data. On this basis, GM is nevertheless still quite large, outranking Israel, Venezuela, and Algeria, although not Taiwan, Indonesia, and Saudi Arabia, as a comparison of sales with GDP misleadingly implies.

---

rations. In later years, *Fortune* added a separate list of the largest service corporations. But the distinction between these two lists is increasingly difficult because more firms are diversifying to include both industrial and service-type production. This causes crossover and ambiguity in the rankings: for example, during the 1980s International

Telephone and Telegraph, Union Pacific, Charter, and Gulf & Western left the top 100 of *Fortune*'s industrial list when they were reclassified as service corporations.

Assets

In theory, a second measure of size, the value of assets, should give a good comparative-size statistic valid between different sectors of the economy. The problem with assets, as every accounting student quickly learns, is that, unlike the items measured in sales data, few assets are actually bought or sold during a given year. As a result, accountants must estimate asset value based on changes in value since they were first purchased. The procedure is called *depreciation,* a complex formula oriented toward taxation, not actual demise of the asset. Smart investors know to investigate closely before trusting the measured assets as the actual value of a company. Despite this drawback, asset value is commonly used in research on diverse sectors of the economy where sales data would be misleading. For example, the debate about the concentration of corporate power discussed below is based on estimates of assets owned by the largest corporations.

Market Value

A third measure of size, used in the *Business Week 1,000*, is based on the combined value of all stock owned in the corporation. This number reflects both the value of funds invested in the corporation when stock was first issued and subsequent changes in the corporation's value based on the rise and fall of the stock price. In theory, the combined knowledge of all stock investors may provide a better measure of corporate values than any single number in the corporate accounts. The drawbacks to stock values as a measure of size are twofold. First, changing stock prices mean that the "value" of the firm changes literally from moment to moment as the stock price varies. Typically researchers must choose an arbitrary day for measuring stock prices; even a short time earlier or later, stock prices may be significantly different.

Second, aside from day-to-day fluctuations, there are uncertainties about the meaning of long-run stock prices, in particular whether this is actually a measure of underlying corporate values. There is ongoing

debate among economists and business analysts about the efficiency of
the stock market, both as an indicator of differences between corporations in terms of their productive capacity and the ability of the stock
measure to measure the economy's overall strength.

In summary, stock prices are a convenient statistic in the sense that
they are widely reported and therefore are readily available in print or
electronic format. The problem is that no one knows for certain what
these voluminous data are telling us.

Employment

Finally, the number of employees is an indicator of size. For organiz-
ing data on varied types of firms, employment is a convenient size
criterion for several reasons. First, counting employees is less ambiguous than using accounting principles to estimate sales or assets. Second, employment data are applicable to all firms, whether incorporated
or not. And third, employment size is a statistic likely to be known by
employees, and thus can be measured in household surveys as well as
business surveys.

Two precautions in using employment data are required. First, employment gives only a general indication of size, differentiating between "large" and "small" businesses, but it cannot be used for comparing
two companies of similar scale. For example, labor-intensive companies such as Fruit of the Loom apparel company had over 23,000
employees in 1988, but was comparable in size as measured by other
criteria to machine-intensive Clorox with only 4,800 employees. Second, researchers must distinguish between business establishments (locations where the business operates) and enterprises (legally
constituted business that may have many establishments). The distinction is important especially in household surveys where respondents
may not know about enterprise employment beyond their workplace
establishment.

Implications

One obvious solution to the problem of too many ways to measure size
is to use more than one statistic; indeed, studies by investors typically
use all the information provided by sales, assets, market value, and
employment. When it is necessary to choose one of the rankings, how-

Box 10.2. **Top of the World** (1993)

Sales	Market Value	Profits
1. Itochu	1. Nippon Telegraph and Telephone	1. Exxon
2. Mitsui	2. Royal Dutch/Shell	2. Royal Dutch/Shell
3. Mitsubishi Corp.	3. General Electric	3. General Electric
4. Sumitomo	4. Mitsubishi Bank	4. AT&T
5. Marubeni	5. Exxon	5. Phillip Morris

Overall, among the top 1,000 firms, Japanese companies account for 48 percent of the market value, while U.S. firms make up 30 percent. These rankings, however, overstated the total Japanese influence for two reasons. First, the Japanese economy has fewer, and therefore larger, corporations, so that they constitute a greater percentage of the top rankings than they do of the total world economy. Second, Japanese stock market prices are higher relative to corporate earnings; in terms of *profits* earned in 1988, U.S. corporations held four of the top five spots.

ever, researchers should ascertain which indicator is most appropriate. For example, investigation of market control within an industry typically looks at sales data, whereas research on the source of profitability—are big firms more successful?—uses asset data, and, as a third option, studies of corporate takeovers are based on market value. A well-justified research project will explain why one size measure was chosen instead of the others.

Are the Big Too Big?

Probably the most important public policy use for data on business size is antitrust law. At issue is government intervention to limit the power of one business entity if it is too big or to restrict the power of several corporations if together they wield too much economic power. Not surprisingly, the criteria for "too big" and "too much economic power" are a sticking point, and the source of much statistical controversy.

Box 10.3. **The Herfindahl-Hirschman Index**

As a key guideline for antitrust enforcement, the U.S. Department of Justice measures market shares by the Herfindahl-Hirschman Index. It includes all firms in the industry, with each firm's percentage market share squared and added together. Thus, an index of 10,000 measures a perfect monopoly (100 percent squared), while 0 measures perfect competition. Guidelines introduced by the U.S. Justice Department indicated that mergers "likely" would be challenged if the index were above 1,800, corresponding to approximately four firms controlling 70 percent of the market, or if the merger would raise the index by an additional 100 points, corresponding to the merger of two firms each with 10 percent of the market. Lower thresholds would bring less scrutiny, down to markets with an index below 1,000, corresponding to four firms controlling about 50 percent of the market, below which merger challenge was "unlikely."

In some cases there was consensus that corporations became too big, as in the nearly total monopoly gained by the American Tobacco Company and the Standard Oil Company. In 1911, both these firms were forced to split into smaller, competing entities. Most antitrust cases, however, involve a middle ground in which no single firm dominates an industry; instead, a few large firms share the market. Antitrust laws are vague about what to do in such situations. The Sherman Antitrust Act forbids the "attempt to monopolize," while the Clayton Antitrust Act forbids business behavior that will "substantially lessen competition." Consequently, the U.S. courts and federal regulators have attempted to develop more specific guidelines for antitrust policy based on measures of market shares of sales.

In recent years federal regulators began using a measure of market shares called the Herfindahl-Hirschman Index (see Box 10.3). Essentially this index has the same impact as the former criteria based simply on market share of sales controlled by the top four or eight firms, a statistic published in the Commerce Department's economic censuses (see Table 10.2 for examples). But these seemingly straightforward guidelines have been complicated in actual practice for two reasons.

Table 10.2

Concentration Ratios (share of value of shipments, 1987)

Industry	Percentage accounted for by four largest firms	Herfindahl-Hirschmann Index
Dog and cat food	61	1,509
Fur goods	16	134
Motor vehicles and car bodies	90	Withheld to avoid discosing data for individual company
Dolls	34	434
Macaroni and spaghetti	73	1,839

Source: Bureau of the Census, U.S. Department of Commerce, *1987 Census of Manufacturing: Concentration Ratios in Manufacturing*, MC82-S-6 (Washington, D.C.: U.S. Government Printing Office, February 1992).

1. What Is a Market?

One fundamental problem in enforcing antitrust rules is determining the relevant market that the firms under investigation are alleged to control. Over the years since the 1890 Sherman Antitrust Act, the U.S. Supreme Count has moved back and forth in defining the level of market control that could be presumed to be in violation of the law. At one extreme, a 1966 decision blocked the merger of Pabst and Blatz beer brewers because they accounted for 24 percent of Wisconsin beer sales, although they constituted only 4.5 percent of the national market over which beer is readily distributed. More recently, the Court has been more permissive, as for example in the 1986 acquisition of Republic Airlines by Northwest Airlines, despite a 90 percent market share in Minneapolis. In this case, the acquisition was approved on the grounds that many passengers who were connecting through Minneapolis could fly via other airports, such as Chicago, where Northwest and Republic had a much smaller market share. A similarly expanded market definition was used in 1988 to approve the merger between Owens-Illinois and Brockway, the second and third largest U.S. glass bottle manufacturers. The merger gave the new firm more than 37 percent of the glass bottle market, clearly violating Justice Department guidelines by raising the Herfindahl-Hirschman Index by more than 600 points.

Nonetheless, the acquisition was approved on the grounds that the actual market for bottles included plastic, metal, and paper containers, for which the two firms had a much smaller market share.

2. What Is Competitive?

Even when the relevant market is identified, antitrust enforcement must still determine *how much* market share will be accepted. Once again, U.S. Supreme Court rulings on the issue have vacillated, shifting from permissiveness during the 1920s, when J.P. Morgan's U.S. Steel, with a 60 percent market share, was permitted to survive, to increased enforcement beginning in the late 1930s. Antitrust enforcement peaked during the 1960s, when, for example, the government blocked the merger of Brown and Kinney Shoes, and between Vons Grocery and Shopping Bag supermarkets, even though the combined market shares in each case were less than 10 percent. By the 1980s, the pendulum swung back in the other direction, epitomized by the 1982 dismissal of a thirteen-year suit against IBM's domination of the computer industry. During the first term of the Reagan administration, the number of challenges brought by the Justice Department and the Federal Trade Commission fell to nearly one-half the average of the previous two decades.

The economic issues about what level of market control constitutes undo influence are complex and beyond the scope of this book. In brief, one highly influential school of thought, identified with the University of Chicago, believes competition will be intense even in a highly concentrated market. In this view, the policy priority should be eliminating government price controls in banking, agriculture, and other industries instead of enforcing allegedly archaic antitrust laws. Yet a great many economists advocate a return to past antitrust enforcement. Economist William Shepherd, for example, former adviser to the Justice Department's Antitrust Division, maintains that today's markets are increasingly competitive *because* of antitrust activity.

Despite over 100 years of antitrust enforcement, there is no consensus about what constitutes the appropriate market for which to measure market shares, nor is there agreement about what level of market shares should be acceptable in any market. The future of market share of sales as a criterion for antitrust action is in doubt. Although the official guidelines still refer to market share of sales, in actual practice during the 1980s antitrust was not enforced by federal regulators, even when concentration indexes were well above the threshold designated as potentially anticompetitive.

The Urge to Merge—Are the Big Getting Bigger?

During the 1980s an unprecedented number of mergers and acquisitions occurred, capped by the 1988 $24.5 billion purchase by Kohlberg-Kravis-Roberts of R.J. Reynolds–Nabisco, two firms combined in an earlier merger. Even taking into account inflation, the value of mergers during the 1980s averaged more than three times the level of the previous two decades. Because of this trend, some policy advisers called for more antitrust regulation. If the mergers or acquisitions occurred within an industry, then the concentration ratios were relevant, as in the case of Northwest and Republic Airlines described earlier. For mergers or acquisitions across diverse industries, however, the absolute size of the resulting corporations is more relevant than market share. In such cases, asset value became the relevant indicator.

Interpretation of asset values has generated an ongoing controversy since a 1932 study by Adolf Berle and Gardiner Means, *The Modern Corporation and Private Property*, measured increased concentration of ownership. But data collected by the U.S. Federal Trade Commission based on corporate financial accounts showed a slight decline in concentration among the top 200 nonfinancial corporations between 1970 and the mid-1980s. These data were used by conservatives to argue that mergers had not harmed the competitive climate. In contrast, economists in favor of government intervention against corporate mergers pointed to data on *manufacturing* corporations (as opposed to all nonfinancial corporations) that showed *increased* concentration of asset ownership among the top 200 firms, rising to nearly 60 percent by the end of the 1980s.

Who is correct? The data on all "nonfinancial" corporations used by conservatives are more inclusive, thus better representative of the entire economy. Nevertheless, the manufacturing data used by the critics may be more consistent over time because these manufacturing industries have not changed as much as those industries included in the nonfinancial category. (In addition, results depend on whether domestic activity alone is considered, for which concentration of ownership by the largest 200 corporations appears unchanged, or whether overseas activity is included, for which concentration of ownership has increased.) Overall, we know there is considerable concentration of ownership, but the long-term trend is a complicated picture, highly dependent on which data are used.

Is Small Beautiful?

Small businesses gained respect during the 1980s when statistics appeared to show that they were the economy's job engine. For example, the U.S. Small Business Administration claimed that "small businesses provided *100% of new jobs* from 1987 to 1992." At a time when large companies were laying off millions of employees, good news from the small business sector appealed to policy makers across the political spectrum.

David Birch, affiliated first with Harvard University and then Massachusetts Institute of Technology, initiated the small business job-creation thesis. Beginning in the late 1970s, Birch exploited a previously unexplored data source from Dun and Bradstreet Corporation's credit reports. Unlike most business data, these credit reports trace the birth, growth, and death of business firms, including information on the number of employees. This research culminated in Birch's 1987 book, *Job Generation in America*, and was the basis for assertions by the U.S. Small Business Administration and other groups that small businesses create the most jobs.

By the 1990s, accumulating evidence began to cast doubt on the role of small businesses. Critics at the Brookings Institution, the National Bureau for Economic Research, and finally, even at Dun and Bradstreet, pointed out flaws in Birch's method. First, the underlying data were subject to substantial error, for example mislabeling a change of ownership as a new business startup. Second, long-term trends were mistakenly extrapolated from recession years in which net new jobs in large firms were negative, so any positive growth in small business jobs appeared to be 100 percent of all new jobs. Since the 1950s, the share of jobs in small business, defined as fewer than 100 employees, has been remarkably stable at about 40 percent of all employment.

Finally, almost all the job growth reported for small businesses occurred in a few new firms that immediately employed more than 100 employees. For example, when the newly created Lotus software company grew quickly to more than 500 employees, these were all counted as small business jobs because Lotus began with fewer than 20 employees. Overall, just 735 firms, or three-tenths of 1 percent of new businesses, generated 75 percent of the new business job gains between 1985 and 1988. In other words, most jobs were not created *within* the small business sector; instead, a few new businesses did spectacularly well, growing up to become quite large employers.

Even though the small business job-creation hypothesis seems to be incorrect, the debate prompted important new research about downsizing in many industries. For example, within large enterprises, there have been more new jobs at small establishments than at large ones. Also, some research suggests that smaller firms may be more innovative, introducing new technology and gaining more patents than larger, more bureaucratic firms. New data sources such as the Dun and Bradstreet data file, available through the U.S. Small Business Administration, will help us better understand these issues.

Line-of-Business Reporting

How much detail should businesses be required to report to government statistical authorities? During the 1970s, a program to increase business disclosure to the U.S. Federal Trade Commission caused so much controversy that the new statistics were no longer calculated, and similar proposals by other agencies were curtailed. As a result, information was not collected that would have been useful for government regulators, financial investors, and academic researchers.

At issue was "line-of-business reporting," the disclosure of financial statistics for different product areas under the control of a single company. Under existing rules, companies are required to disclose only limited information about multifaceted operations; most financial data could be reported in consolidated form, that is, a single number encompassing the entire business firm. A leading proponent of line-of-business reporting pointed to the example of the General Electric Corporation, which reported much of its financial data to the SEC under the category "consumer products," not further divided into refrigerators, light bulbs, televisions, hair dryers, or other items made by the corporation. Similarly consolidated statements are the most detailed public information available for other large U.S. corporations, most of which also have diversified production.

The proposal for line-of-business reporting was initiated by the U.S. Federal Trade Commission as part of its antitrust enforcement to assess corporate control in individual markets. Private investors also argued for increased disclosure because existing practices enabled diversified corporations to hide losses by unsuccessful parts of their companies. Since 1976, the Financial Accounting Standards Board has required corporations to report separate accounts for business segments that constitute more than 10 percent of sales. The U.S. Securities and Exchange Commission has been lax in enforcing disclosure, however, so investors complain that they cannot accurately assess corporations such as Kodak that lump together earnings from products as different as cameras, batteries, and copiers under the single reporting segment "imaging."

Opponents of increased disclosure succeeded in preventing extensive overhaul of line-of-business reporting. Arguments against the plan were threefold. First, critics maintained that disclosure would not provide accurate information because of inconsistencies in the Standard Industrial Classification (see Box 10.4) proposed for line-of-business reporting. Second, critics argued that corporate accountants could not accurately measure how overhead costs are distributed among different parts of a business. Third, and most important for the defeat of the proposal, corporations opposed disclosure on the grounds that it would breach financial confidentiality, providing data to possible business competitors.

One hundred and eighty companies filed lawsuits against the Federal Trade Commission's line-of-business reporting program. Even though the Supreme Court ruled in favor of the commission in 1978, the program was halted until Federal Trade Commission staff could prove that the benefits of the data exceeded the costs of collecting it. Eventually, the line-of-business data, covering almost 500 corporations, led to a large number of published studies and the data are now available to individual researchers on special application to the Federal Trade Commission.

The debate about line-of-business reporting is illustrative of a tug-of-war that frequently takes place between government regulators and the business world. In this case, as in other disputes, the experience of the past two decades has been soundly against increased disclosure. Ongoing political debate will determine whether additional information will be collected in the future.

Box 10.4. **Standard Industrial Classification**

Consistent classification of U.S. industry is so important that responsibility is entrusted to the president's Office of Management and Budget's Statistical Policy Office. They oversee the Standard Industrial Classification (SIC), a numerical coding used throughout the government and in most private-sector research as well. In the SIC, four digits refer to specific industries; for example, 2098 is macaroni and spaghetti makers. The first two digits are larger aggregates; in this case, 20 is for food and kindred products manufacturers. The U.S. Census Bureau adds three more digits to create product-line codes. For example, 2844515 is "suntan and sunscreen lotions and oils" in the "toilet preparation" industry, SIC code 2844.

The major problem with the SIC is that its codes are outdated. For example, until recently, microwave components were included in a catchall category, 3679, "Electrical Components Not Elsewhere Classified," along with phonograph needles and radio headphones. Service-sector classification is especially obsolete with major industries often categorized in a single four-digit code. Thus, *all* eating places fall under code 5812, while the older food manufacturing industry is divided into many four-digit codes, for example, with a separate code for macaroni and spaghetti products. Researchers and marketing groups (who use SIC codes to target advertising) claim that they are handicapped by these out-of-date categories. But budget restraints have prevented the much-needed overhaul of SIC codes, reducing the Statistical Policy Office to a staff of fewer than ten professional employees in 1987 who had time to recommend only minor changes in the classification system.

How Much Profit?

Even without line-of-business data, considerable information is available about corporate finances. One frequently studied subject is profits, a term that has different meanings to different users. A recent controversy about profits illustrates potential pitfalls that can occur when a term is not defined precisely.

Are Profits Too High?

American corporations have paid for newspaper and magazine space to respond to what they perceive as widespread misperception on the part of the public about the level of corporate profits. Opinion polls show that the public estimates typical profit rates at nearly 30 percent, whereas according to the Chevron Oil Corporation in one advertisement, profits averaged only 5 percent.

The number reported by Chevron is profit as percentage of sales, based on a statistic in corporate reports called "net income as a percentage of sales." Indeed, for many corporations this figure is no more than 5 percent. This statistic has limited applicability for comparative purposes, however, because sales cannot be compared between different sectors of the economy. (See earlier on sales as a measure of corporate size.) For example, the profit rate on sales can be misleadingly low if the business has a fast turnover that enables high profits to be earned despite a low profit rate. As an alternative, business analysts calculate profits as a percentage of how much has been invested in the firm, a profit rate that averages over 10 percent. For example, in 1988, Chevron's profit as percentage of stockholder equity was 12.3 percent. It is this second definition of profits that the public probably had in mind in the opinion polls because it is similar to the concept of the rate of return received on individual investments. (The survey questions asked specifically about profit as a percentage of sales, but this qualification was likely ignored or not understood by many respondents.) Moreover, the public probably also used an entirely different concept of profits that included pay and other benefits accruing to high-level management. In standard corporate accounting these are considered "employee costs" and are never counted as profits. Unlike small businesses, with which the public was more familiar, where managers and owners are the same people, corporate accounting limits the concept of profit to earnings paid as dividends or retained for corporate use. For example, in 1989, Craig O. McCaw, chairman of McCaw Cellular Communications, was the highest paid of all U.S. corporate executives with $53.9 million in salary, bonuses, and stock options—even though in strict accounting terms his company earned no profits.

In summary, Chevron used a standard definition of profits in its advertisement, although the corporation chose to measure profits as a percentage of sales, a procedure that minimized their apparent profit rate. The public had a much looser sense of what should be included in profits and misunderstood the accounting definition. Yet the public was correct in the sense that profits are best measured as a proportion of what has been invested. The contrast between these two uses of the same concept is instructive about the need for caution when strict accounting terms are compared with everyday usage.

How Now Dow?

The Dow Jones Industrial Average (DJIA) is probably the most commonly reported of all economics or business statistics, but few viewers of the nightly news know either the meaning of the "Dow" or its limitations. The Dow Jones Industrial Average is simply the total stock prices of thirty representative stocks (corrected for the minor detail of stock splits and changes in the thirty representatives). For example, on June 26, 1989, the DJIA, or the Dow, was 2511: the total stock price of General Motors, McDonalds, and twenty-eight other of the largest U.S. corporations (multiplied by a correcting factor of 0.659).

Stock market experts agree that the Dow is a poor gauge of the overall market. By simply adding each stock price, the Dow gives greater weight to higher-priced stocks. For example, IBM's stock price, approximately $100 during the late 1980s, counted more strongly in the Dow, exerting a strong 80-point downward pull in the Dow between 1987 and 1989. On the other hand, the Exxon Corporation had much less effect because its stock sold for about half as much per share, even though Exxon is comparable in size to IBM. An additional drawback to the Dow Jones Industrial Average is its coverage of only thirty companies. The choice of thirty stocks stems from the Dow's origin in 1884 as an easily calculated measure of overall stock activity. Today, with computers, it is possible to include many stock prices, and to weight them by corporate size. Stock indexes such as the New York Stock Exchange Index and the Standard and Poor's Index use these more sophisticated techniques (See Figure 10.1).

Picking Stock Winners

Can anyone predict which stocks will do well? Or, as some researchers argue, do stock prices move so randomly that monkeys throwing darts at the stock page would do as well as stock advisers—or even better once we subtract the fees charged by human stock pickers? It seems common sense that *some* experts predict stocks well; after all there are some investors who become fabulously rich. It is also true that if we have a large number of monkeys, a few of them also will succeed.

Figure 10.1. **Dow Jones versus the Overall New York Stock Exchange.** Changes in DJIA compared with the NYSE composite index for a typical week.

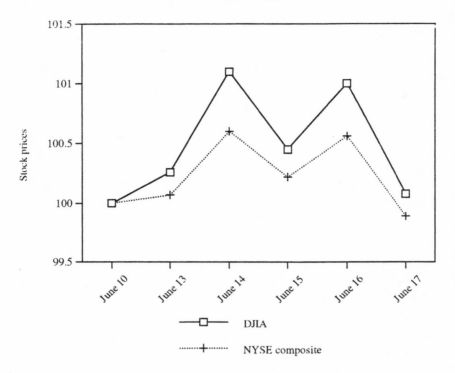

Source: *The Wall Street Journal,* June 10–17, 1994.

Since there are thousands of stock advisers, perhaps we should not be surprised that some do well.

To separate luck from skill, analysts measure the repeat success of investment advisers: do they accurately predict the market year after year? Business magazines often feature the record of last year's top predictors with sobering results; most successful advisers fail to maintain their success from one year to another.

In a similar test, the *Hulbert Financial Digest* tracked the advice of investment newsletters that did well one year to see how they did the following year. Between 1981 and 1992, investors who followed the advice of previously successful newsletters did poorly and would have done six times better by following the random choices made by mon-

Table 10.3

The First Shall Be Last: Mutual Fund Rankings (*Business Week* "top performers"; mutual growth funds with highest rating, 1987–91)

	1991 Performance (rank out of 245 funds)	1992 Performance (rank out of 233 funds)
Fund A	50	218
Fund B	2	99
Fund C	27	117
Fund D	77	228
Fund E	95	200
Fund F	29	31
Fund G	236	41
Fund H	113	181
Fund I	18	214
Fund J	20	205
Fund K	36	153
Fund L	3	196
Fund M	10	219
Fund N	24	220
Fund O	244	185
Fund P	28	150
Fund Q	61	192
Fund R	85	91
Fund S	4	226

keys. Interestingly, following the advice of the previous year's *losers* led to better earnings than following the previous year's winners' advice—but still not as lucrative as the monkey's choices. Hulbert concludes: "one-year performances are an unreliable guide to the future."

For long-term investment, the picture is more complicated. Carefully adjusting for fees charged and the risk an investment incurs, several researchers find a small positive correlation in the earnings of investment funds over many years. Thus, by choosing funds carefully there are potential long-term gains, about 2 percent per year. Princeton economist Burton Malkiel disputes these findings on the grounds that these studies omit very unsuccessful funds that went out of business.

When the failed funds are included, he concludes that the overall fund record is less than could be obtained by investing at random. In sum, the predictability—or randomness—of the stock market remains an unresolved research problem. We know that it is not *very* predictable; short-term success is ephemeral and long-term success is, at best, relatively slight. This is not an argument against investment advice altogether, but rather a warning about those who promise short-term gains from individual stocks. Advisers may be able to predict the riskiness of various investments and the likelihood of short-term versus long-term earnings.

> *Data Sample:* Market recommendations based on astrology, as advised in Crawford Perspectives, earned a ranking of 7 out of 65 in Hulbert Financial Service's 1992 study—an embarrassment to newsletters that claim to use more scientific principles.

Summary

The examples reviewed in this chapter suggest two common problems that apply to many business statistics.

First, because most business statistics come from data reported by corporations themselves, there are limits on how much information is available. As shown in the dispute over line-of-business reporting, corporations have not been willing to disclose additional information above what is already required by law. Consequently, researchers and government regulators must rely on imperfect statistics, which is sometimes a considerable handicap.

Second, on a more positive note, these corporate reports are subject to strict accounting procedures. It is true that investors sometimes complain about corporate attempts to hide unfavorable information, as in the case of misleading language in annual reports. But overall, researchers using business statistics are more fortunate than most data users in the sense that few other data sources are subject to such intensive review by outside experts or to such well-established reporting criteria. The problem is that these strict accounting procedures can be misinterpreted. For example, accounting rules for depreciation are the source of problems in measuring asset values and profitability. Users of these statistics need to be aware that depreciation often is measured with an eye toward the corporation's tax liability, rather than with any concern for creating a consistent data base for research purposes.

In conclusion, business is probably the most completely documented field covered in this book, in terms of both the volume of data and their interpretation by experts. As with many other social science data, a telephone call to the appropriate corporate or government official often will clarify problems encountered with these numbers. Researchers also should not overlook public libraries, which often have extensive holdings of business publications, including many that are too expensive for an individual to buy.

Case Study Questions

1. One of the arguments in favor of line-of-business disclosure is that it is needed to answer important research questions. Describe a research project that would require line-of-business information. Describe public policies that might be changed based on this research project.

2. Design an advertising campaign for a business that would make use of SIC data. Be specific about how many digits you need in the SIC.

3. The 1985 *Economic Report of the President* argues that measures of the concentration of corporate assets are "deceiving because it masks substantial turnover in the rank and identity of the largest firms. For example, of the 500 largest industrial firms [in 1955] . . . only 262 remained in the top 500 in 1980." Evaluate this claim.

4. On September 30, 1994, the Dow Jones Industrial Average was *down* by 0.30 percent, while the New York Stock Exchange index was *up* by 0.14 percent. Explain the difference.

5. Traditionally, economists have used the *Fortune 500* industrial corporations as the sample for investigating the relationship between profitability and differences in types of corporate ownership. What kinds of companies were omitted from this research effort? Why might these omissions bias the research results?

6. In a 1963 antitrust suit, the U.S. Supreme Court ruled against the merger of the Aluminum Company of America (Alcoa) with a much

smaller aluminum company called Rome. The following market shares
for Alcoa were cited in the case:

> Aluminum bare conductor wire and cable: 27.8 percent
> Aluminum and copper bare conductor wire and cable: 10.3 percent
> Aluminum and copper bare and insulated wire and cable: 1.8 percent
> (Rome's market share was 2 percent or less in all markets.)

Using these data, construct cases both for and against the merger. (The
Supreme Court ruled against the merger.)

Chapter 11

Government

By this point in the book, readers should be convinced that few social statistics are to be taken at face value. Thus it will come as no surprise that there is controversy about statistics concerning the operations of the U.S. government itself. And again, there is little debate about the sincerity of those who gather the data. In fact, many of the problems were first identified by government statisticians. This chapter reviews disputes about military spending, welfare spending, the U.S. deficit, and the money supply. Important policy decisions depend on how we measure each of these variables. In addition, a final section reviews problems raised in earlier chapters about inflation and currency-exchange rate adjustments. Again, the difficulty for researchers is choosing the correct statistic from the many numbers published by the government.

Data Sources

Data collected by the U.S. government about the government are readily available. Statistical publications are inexpensive; voluminous information is distributed to Federal Depository libraries, and federal agencies generally are receptive to direct inquiries.

U.S. Budget

Detailed analysis of spending and taxation is contained in the annual Budget of the U.S. Government submitted by the president to Congress

Where the Numbers Come From

Organizations	Data sources	Key publications
Office of Management and Budget, Executive Office of the President	Proposed budget of the United States	*The Budget of the United States Government*
Social Security Administration, U.S. Department of Health and Human Services	Social security and other program payments	*Social Security Bulletin; Public Assistance Statistics*
Bureau of Labor Statistics, U.S. Department of Labor	Consumer Expenditure Survey and other BLS surveys	*Monthly Labor Review; Consumer Price Index, Detailed Report; Producer Price Indexes*
Bureau of Economic Analysis, U.S. Department of Commerce	Deflators from national income and product accounts	*Survey of Current Business*
U.S. Arms Control and Disarmament Agency	Worldwide military expenditures	*Worldwide Military Expenditures and Arms Transfers*
Stockholm International Peace Research Institute	Worldwide military expenditures	*SIPRI Yearbook*

For summary information, see *Economic Report of the President.*

in January and then revised substantially during the year. It is a massive book with additional volumes of appendix, special analyses, and historical tables. Summary data are published in a more manageable "United States Budget in Brief," the annual *Economic Report of the President*, and the July issue of the U.S. Commerce Department's

Survey of Current Business. These data are published in "fiscal years." From 1844 until 1976, the fiscal year ran from July 1 to June 30; in 1976, it was changed to run from October 1 to September 30. Thus, fiscal year 1995 included October 1, 1994, through September 30, 1995. The slight differences from the calendar year are overlooked for most research purposes.

Money

The money supply is measured by the board of governors of the U.S. Federal Reserve. Both its short-term estimates and longer-term official figures are widely available in official government publications, with analysis in many business periodicals.

> *Data Sample*: The U.S. Federal Reserve estimated a daily average of $8.1 billion in travelers checks in December 1992, up from $6.9 billion in December 1989.

Prices

Most inflation data are collected by the U.S. Labor Department's Bureau of Labor Statistics for its own price indexes, numbers that also form a large part of the U.S. Commerce Department's inflation adjustments for GDP accounting. The Bureau of Labor Statistics surveys more than a million price quotations to compute consumer and producer price indexes for a large number of products and geographic regions. These data are widely publicized: up-to-date estimates are available on telephone recordings, while historical data are published in several government documents.

Currency values are determined by market exchanges around the world and are widely publicized in newspapers and business periodicals. Composite exchange rates measuring values relative to several currencies at one time are calculated by central banks, including the U.S. Federal Reserve and the Bank of England.

> *Data sample:* The Consumer Price Index for all urban consumers for school books and supplies rose to 204.6 in June 1994 from 196.4 in June 1993, an increase of 4.2 percent.

Controversies

How Much for the Military?

Two fundamental questions arise in assessing military spending. First, what is the total level of U.S. military spending? And second, how does U.S. military spending compare with other countries' spending? These questions affected policy debates both when military spending was rising and when it was reduced.

The U.S. Military Budget

Even with the end of the Cold War, U.S. military spending is in the hundreds of billions of dollars. The actual total is measured several ways. Traditional U.S. government budgets include only Defense Department spending, the number typically reported as the level of "military" spending, $260 billion in 1995. But this measure leaves out more than $100 billion in spending on military assistance to other countries, nuclear weapons constructed by the Energy Department, spy satellites launched by NASA, veterans' benefits administered by the Veterans Administration, and interest on the debt accrued during past wars. The defense establishment recognizes some of these issues in alternative measures of military spending. For example, NATO estimates include aid to other countries, whereas CIA estimates include defense-related spending outside the Defense Department but leave out military assistance. If the research purpose is to ascertain total resources designated for military use, then corrections to official data are necessary.

Third World Military

Even trickier to measure are military expenditures in less developed countries. Not only is there less publicly available information, but researchers also face substantial problems of definitions. In many less developed countries there is considerable overlap between military and civilian expenditures, including police forces, roads, bridges, and power plants built or controlled by the military. Comprehensive time-series data are available from several expert sources including the U.S. Arms Control and Disarmament Agency and the Stockholm International Peace Research Institute. These groups rely on a combination of official publications, intelligence reports, and media sources.

Soviet Military Spending

In addition to the problems cited earlier, the interpretation of a country's military spending depends on the accounting unit used to measure it. Should the military costs be counted in dollars? in the local currency? Or should military weapons be compared with each other based on their physical capabilities, independent of cost? An ongoing debate about military expenditures in the former Soviet Union illustrates these conceptual difficulties.

According to some conservative military analysts, an "intelligence blunder" by the CIA caused Soviet military spending to be underestimated during the 1970s and early 1980s. In this view, the Reagan and Bush administrations were justified in increasing U.S. military spending because the Soviet Union had outspent the United States by over $400 billion. Many of the data remain classified, so independent researchers cannot assess all the competing claims. Nonetheless, experts outside the CIA maintain that enough is known to question the assertions made by Presidents Reagan and Bush.

One source of controversy is the method used to compare prices in the centrally planned Soviet economy versus prices set primarily by markets in the United States. For example, Soviet soldiers who were drafted earned considerably less than U.S. soldiers who had been hired in a competitive labor market after 1973. Should we value the Soviet army at its cost to the Soviet government or at the far larger amount that it would have cost to raise such a large army in the United States? The problems were even greater for military hardware, for which there were often no Soviet prices whatsoever because weapons were not bought or sold in any market. Even in the United States, much military hardware is purchased in noncompetitive markets, which, as recent scandals revealed, can cause extraordinarily high prices. These costs make it difficult to assess the military's use of real resources—as opposed to its use of government budget dollars. According to the critics, for this reason alone the CIA overstated Soviet spending by more than $200 billion because it relied too much on U.S. prices rather than actual costs in the Soviet Union.

If the critics are correct, official estimates exaggerated the Soviet threat, leading the United States into an unnecessary arms race that cost many hundreds of billions of dollars and endangered the entire earth. One could hardly make a more convincing case for the need for researchers to understand carefully the data that lie behind policy decisions.

How Much for Welfare?

In common usage, "welfare" means assistance to the poor or, in more technical terms, "means-tested" transfer payments, that is, programs for which recipients must prove they are poor. But a broader definition of welfare includes social programs available to everyone, such as social security, publicly funded health care, and public education. Several recent policy debates depend on which definition is used.

Does Welfare Work?

Charles Murray's 1984 book, *Losing Ground*, claimed that greatly expanded government programs for the poor, beginning with the War on Poverty in 1965, actually made matters worse for the supposed beneficiaries. In Murray's view, poverty had declined *until* the government introduced misguided programs that created disincentives for the poor to work and maintain stable families.

Critics pointed out that "social welfare," as measured by Murray, included a number of programs, not all of which are designed to help the poor. For example, between 1970 and 1984, means-tested spending counted for only one-seventh of the rise in total transfer payments. Most of the rest of the rise was an increase in programs for the elderly, for whom poverty indeed was reduced. In this view, means-tested programs have always been so underfunded that it is no surprise that poverty for groups other than the elderly has not been significantly reduced.

Whichever policy advice one supports for the welfare system, the debate illustrates the need to specify carefully what constitutes welfare spending. Failure to do so seriously undermined the credibility of Murray's findings.

Welfare for Everyone?

By the broad definition of welfare as including all social programs, the United States spends over 10 percent of national output on welfare, or more than $500 billion in 1990, a statistic used both to criticize and to defend government spending.

In a widely quoted analysis, economist Gordon Tullock argued in 1981 that there was sufficient federal transfer money to give all poor families a yearly income of $48,000—*if* all the funds were distributed to the poor. Of course, many of the most expensive government programs go to nonpoor recipients, most importantly, social security and Medicare. In Tullock's view these programs specifically, and government intervention generally, do not help those in need of welfare, but instead transfer resources to politically powerful groups.

Other researchers use the expanded definition of welfare to argue in favor of government programs. In this view, welfare works best if it is available to everyone and does not stigmatize the poor. For example, social programs in Sweden are about triple their U.S. level (as a percentage of the total economy), providing a wide range of benefits, including health care, child care, higher education, job training, and retirement pay. Such expensive programs were justified not as a handout to the needy, but as the right of every resident.

These two views on government transfers show the importance of connotation in a politically loaded word such as welfare. In Tullock's view, welfare spending is a transfer from one group to another, sometimes to those not in need, whereas advocates of the Swedish model see welfare spending as a means to secure widespread social benefits. Researchers need to be aware of these quite different meanings.

How Big Is the Deficit?

In a national survey, U.S. citizens identified "the deficit" as the major problem facing the country, and nearly all national political candidates present plans to bring the budget into balance. Indeed, the official U.S. deficit, the difference between federal government spending and revenues, topped $100 billion for every year between 1980 and 1995, so the national debt, the total of past deficits, reached $4,000 billion (see Figure 11.1). When President Clinton announced in his 1992 Inaugural Address that we must "cut our massive debt," he likely meant that we should cut the deficit, since only a budget surplus would reduce the debt, something that has not occurred since 1969. One consequence of the pressure to bring the budget into closer bal-

Figure 11.1. **U.S. Federal Deficit.** Total deficit, on and off budget, for fiscal year.

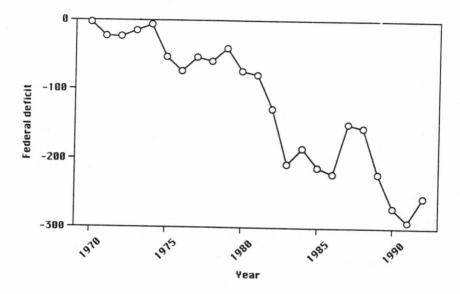

Source: U.S. Department of Commerce, *Economic Report of the President, 1994* (Washington, D.C.: U.S. Government Printing Office, 1994), p. 359.

ance has been to disguise the actual state of the government's finances. Three deliberate manipulations were practiced.

Selling off Government Assets

Several times during the 1980s, the Reagan administration improved the apparent budgetary balance by planning to sell U.S. government assets. The 1982 Asset Management Program called for the sale of federal property, including large blocks of public lands. The prospective sale of the government-owned freight railroad system, Conrail, was included as revenue for the 1986 budget, and then again in 1987 when the sale was blocked for 1986. Finally, the 1988 budget included projected revenues from the sale of debts owed the government, including farm and school loans, that were to be sold to private investors for collection.

Whatever the advantages or disadvantages of public ownership for these assets—for example, environmentalists fought bitterly against the sale of public land—the sale of government assets was criticized by accountants as a one-shot injection of revenue. The deficit would fall only once and reappear the following year. In the private sector there are strict rules to prevent companies from using the sale of assets to cover up deficits.

Shifting Targets

In 1985, the U.S. Congress passed the Gramm-Rudman-Hollings Act, a mandate for continuous reductions in the deficit and a balanced budget by 1991. The Congress and the president never failed to meet each year's goals—but they also failed to cut the deficit anywhere near the Gramm-Rudman-Hollings intentions. Instead, gimmickry provided the false appearance of fiscal responsibility. One simple procedure was to shift the military payday and some farm-support programs back into the previous year's budget. Since only this year's budget needed to be certified under Gramm-Rudman-Hollings, there was no penalty for worsening the previous year's budget. Of course, the change did not save the government a penny.

Off-budget Items

The major discrepancy in the federal budget involves moving items in or out of the official budget. The principle for excluding some items is to separate ongoing government programs from special funds such as school loans for which expenditures and repayment may not be expected to balance in any given year. But because Gramm-Rudman-Hollings applied only to on-budget items, several expensive items such as the federal government's bailout of savings-and-loan institutions were kept off-budget. For example, in 1988 this bookkeeping trick reduced the apparent deficit by about $35 billion.

Fortunately for researchers, many of these budget shenanigans have been relatively small, at least relative to the more than $100 billion deficits. The major exception is the surplus in the social security trust fund, government "debt" that actually is owned by the government itself. For most research purposes, we want to look at the debt held by the public, about $1 trillion less than the total $4 trillion debt in 1994. In most economists' estimations, even without changing the trend in government spending and taxation, the social security surplus will absorb all current and past deficits some time early in the twenty-first century. A few years later, however, increases in social security payments as the baby boomers retire will turn the surplus into a deficit (see chapter 2 on this point). On the other hand, greater than expected off-budget items such as the savings and loan insurance program, or increased losses from government loans, could add to the deficit. Researchers need to look at both official and off-budget items to understand the total financial picture of the U.S. government. Although this difference is often overlooked in popular accounts of the budget, and in congressional compliance with Gramm-Rudman-Hollings, both sets of data are available, most readily in the annual *Economic Report of the President.*

A Debt Monster?

The U.S. federal debt, topping $4 trillion in the 1990s, is a number guaranteed to shock. The debt clock in New York City's Times Square ticked off more than $1 million every minute, totaling more than $30,000 in accumulated debt for every U.S. family. Many economists agree that the deficit is a serious problem and call for policies of more taxes or reduced spending to decrease the deficit. But a contrary position is put forward by a number of influential economists, including 1988 American Economic Association president Robert Eisner and best-selling author and economist Robert Heilbroner. In their view, the fiscal problem of the U.S. government may be too little, not too much, debt.

Eisner and Heilbroner recommend several accounting corrections to the traditional definition of the debt. For example, they maintain that government accounting overstates the debt because it does not decrease the value of the debt when inflation occurs. But the major adjustment advocated by Eisner and Heilbroner is to separate government investments from other government expenditures. Analogy is made to the private sector where borrowing for investment purposes is recognized as vitally necessary. If no one incurred debt for investment, our economy would collapse: there would be no home building, no telephone system, no railroads, no other projects that require long-term financing. Of course, not all borrowing is good. For example, the bank likely will frown on a loan for a vacation or other forms of consumption. But loans for housing or new equipment for a business are more likely to be approved because debt is being used for what economists call *capital*. These expenditures should be financed through borrowing, or we would waste time accumulating funds to pay for investments that could have been generating new economic activity.

Because many government expenditures such as bridge and road building clearly qualify as investment, Eisner and Heilbroner argue they should not be counted as a harmful part of the deficit. For 1992, Eisner attributes about $172 billion in federal government expenditures to net investment, that is, total investment less what is needed to replace worn-out older investment. If we also include state and local expenditures for education, then, according to Eisner: "the entire government budget deficit would disappear. And with it would have to go the oft-repeated charge that our budget deficits mean we are reckless with our future."

Critics object to these revised numbers on several grounds. First, they point out that deficits became a major problem after 1980 primarily because of increased military and social security spending, neither of which is an increase in investment. Eisner responds that earlier budgets, seemingly in balance, actually were in tremendous surplus because of undifferentiated investment expenditures. Thus, increases in expenditures, although for consumption purposes, simply brought the budget into closer balance, not the deficit measured in traditional accounts.

Second, critics challenge Eisner's assessment of what constitutes investment. For example, Charles L. Schultze, chief economic adviser to President Carter, measures far less net investment in the federal budget, only an estimated $7 billion in 1989. Eisner and Heilbroner agree that investment is tricky to measure and suggest that the federal government might follow the corporate model and keep a separate capital budget. In fact, many local governments already do so. But other noted economists oppose extension of the concept to the federal government because politicians would be too likely to manipulate the process to spend money without collecting taxes. Brookings Institution economist Henry J. Aaron points out that there is no independent accounting authority as exists for private corporations to ensure proper bookkeeping.

The choice of deficit numbers appears to be guided by political perspective. Those opposed to government spending tend to point to the traditional high deficit numbers, while Eisner and others, who have long urged more public programs, use much lower deficit estimates. Researchers need to look at several ways of measuring the deficit, choosing the appropriate statistic depending on the research project. For example, in comparing the relative advantage of spending priorities between the public and private sectors, we need to separate investment from other expenditures. Without a widely accepted U.S. government capital budget, the task is difficult, but the presence of a government deficit is in itself insufficient reason to favor private-sector spending over public spending.

Taxes

It seems a simple matter to understand taxes. After all, tax rates are public knowledge, and there are complete government records about the amount and kind of taxes collected. But two factors complicate recent analysis of the U.S. tax system: first, how to measure the "fairness" of tax cuts, and second, how to measure who actually bears the burden of the tax system.

Capital Gains Tax Cuts

A debate took place during the 1990s about the advisability of cutting the capital gains tax, that is, the tax on profitable sales of assets such as stock or property. In his 1992 State of the Union address, President Bush maintained that "60 percent of the people who benefit from lower capital gains have incomes under $50,000." But the Congressional Joint Committee on Taxation found that more than 80 percent of the benefit would go to those with incomes *over* $100,000. The discrepancy occurred because many low-income taxpayers owe capital gains and thus could benefit from the tax cut, but only by a very small amount, about $300 for the $30,000 to $40,000 per year income range. High-income taxpayers were fewer in number, but accounted for a lion's share of the capital gains. For example, those with incomes over $200,000 would average more than $8,000 in savings.

A second problem in measuring capital gains is the use of "ordinary" versus "total" income. Former Assistant Treasury Secretary Paul Craig Roberts found that taxpayers with incomes under $20,000 would benefit as much as those with incomes over $200,000. Other researchers pointed out that these income classifications were based on "ordinary" income (although in some reports the qualification was missing). "Ordinary" income excludes capital gains, which one critic charged is like "justifying a tax break for investment bankers on the grounds that if you don't count their income from investment banking, investment banks don't make much money." In addition, Brookings Institution economist Joseph Pechman points out that many wealthy individuals are able to use tax shelters to show low or even negative incomes on their tax returns. By not counting low incomes caused exclusively by such "losses," Pechman finds that contrary to the *Wall Street Journal*'s claims, capital gains received by those with incomes under $20,000 is only one-third the capital gains received by the over-$200,000 income earners.

The lesson for researchers in this debate is to look closely at what is called fair. One can construct a case for the definitions of fairness used to defend the capital gains tax cuts. But an average citizen likely would interpret fairness differently from how it was used by government defenders of the tax cuts.

Who Bears the Tax Burden?

The overall distribution of taxes among income groups is measured by what economists call the *progressivity* of the tax system. Taxes are progressive if tax rates increase for higher-income groups. (Tax rates are regressive if they fall as one moves up the income ladder.) The most frequently cited studies of U.S. taxes were conducted by Brookings Institution economist Joseph Pechman, who also investigated the capital gains tax described earlier. Pechman's research illustrates the problems in measuring the tax rate for different income groups.

At the Brookings Institution, Pechman used a data set called the MERGE files, which combined Internal Revenue Service tax returns with Census Bureau data on the characteristics of households. (Because neither the Internal Revenue Service nor the Census Bureau allows individuals to be identified specifically, a computer program "matched" tax data with similar households from the Census Bureau; in large numbers the procedure approximates what would happen if both tax and census data were available for the same households.)

The major challenge to Pechman and other researchers using the MERGE files was determining the allocation of taxes that can be passed on to parties other than those from whom the tax is collected.

Consider social security taxes. Most economists agree that workers bear the burden not only for the approximately 7.5 percent taken out of their paychecks but also for the equivalent sum paid by employers that is likely passed on to workers as lower wages and salaries. Similar problems occur in assessing the impact of other taxes such as the sales tax, some of which may be absorbed by sellers, property taxes that may be passed on to renters, and corporate income taxes passed on to consumers in higher prices.

The 1986 Pechman study included eight variations of possible assumptions about the ultimate bearer of the tax burden. For example, one variant assumed that employees ultimately paid the employer portion of social security taxes and that property and corporate taxes were paid by property owners and stockholders rather than passed on to consumers. By these assumptions, the tax system was most progressive, ranging in 1980 from about 20 percent taxation for the poorest one-tenth of the population to about 27 percent for the top one-tenth. Other assumptions measured far less progressivity, or in some instances a regressive system in which the total tax rate is higher on the poor than on the rich. According to Pechman, these results show that "the tax system has very little effect on the distribution of income" and that the United States could increase the progressivity of the tax system "without punitive tax rates that will hurt economic incentives."

On the other side, supporters of President Reagan's tax cuts in the 1980s maintained that the tax system hurt incentives because tax rates were in fact far more progressive than Pechman had found. A persistent critic of Pechman's findings was Edgar K. Browning. In a 1976 study for the American Enterprise Institute, Browning and his colleagues measured considerable overall progressivity in the tax system, ranging from less than 12 percent for the lowest-income group to more than 38 percent for the top-income group.

One reason Browning measured more progressively was that he took into account the effect of transfer payments such as social security, Aid to Families with Dependent Children, and food stamps. Browning pointed out that including these programs, which are untaxed, causes the tax system to become more progressive because the poor receive income that is not taxed. In a 1986 debate with Browning, Pechman accepted this revision, but rejected Browning's claim that the overall trend in tax system was toward progressivity. According to Pechman, gains from transfers to low-income earners were offset by increases in social security taxes. Moreover, reductions in taxes for high-income groups caused taxes for the top 1 percent to fall from 39.6 percent in 1966 to only 25.3 percent in 1985.

In textbooks and popular media articles, tax rates are often presented without any discussion of these controversies about how to measure the tax burden for different income groups. Some conclusions are not disputed, such as the progressivity of the federal personal income tax over the range of low to middle incomes and regressivity of the social security tax between middle- and high-income groups. But most other estimates require assumptions that change the effective tax rates. In assessing the state of the current tax system and in understanding the effect of new tax rates, researchers must pay careful attention to controversies about the underlying assumptions.

Measuring Money

In the United States, both measurement and policy making for financial affairs rests primarily with the Federal Reserve System, a quasi-independent branch of government. (Similar central banking organizations exist in most other countries.) The Federal Reserve, or Fed, as it is more commonly known, runs its own statistical-gathering operation, gathering data on national production (see chapter 7) and financial affairs, most importantly, measurement of the money supply.

What Is Money?

Economists use the word *money* in a far more complex manner than everyday usage would suggest. As defined by economists, money includes not just the coins and currency commonly called money but also bank deposits that exist only on bank accounting sheets. The measurement challenge is determining which bank accounts should count as money. At stake are important economic policies, as well as many research projects that require a measure of the money supply.

Federal Reserve publication of money data began during the 1940s, based on surveys of banking institutions. Today, daily reporting from approximately 10,000 large banks is supplemented by less regular reporting from smaller banks. Beginning in 1960, these numbers have been published as "monetary aggregates." Since then, money supply statistics have been expanded and redefined to take into account the changing financial system, as well as changing economists' views about the most appropriate measure of money. As of 1990, the two major definitions were labeled simply M1 and M2, based on the ease with which funds can be spent, a criterion called liquidity. M1, about $1,100 billion in 1994, includes only coins, currency, and checking accounts, funds readily available for use; M2, about $3,600 billion in 1994, includes these money supplies plus savings accounts and money market accounts, funds less likely to be spent in the near future on goods and services.

At times the Federal Reserve has used M1 and M2 as key policy targets. For example, during the early 1980s the Federal Reserve set quite restrictive goals for M1 and M2 in an attempt to lower the inflation rate. In theory it should have been possible to control inflation by increasing the money supply at a noninflationary rate. Economists are divided about the efficacy of this experiment: inflation was reduced, but at enormous cost in unemployment and lost production. There is general agreement, however, that measurement problems made it difficult to use the money supply as a policy target.

At almost precisely the same time that the Federal Reserve started to target the money supply, the relationship between the money-supply measures and the overall economy became especially erratic. Because of bank deregulation initiated during the late 1970s, there was an unprecedented movement of money into new types of bank and money market accounts. As a result, M1 and M2 fluctuated when funds moved between bank accounts, confounding attempts to use them as indicators of the inflationary pressures in the underlying economy. Most economists and financial analysts applauded the 1983 decision by the Federal Reserve to abandon its single-minded attention to money-supply statistics and to expand its targets to include a number of economic variables such as interest rates and the growth in economic production.

Missing Currency?

Do you have $1,000 in your pocket? Probably not, although more than this amount of U.S. coins and currency is in circulation for every U.S. adult. Not all of this cash belongs to individuals; some cash lies in vending machines, business cash registers, and banks. But economists believe these locations account for little of the currency excess. Instead, much of the missing money is likely held by drug dealers and other members of the underground economy, who hold on to large amounts of cash because of disclosure rules when these sums are deposited in banks. No one knows how much money can be accounted for in this way. A second location for the missing money is currency held by foreigners, especially in Latin American and Eastern Europe, where dollars are valued as a stable form of money. Although economists can only guess how many dollars circulate underground and overseas, the consensus is that only about 16 percent, or $28 billion of the total $177 billion in 1986, could be accounted for by household and business demand. According to Internal Revenue Service research, probably another $9 billion circulates underground, leaving about $140 billion in the hands of foreigners.

A number of important issues are at stake in tracking this money. As described in chapter 7, the appropriate response to the underground economy depends on its size, often estimated by the value of unaccounted-for currency. Dollars that flow overseas create a temporary windfall for the United States because imported products can be bought without foreigners using the money to demand U.S. products. For both the United States and recipients of dollars, the dollar flow makes it difficult for monetary authorities to measure and control the money supply.

In summary, the problems in measuring the money supply are both conceptual—what to include in the money supply?—and practical—where is the missing currency? The interpretation of money-supply statistics is an ongoing controversy among economists. These disputes illustrate the lack of precision, even in a statistic that one might think could be measured accurately.

Inflation

One of the most common problems in social science research and policy making is how to adjust variables for the effect of inflation. Although inflation adjustments are readily available from U.S. government agencies, the correct use of these adjustments is critical for accurate research as well as for appropriate inflation indexing in many labor union contracts, the social security system, and the income tax.

The most commonly used inflation rates are measured by the rates of change in the U.S. Commerce Department's Personal Consumption

Expenditure's deflator (PCE) and the Labor Department's Consumer Price Index (CPI). Usually these statistics move up and down together, measuring approximately the same rate of inflation. For example, the oil-shortage inflation of the late 1970s caused the inflation rate measured in both the PCE and the CPI nearly to double, reaching 10.7 and 13.5 percent respectively in 1980. The difference between the two inflation rates is indicative of a fundamental problem that has caused bitter policy disputes about the best way to measure inflation.

The Cost of Health Care

During the early 1990s, inflation in health care was 9.9 percent according to the CPI but only 5.9 percent in the PCE. The difference occurred because cost increases that continued to be counted in the CPI caused a lower PCE when people shifted level of service, for example away from hospitalization to less expensive ambulatory care. Should we measure inflation by what people actually purchase—the PCE approach —or by what people *would have* purchased had inflation not occurred —the CPI approach? For changes in overall prices, the difference in these two approaches has been relatively minor since 1982, no more than few tenths of a percentage point. For specific items such as health care, however, researchers need to select carefully which price index is appropriate.

The Cost of Housing

Because housing constitutes the largest single component of consumer spending, problems in measuring housing costs have a large effect on inflation rates. During the 1970s, the divergence of the CPI and the PCE was caused primarily by changes in housing costs. As a result, in 1983 the U.S. Labor Department's Bureau of Labor Statistics introduced a new CPI that subsequently was adopted for almost all research purposes and used for indexing the federal income tax, social security payments, and other government programs.

The new CPI made several noncontroversial adjustments such as a more representative sample of housing prices and incorporation of adjustable rate mortgages. But the major change was to measure housing costs by their rental equivalence, that is, estimating how much it would cost to rent homes that actually are purchased. In this way, the bureau hoped to smooth out the effect of fluctuating interest rates and to leave out the investment component of housing expenses. Economist Robert Pollin and housing expert Michael Stone maintain that the underlying problem still has not been solved. In their view, political expediency created the new CPI so that employers and the government could avoid pay and benefit increases that had been tied to the old CPI. Pollin and Stone point out that home purchases are not simply investments but are the predominate way in which U.S. households pay for a place to live. Consequently, an accurate cost of living index will include home purchase costs as well as rental equivalence.

In the years since the new CPI was introduced, these problems receded somewhat. Falling interest rates meant that there was less difference between the new rental equivalence and the old homeownership cost estimate. As a result, the new CPI has been only slightly different from the old CPI, and programs adjusted to the CPI were not greatly affected by the new method. If we apply the new CPI retroactively, however, then it can dramatically affect our data. For example, the U.S. Census Bureau's "alternative poverty line," using the new CPI back to 1967, reduces the poverty level for a family of four by more than $1,000. This change would have affected the eligibility of millions for government programs such as food stamps, Medicaid, and Head Start.

The new method for measuring poverty was not adopted, in part because of protests against its inequities. Nevertheless, the proposal underscores the importance of how inflation is measured. In this case, about 3.5 million people would have been "lifted" out of poverty simply because of seemingly minor differences in the measurement of housing costs. Those involved in public programs, and researchers (see Box 11.1) need to understand the potential effects of alternative inflation statistics.

Currency Rates

Converting currency values between countries is a common social science problem, providing a challenge in the interpretation of data from different countries. Many comparisons depend critically on how prices are converted to a common currency.

The Problem of Many Currencies

Newspaper and magazine financial pages show the daily ups and downs of world currencies relative to one another. For example, on

---

Box 11.1. **CPI or PCE: Watch Out!**

When economists Bennett Harrison and Barry Bluestone published research showing an increase in low-pay jobs during the late 1970s and
early 1980s, critics charged that the results depended on use of the old
CPI, a deliberate deception according to one newspaper account. Nonspe-
cialist readers who probably had never heard of the different inflation
indexes were regaled with the advantages of the PCE and the new CPI.
Eventually Bluestone and Harrison were able to affirm their main findings.
Recalculation using the new CPI, and other research using the PCE, measured a predominance of low-pay jobs. In the meantime, however, their
credibility and policy advice were called into question. Congress's Joint
Economic Committee, sponsors of Bluestone and Harrison's original study,
instructed future researchers to use both the CPI and the PCE. Such
caution is warranted for studies of income and other money amounts
measured over time. A repeated lesson in this book has been the need for
researchers to demonstrate the robustness of results under different assumptions.

October 13, 1994, the U.S. dollar was up slightly against the Canadian
dollar, but down relative to the German mark. But many research
projects require a statistic for the *overall* movement in the dollar. Common sense suggests that in measuring the value of the U.S. dollar we
should count currency changes more for top trading partners, such as
Japan and Canada, than changes relative to Swedish or Spanish currencies, with whom the United States does less trade. In fact, just such
"trade-weighted indexes" are calculated by the U.S. Federal Reserve
Bank and the Bank of England. But differences in the methods for
calculating these indexes cause research and policy-making confusion.

During the 1980s, the most commonly cited index was the Federal
Reserve Board weighted value based on trade with ten countries: Germany, France, the United Kingdom, Belgium, Italy, Sweden, Spain,
Switzerland, Canada, and Japan. This short list was sensible in 1972
when these countries accounted for most U.S. trade. But increasing
trade with Korea, Mexico, Taiwan, and Brazil quickly made the index
obsolete. When the dollar fell by 32 percent in 1985 and 1986 (based
on the traditional index), U.S. imports should have declined because of
higher prices for goods produced in other countries. Instead imports

went up. The apparent paradox was explained in part by an *increase* in the value of the dollar relative to countries not counted in the Federal Reserve index.

For some purposes, such as studying money management, the traditionally weighted index makes sense because international speculation occurs mostly between the ten major currencies. But for research on trade, as for example understanding the failure of the trade deficit to fall in 1986, alternative trade-weighted indexes are needed, such as the one developed by an economist at the Dallas Federal Reserve Bank that includes all 131 countries trading with the United States. But even this more complete statistic will fail if it is not continually updated to take into account future changes in which countries trade with which others.

The Problem of Fluctuating Exchange Rates

After the 1973 introduction of floating exchange rates for most of the world's currencies, researchers faced an ongoing problem comparing well-being between countries. When the dollar is falling, as it did relative to the Japanese yen during the early 1990s, Japan appears to gain income as measured in dollars, although except for lower prices for a few imports, Japanese citizens were not better off. The problem is that comparative prices can be whipsawed by fast-changing exchange rates at the same time that the volume of goods and services is unchanged. In order to focus on actual production, as opposed to comparative price changes, economists recommend a statistic called "purchasing power parity" adopted by the International Monetary Fund and the World Bank in 1993 for its national income comparisons.

Purchasing power parity statistics have the most dramatic effect on the measurement of well-being in Asian economies. Which country has the best development strategy: Korea with its largely homegrown technology or Malaysia with its reliance on foreign enterprise? Based on exchange rates, Korean surpasses Malaysia in national income. But purchasing power parity measures the two countries as nearly equal. Thus, in 1994 a Big Mac hamburger cost more than twice as much in Korea as in Malaysia, indicating that Korea's larger national income overstated the actual well-being of its citizens.

China provides the most extreme case. Exchange rates used in most textbook accounts measured China's income at under $400 per person per year as of the early 1990s. But adjusted for actual prices in China, including rents kept to a few dollars a month by government regulation, the purchasing power for every person is many times that level. Using the new method, the International Monetary Fund moves China from the world's number-ten economy to number three, at $1.66 trillion, ahead of Germany and France, and just behind Japan at $2.37 trillion. (The U.S. remains number one in both statistics at more than $5 trillion.) Based on energy consumption and health standards, geographer Vaclav Smil argues that the true measure of China's income is somewhere in between the two estimates. At issue is the assessment of China's role in the world; unanticipated fast economic growth means that China may already be the world's second-largest market—and the world's second-largest resource user and polluter.

The Problem of Unofficial Exchange Rates

A final problem in currency conversion is the existence of unofficial or black-market exchange rates. In a dramatic case, during the 1989 economic dislocation in East Germany, black market rates were more than ten times as high as official rates. Comparisons of East and West German production varied by a several-fold factor, depending how one compromised between these vastly different exchange rates. More market-oriented economies in Eastern Europe will ease this statistical conundrum; indeed, one motivation for introducing market prices is to facilitate trade with other countries. But in any situation where currency exchange controls exist, as for example in many Latin American countries, there may be unofficial money exchange. Research that looks at only the official rate may not accurately measure the actual price differences between countries.

Implications

Correcting prices for the effects of inflation and different currency values is a problem in research on a wide range of issues. Cost data on health, housing, and crime, as well as economic data on incomes, businesses, and government, usually must be adjusted for inflation if different time periods are compared or for currency values if different countries are compared. The controversies described here serve as an introduction to these adjustments and as a caution to their use. The overall lesson is that researchers should investigate alternative measures of inflation and currency value that would demonstrate how results change when different adjustments are used. Alternatively, if one measure of inflation or currency value is considered to be more accurate, then its use should be carefully justified.

Summary

Data covered in this chapter have the advantage of accuracy in the sense that the numbers come from complete counts rather than surveys. Even inflation measures that do rely on survey data are derived from such massive samples that sampling error is not an issue. Instead, the problem for researchers is choosing which numbers to use. In the case of government budgets, inflation rates, and currency values, there is a choice between conflicting official statistics. For military spending and the deficit, official data are challenged by alternative data based on quite different accounting techniques. Finally, "welfare spending" and "fair taxes" have been shown to generate different statistics and opposite conclusions depending on how the terms are defined.

As this chapter demonstrates, "official government data" are not the only data available; nor are they always the most appropriate. But when an alternative statistic is used, explicit discussion of the choice is necessary. For example, Robert Eisner's use of alternative measures for the debt and deficit, although perhaps reasonable, require careful justification if they are to be used by other researchers. The best solution is to test research hypotheses based on varying assumptions. In the case of inflation adjustment where several indexes are available, research results are far more convincing if they do not change significantly when alternative statistics are used.

Case Study Questions

1. The proportion of the U.S. money supply in $100 bills increased from 42 percent in 1982 to 49 percent in 1989. What might explain this change?

2. Studies of taxes often focus on federal taxes. But state and local taxes often take a bigger bite out of income, especially for low-income groups. Estimate the regressive or progressive effect of state and local taxes where you live.

3. Most state and local governments separate their current budgets from capital budgets that are reserved for spending on long-lived projects such as roads and buildings. If the U.S. government were to issue a capital budget, list the types of items that would be included. How would this new budget technique affect the measurement of the U.S. budget deficit?

4. The proportion of the U.S. budget designated as investment depends critically on whether military spending is counted as investment or as consumption. Which components of military spending might be counted correctly as productive investment?

5. The CPI's methodology has changed over time, for example, in 1983 to count housing differently and in 1987 to take into account different product purchases. But these changes are not used to revise *past* official estimates for the CPI. Why would such changes cause a legal and administrative nightmare?

	Old (1972–73)	New (1982–84)
Housing	38.1%	42.9%
Food	19.0%	16.2%
Fuel and utilities	7.5%	7.9%
Medical care	6.9%	5.4%

6. In 1987 the Consumer Price Index was revised to take into account changing household spending patterns, measured for 1982–84, replacing the old patterns based on a 1972–73 survey. Some of the spending patterns are listed above.

   a. Can you suggest reasons why these categories shifted in importance?

   b. Explain the surprisingly downward trend in the medical care proportion of spending. (Hint: Overall, many medical costs are paid by government, and employer-sponsored medical insurance is not counted as a consumer expense.)

   c. How might spending patterns differ for the elderly? How could this difference cause social security increases based on the CPI to be too high or too low?

Chapter 12

Public Opinion Polling

Public polling is a twentieth-century science first developed as a method to predict elections, then expanded to include opinion polling on a wide variety of issues. Today many businesses hire pollsters to take the public pulse about their products and the advisability of introducing new items. Many political and business polls are proprietary, released to the public only when it serves the purpose of the poll's subscriber. Nonetheless, enormous numbers of election and public opinion polls are available to researchers. These include several decades of data predicting elections and then analyzing voter behavior afterward. In addition, private and university-affiliated opinion surveys are designed to trace public opinion over long periods of time. They cover most current public policy issues, ranging from support for the U.S. president to the public's general happiness. All are well indexed and readily accessible for research use.

Data Sources

Private Polling Organizations

The U.S. polling industry comprises more than 200 private companies including the household names Gallup, Harris, Roper, and Yankelovich. The major pollsters have contracts with media sources; the Roper poll conducts regular polling for *Fortune* magazine, while Gallup polls for *Newsweek* and Yankelovich for *Time*. Beginning with the 1960 election, pollsters have assisted every major U.S. presidential cam-

Where the Numbers Come From

Organizations	Data sources	Key publications
American Institute on Public Opinion	Gallup poll	*The Gallup Poll; Gallup Report*
Roper Center for Public Opinion Research	Most major U.S. polls and polls from seventy other countries	Guides to *Roper Center Resources*
Harris Poll Center	Harris poll	*Sourcebook of Harris National Surveys*
Survey Research Center	Center for Political Studies surveys	*American National Election Studies Sourcebook*
National Opinion Research Center	General Social Survey	*GSS Social Change Reports*; *General Social Surveys: Cumulative Codebook*

paign. Peter Hart and Patrick Caddell are well-known pollsters for Democratic candidates, whereas Robert Teeter and Richard Wirthlin traditionally advise Republicans. Even on the local level, political candidates typically spend 5 to 15 percent of campaign funds on polls.

> *Data Sample*: A 1991 Gallup poll found that 47 percent of U.S. respondents chose a "creationist" explanation for the descent of humankind: "God created man pretty much in his present form at one time within the last 10,000 years." Only 9 percent chose a secular version: "Man has developed over millions of years from less advanced forms of life. God had no part in this process"; while 40 percent preferred: "Man has developed over millions of years from less advanced forms of life, but God guided this process including man's creation."

Media Polls

CBS entered the market first in 1967 with its own election polling unit and created a partnership with the *New York Times* in 1975 that soon became the major force in media polling. Similar collaboration has been established between ABC and the *Washington Post* and NBC and the *Wall Street Journal*. A study of media polling by the Roper Center measured an increase to more than 4,000 questions per year in 1990 from about 1,000 poll questions asked by news organizations in the mid-1970s.

Research Centers

The Center for Political Studies at the University of Michigan's Survey Research Center collects economic data from consumers and voting and attitude data in the National Election Studies conducted every other year by the Center for Political Studies.

> *Data Sample*: In the 1986 American National Election Studies, low-income respondents who identified themselves as "strong Republicans" fell to 6 percent from 14 percent in 1952. "Strong Democrats" stayed at about 25 percent of the low-income group.

The National Opinion Research Center (NORC) at the University of Chicago collects data for the U.S. government including the National Longitudinal Survey (see chapter 5). The NORC's General Social Survey, conducted since 1972, is a major data source for public behavior, attitudes, and happiness with various aspects of life. It contains a core of replicated questions that enable researchers to track changing attitudes over time.

> *Data Sample*: In the General Social Survey, respondents answering yes to the question "Have you seen an X-rated movie in the last year?" increased to 24.8 percent in 1986 from 15.0 percent in 1978.

Controversies

Predicting Elections

In 1936 a poll taken by the *Literary Digest* was sensationally wrong, predicting a 14 percent margin for Alf Landon over incumbent President Roosevelt, who won with an even larger margin than the *Digest* predicted for Landon. This tremendous error cast a shadow of doubt on political polling that has yet to disappear and that caused the *Digest* to go out of business the following year.

Strangely, the straw poll methodology that killed the *Digest* was successful in four previous presidential elections, even predicting Roosevelt's 1932 margin with only a 0.7 percent error. What went wrong in 1936? The *Literary Digest* poll was exceptionally large, with ballots sent to more than 10 million households. But large samples are not necessarily better; the *Literary Digest* poll suffered from sample bias because names were drawn from telephone books and auto registration lists, a group decidedly better off than the typical depression-era voter. Even with its biased sample, the *Digest* poll would have correctly projected Roosevelt the winner *if everyone had returned the survey*. Of the 10 million ballots distributed, only 2 million were returned, most in support of Landon, whereas those who did not return the *Digest* ballots were overwhelmingly Roosevelt voters. From 1920 to 1932, the sample bias toward wealthier Republicans was offset by a higher response rate from Democrats who wanted to voice their opposition to incumbent Republican presidents. In 1936, the two biases reenforced each other when disgruntled Republican subscribers responded in higher numbers than the Democratic majority.

The *Literary Digest* fiasco shows how political polling can go wrong. Lesser known is the stunning success of George Gallup, who offered money back to his poll subscribers unless he was more accurate than the 1936 *Digest* poll. Gallup won his audacious gamble by predicting a Roosevelt victory, albeit by a 7 percent too small margin. Even though Gallup's sample was a fraction the size of that used by the *Digest*, it was less biased because of a quota system that guaranteed representative proportions based on economic class, age, gender, and political preference. In 1948, however, Gallup received his comeuppance when he, along with most other pollsters, predicted that Harry Truman would lose to Thomas E. Dewey. Compared to 1936, Gallup came closer to the actual vote in 1948 with just a 5 percent error, but this was small consolation for missing the winner.

Sampling in the 1990s

Are polls today superior to 1936 or 1948? The answer is, "usually": because of superior sampling methods, modern polls rely on a sample of about 1,000 individuals. Statistical theory suggests that the error caused by random chance in these polls should be plus or minus three percentage points in nineteen out of twenty elections. This error often is misreported as *the* margin of error. Even though there have been no miscalls of national elections since 1948, the actual accuracy has been far less accurate than would be expected based simply on random sampling error alone. Far more than one in twenty polls is outside the theoretical confidence intervals, and no single poll has a success record entirely within this range.

Margin of error in recent presidential elections was as follows:

1980: Reagan over Carter
    NBC/Associated Press, 3%
    ABC/Harris, 5%
    Gallup, 7%
    CBS/*New York Times*, 9%
1984: Reagan over Mondale
    Gallup/*Newsweek,* 1%
    CBS/*New York Times,* 3%
    Washington Post/ABC, 4%
    Harris/NPR, 6%
    Gordon Black/*USA Today,* 7%
    Roper, 8%
1988: Bush over Dukakis
    CBS/*New York Times,* 1%
    Washington Post/ABC, 2%
    Time, Yankelovich–Clancy–Shulman, 2%
    NBC/*Wall Street Journal,* 3%
    Gallup 4%
1992: Clinton over Bush
    NBC/*Wall Street Journal,* 1%
    Gallup/CNN/*USA Today,* 2%
    ABC News, 2%
    CBS/*New York Times,* 4%
    Washington Post, 5%
    Los Angeles Times, 5%

Today, most opinion polling is conducted by telephone, a shift from the early Gallup and Roper polls, when pollsters traveled around the country interviewing people face to face. The reason for the change is cost; as one pollster explains, "only the federal government can come up with the bucks for in-person interviewing." Because more than 90 percent of the population can be reached by telephone, the bias toward the well-to-do of the 1930s *Literary Digest* poll is avoided. Even those who have unlisted phone numbers are included in most surveys by randomly choosing telephone numbers. For example, the Gallup poll chooses the first digits of phone numbers to assure geographic representation and then randomly selects the last digits to include both listed and unlisted numbers.

The major problem for modern pollsters is an increase in the refusal rate, apparently because respondents confuse legitimate polls with the large number of telephone sales pitches. In Los Angeles the refusal rate reached as high as 65 percent in a 1990 pre-primary *Los Angeles Times* poll, greatly increasing the risk of misinterpretation when the results were extrapolated to the population as a whole. Although California rates are higher than the average for the United States, the state's extensive telemarketing and increasing cultural diversity may be a harbinger of difficulties pollsters will face elsewhere. Three major media polling organizations made their 1990 and 1991 confidential telephone records available to survey experts Henry E. Brady and Gary R. Orren, who found that about 15 percent of calls were broken off or refused and an equal number encountered no answer, a busy line, or an answering machine.

Many polls correct for nonresponse by weighting the final results to compensate for those who refused to participate. For example, those respondents who say they were not home on the *previous* evening may be counted again as proxies for those who were not home on the day of the survey. The assumption is that individuals who were not home previously share similar characteristics with those who cannot be reached for the survey. Similarly, pollsters often adjust survey data for misrepresentative samples, adjusting the total to include the known proportion of men and women, Republicans and Democrats, or those likely to vote. This adjustment can change poll outcomes, as for example in a 1986 *Columbus Dispatch* poll for the governor's race that showed former Governor Rhodes ahead—until adjustment caused incumbent Governor Celeste to take the lead, a difference that may have altered fund-raising prospects as well as the upcoming vote. To the credit of the newspaper, readers were told that "results were adjusted, or weighted," but we did not learn that the adjustment reversed the predicted election outcome.

Box 12.1. **Black Candidates/White Voters**

Some of the largest election polling errors occur when black candidates face a white opponent. For example, California's Tom Bradley and New York City's David Dinkins both lost elections that the polls indicated they might win, and Virginia's Douglas Wilder won with only 51 percent after polls showed him with a substantial lead. One theory was that white voters, sensitive to charges of racism, misrepresented their voting intentions by telling survey takers they would vote for the black candidate. Henry E. Brady and Gary R. Orren argue that the effect is more subtle, a result of previously undecided white voters who disproportionately made a last-minute decision to vote for the white candidate. Evidence for such switching also occurred in a 1989 Chicago mayoral election when undecided *black* voters supported black independent Timothy Evans at the last moment, making a closer race than had been expected against white Democrat Richard Daley.

Race of the interviewer can also skew results, as occurred in polls of President Reagan's 1985 popularity. Most observers were incredulous when a CBS News/*New York Times* polls showed 56 percent black support for the president, more than double the level of support he received only one month earlier in an ABC News/*Washington Post* poll. One problem was a 9 percent sampling error in the CBS/*Times* poll because only 150 blacks had been interviewed, rather than the standard 1,000 or more in other polls. Also the ABC/*Post* poll used black interviewers who began with an explanation that they were conducting a survey of blacks, probably causing respondents to take an ethnically conscious perspective that was more critical of the president than the CBS/*New York Times* poll. These examples show how the social dynamics of the interview process can change survey results. When an election includes sensitive issues such as race, we need to be prepared for the possibility of increased survey error.

Weighting is standard practice, used in the recent presidential election polling by Gallup, ABC/Harris, and CBS/*New York Times*. Clearly weighting is better than the original sample, biased because it includes only those who have telephones, were at home, and were willing to talk. But as in the case of the election race between Rhodes and Celeste, researchers need access to the original polling methodology to assess the significance of weighting, and few polls publish such information.

Exit Polling

Television and radio news predict results on election day through "exit polls" in which respondents are surveyed outside voting sites. The method has been tested extensively so that pollsters can choose a sample of election precincts that will give an accurate picture of the entire voting public. The major problem is that 30 to 50 percent refuse to answer, sometimes in protest against the ability of the media to predict elections before all citizens have voted. Because refusal rates are higher for some groups, such as older people, exit polls may provide a biased picture of the electorate unless the results are weighted to take into account those who do not participate. Exit polling is so expensive that in 1990, ABC, CBS, CNN, and NBC created a combined operation called Voter Research and Surveys, a dangerous precedent according to some critics because there will be only one data source.

Polling Standards

The fine print at the bottom of media polls often reads like the following example:

> The Gallup Organization interviewed a representative national sample of 606 adults by telephone March 26 and March 27. The margin of error is plus or minus 5 percentage points. Some "Don't know" responses were omitted.

The National Council on Public Polls and the American Association for Public Opinion Research have adopted principles of disclosure, encouraging pollsters to include reference in their polls to the survey's sponsorship, date of interviewing, method of interviewing, population sampled, sample size, complete question wording, and percentages on which conclusions are based. Although most pollster press releases comply with these requirements, media reports usually edit out some of this information. Television news provides the scantiest background help, and newspapers often omit important details; for example, sampling error is left out 84 percent of the time. Researchers need to be prepared to contact the survey source itself for a poll's complete background information.

Political Bias

Even with full disclosure, we know it is possible for polls to be biased. Pollsters are able to promise candidates, "Tell me the results you want, and I can get them." Polling expert Charles Roll recounts how New York Senator Charles Goodell, running a poor third according to a newspaper poll, was offered the services of another polling firm that promised to show him ahead. Political candidates, ill served by inaccurate polls, may be offered two poll results, one for public relations and one to report how things really are. Even independent polls are subject to manipulation, as occurred in 1968 when Richard Nixon vied with Nelson Rockefeller for the Republication nomination. Embarrassed by repeated polls showing Rockefeller as the candidate more likely to beat Democratic nominee Hubert Humphrey, it is alleged that Nixon arranged to be endorsed by former President Eisenhower just before the next Gallup poll would be conducted. Indeed Nixon's support jumped, and according to some observers, this knocked Rockefeller out of contention for the nomination.

As noted earlier, pollsters often work exclusively for one political perspective, a source of potential bias. For example, Louis Harris worked extensively for the Kennedy brothers, including campaign surveys for John Kennedy's 1960 nomination campaign. During the 1980 primaries, when Harris published three syndicated columns a week, critics charged that he featured polls that showed Edward Kennedy leading, even if insignificantly, and did not report his polls that showed incumbent President Carter with as much as a 30 percentage point lead.

Other pollsters may not proclaim their political bias as brazenly as the Harris poll, but researchers need to be aware that pollsters have political or even economic ties to candidates. They may not use obviously inaccurate survey techniques, as did the pollster who promised "any result you want," but when pollsters write their own columns, their selection of polls introduces a bias to their reporting. Researchers need to consult the full set of polls that usually are available from the pollsters but are not all featured in the media. (See sources in Where the Numbers Come From.)

Horserace Journalism

The most unbiased poll will influence election results if voters jump on the bandwagon, voting for the apparent election winner. Or the reverse

may be true: voters empathize with the underdog, voting for the candidate who is behind in the polls as a protest against those with political
power. Considerable research evidence indicates that both effects occur.

Surveys taken after an election typically count more respondents
claiming to have voted for the winner than actually occurred, a potentially serious problem for research based on the National Election
Studies and other postelection surveys. The error is especially high for
House of Representative elections, for which political scientist Gerald
C. Wright finds about 20 percent of those on the losing side say they
voted for the winner. Also, 25 to 30 percent of nonvoters claim to have
voted, introducing another bias if these respondents also claim to have
voted for the winner more often than those who actually went to the
polls. Misreporting is slightly less serious for Senate races and quite
low for U.S. presidential elections, with the exception of 1964 when an
additional 6 percent failed to report their vote for Barry Goldwater in
his overwhelming loss to incumbent Lyndon Johnson.

The reasons for misreporting include the eagerness of respondents
to be on the winning side and, for those who do not remember much
about the election, better name recall for the winner. If a bandwagon
effect exists after elections, then likely it exists in preelection polls as
well, increasing support for the candidate who is reported to be most
popular. For example, polling expert Herbert Asher argues that the
bandwagon effect may have helped Governor James Rhodes win re-
nomination in the 1986 Ohio governor's primary when early polling
gave him 70 percent support. In Asher's view, opposition candidates
might have done better if media reports had not focused on the "inevi-
tability" of Rhodes's victory.

The opposite, or underdog, effect—support for the apparent losing
candidate—shows up in the common tendency of political races to
tighten during the last days of a campaign. In particular, non-
incumbents are able to gain ground by picking up the undecided votes.
Thus the Mason-Dixon Political/Media Research polling firm maintains that "incumbents who fail to get more than 50 percent in late polls
usually lose." For example, one week before the 1993 New Jersey guber-
natorial election, incumbent Jim Florio's 46 percent support was insufficient, despite a 13 percent lead, because so many voters were
undecided. Indeed, he lost to challenger Christine Todd Whitman.

Because the bandwagon and underdog effects may counteract one
another, measuring the net result would require an enormous study,

tracking voter reaction over time, separating these effects from other swings in voter preference. One study, proposed in 1950 but abandoned because of cost, would cost about $500,000 in today's buying power. As a result, political scientists believe that both bandwagon and underdog effects occur, but they are uncertain about their total effect.

Implications

For some political critics, the problem with polling runs deeper than bandwagon or underdog effects. In this view, polling has become so prevalent that instead of studying the pros and cons of candidates' positions, the media become fixated on who is ahead. Would we better off without so many polls, perhaps following the lead of other countries, banning polls just before election time? The main line of defense for polling is that it forces all commentators on the political process to analyze data, rather than rely on biased surmises. There are many examples from U.S. political history of claims for political majority that were disproved by the polls. Supporters of Senator Barry Goldwater's 1964 nomination insisted that there was a majority waiting to be heard, which was evident in letters to the editor that supported Goldwater's conservative cause. Yet polls at the time of Goldwater's nomination anticipated his defeat in the subsequent presidential election.

Polling also gives us the power to learn why a candidate won. Repeatedly, polls found that Ronald Reagan's overwhelming popular votes did not represent support for his stands on many key issues, such as women's rights and abortion. The case for polling is best made by the research lacuna caused when no polls are taken, as occurred in Jesse Jackson's surprise victory in the 1988 Michigan Democratic caucuses. Was there a groundswell of support for his views from a rainbow coalition, as his campaign argued, or was the victory an aberration caused by a small turnout in a caucus environment? In this instance, a definitive answer based on polling might have changed the course of the 1988 nomination process. Because no poll was taken, the election was reported as an inconsequential curiosity.

Question Wording

Survey experts identify question wording as the most critical factor in poll results—and the one most easily manipulated to gain desired re-

---

Box 12.2 **Dial 900**

Pay calls to express political and other views are common on television. After the 1980 Carter–Reagan debate, 727,000 calls at 50 cents per call gave candidate Ronald Reagan a two-to-one margin over President Jimmy Carter. The poll was biased in favor of Reagan because his supporters were more likely to afford the calls and because they were more likely to live in the West, where the poll took place earlier in the evening. Despite criticism from polling experts, ABC and other networks continued to conduct 900 polls on issues such as the Persian Gulf War. No serious researcher uses the 900 poll results as an accurate public opinion indicator, but television's reporting of 900 poll results may itself influence public views.

---

sults. Sometimes the effect is dramatic, as in the following examples. The General Social Survey asks respondents if "we spend too little on"

Assistance to the poor, 65%
Welfare, 20%

Assistance to big cities, 18%
Solving problems of big cities, 48%

Assistance to blacks, 27%
Improving condition of blacks, 37%

These are predictable wording effects, well known to pollsters. Welfare has negative connations, as do words such as "big business" or "big labor"; positive verbs, such as "solving" or "improving," increase the popularity of an answer.

In some cases, the effects of question wording are subtle. In a poll conducted by Louis Harris for the Aetna Insurance Company, at issue were limits to liability suits that allegedly caused excessive monetary payments awarded by juries to successful litigants. Aetna and insurance lobbyists were pleased at the Harris poll results, which apparently demonstrated that an "overwhelming majority of Americans support a number of specific reforms to improve the nation's civil justice system," including limits on jury awards. But a follow-up study by Ohio State University professor Jon A. Krosnick found that a simple change in question wording altered the results. In the original Harris poll a majority found the legal changes "acceptable." But when Krosnick asked respondents if they "supported" these changes (the verb actually used in Aetna's summary of the Harris poll and repeated in the *New York Times*), there was no longer a majority in favor.

Implications

Sociologist James Wright argues that when carefully interpreted, polls actually do tell us what the public thinks—even when changes in question wording give apparently contradictory answers. In a study of surveys on gun-control legislation, Wright examined reports by the National Rifle Association (NRA) that "majorities of American voters believe we do *not* need more laws governing the possession and use of firearms" and the conclusion of the Center for the Study and Prevention of Handgun Violence that "the vast majority of the public . . . want handgun licensing and registration."

> "Attitudes of the American Electorate toward Gun Control" prepared by Decision Making Information, commissioned by the National Rifle Association
>
> Agree that there are too many laws governing firearms, 13%
> Agree that present laws are about right, 44%
> Total supporting the status quo or fewer laws, 57%
>
> "An Analysis of Public Attitudes toward Handgun Control" prepared by Cambridge Reports commissioned by the Center for Study and Prevention of Handgun Violence
>
> Favor requiring a permit of license in order to buy a handgun, 82%
> Favor the registration of handguns, 84%

Wright maintains that these apparently contradictory findings can be reconciled. Although the National Rifle Association press release gives the misleading impression that people oppose additional gun control, technically they are correct that many people believe "the present laws are about right." This is consistent with the Center's finding that most respondents wanted stricter enforcement of *existing* laws. Similarly, the NRA emphasizes majority opposition to "a law giving police the power to decide who may or may not own a firearm." Again, this opinion is consistent with the Center's finding that the public overwhelmingly supports gun registration, but this is not the same policy as giving the police the power to decide who may own a gun. Wright maintains that the apparent contradictions on gun control arise not from polling but from selective interpretation that reduces a complex issue to a simple "for" or "against" gun control. In Wright's view, we gain a full picture of the public's gun-control views by looking at the precise wording used in both polls.

Careful attention to question wording also explains apparently conflicting attitudes on other contentious issues, such as abortion rights. A CBS poll found more than 70 percent supporting the "right of a woman to have an abortion," but a Harris poll found the public evenly split on "legalized abortion." Such results provide simplistic propaganda for both sides in the dispute, but not the sophisticated views of thoughtful respondents. Michael Kagay, *New York Times* director of polling, concludes: "When people want to make such distinctions, pollsters should too—if they are to give an accurate picture of public opinion." A 1989 *New York Times* poll found only 10 percent of U.S. respondents opposing abortion in all circumstances and only 21 percent permitting abortion in all circumstances. Given the opportunity, most respondents reported a shaded position in between these two extremes.

These examples demonstrate the critical nature of question wording. The American Association for Public Opinion Research standards recommends disclosure of full question wording, a requirement that is not always followed. A study of Detroit newspaper polls between 1968 and 1984 found exact question wording reported only about 28 percent of the time and showed no sign of improvement during the sixteen-year period.

Question Order

Survey results often report exact question wording but rarely tell us the *order* in which questions were asked, a difference that can affect the outcome. On October 13, 1982, the *New York Times* reported Toby Moffett in the lead over incumbent Senator Lowell Weicker of Connecticut, while the *Hartford Courant* found Weicker—the eventual winner—ahead by sixteen percentage points.

To pollsters Irving Crespi and Dwight Morris, the results were extraordinary because both polls used large samples and similar questions. Even the keypunching of the data was double checked and verified. Careful detective work revealed a subtle difference—and a warning to poll users. The *Courant* poll asked respondents for their vote in the Senate race first, then in the governor's contest; the *Times* reversed the order, thereby inadvertently skewing the results between Moffett and Weicker. Apparently voters who had first indicated a preference for Democratic Governor O'Neill were reluctant to admit that they planned to vote for the Republican Weicker. A large number of middle-of-the-road voters supported the moderate Democrat O'Neill and moderate Republican Weicker—but did not want to appear inconsistent to the poll takers.

A second problem involving question order occurs when polls first ask respondents if they know about a candidate before asking further questions. In 1992 surveys about Ross Perot, respondents who first admitted lack of knowledge about Perot were less likely to indicate support for him than in a poll that simply asked for whom they would vote. Similar results occurred in 1984 when voter support for incumbent President Reagan dropped considerably if it followed questions in which the respondent was asked to rate the president's performance.

A third problem occurs when prior questions alter a respondent's opinion on subsequent questions. The National Crime Survey (see chapter 6) measures more crime victimization if preceded by attitude questions about crime that apparently stimulate memory and willingness to report more personal experiences. Similarly many Hispanics change their answer to the Census Bureau's race and ethnicity questions (see chapter 2) depending which is asked first. In the 1990 census, many Hispanics chose "other race" rather than "white" or "black" to the question about race and then indicated Hispanic origins in the follow-up ethnicity questions. If the questions were reversed so that people were first asked to identify themselves as Hispanic, then respondents identified their race as "white." Apparently, Hispanics who wanted a separate minority identity felt uncomfortable calling themselves white unless they already knew they had been able to choose the Hispanic label.

Finally, when a poll asks for a choice of answers, the order of the answers leads to considerable bias. Researchers document a substantial "recency" bias in which respondents tend to choose the answer listed last. Thus a 1988 Roper poll found a swing of eight percentage points if Vice-President Bush was listed before, rather than after, his opponent, Governor Dukakis. To complicate matters there is also a "primacy" effect in which respondents choose the response listed first. For example, in a Survey Research Center study of whether "the government" or "each person" should be responsible for adequate housing, respondents were far more likely to choose "each person" if it was listed first.

These examples show the tremendous complexity of question-order effects. Because these effects are so unpredictable, an accurate interpretation of surveys requires that the format be varied to see if there are important order effects. Once again, such tests rarely are reported in survey results.

Moral Majority: Agree or Strongly Agree?

Because few opinions fit comfortably in a yes or no framework, pollsters usually provide a range of answers ranging from "strongly agree" to "strongly disagree." The problem arises when researchers attempt to summarize this continuum by categorizing different opinions into what pollsters call "cutting points." For example, support for a position may include just those who "strongly agree" or those who "strongly agree" *and* "agree." The change in cutting points may lead to different conclusions, as in a dispute about public support for the Moral Majority, a conservative religious coalition.

Using 1977 data, sociologist John H. Simpson estimated more than 30 percent U.S. support for the Moral Majority, defined as those who opposed sexual relations between adults of the same sex, opposed the legal right to abortion for any reason, believed women should stay home and take care of the family, and favored required Christian prayer in school. In a rejoinder based on the same data, sociologists Lee Sigelman and Stanley Presser measured only 9 percent support for the Moral Majority view. The difference depended on the definition of cutting points for only one question:

> "It is better for everyone involved if the man is the achiever outside the home and the woman takes care of the home and family."

> Strongly agree *or* agree, 65% (Simpson definition)
> Strongly agree, 18% (Sigelman and Presser definition)

Using the cutting point "strongly agree" as evidence for support of the Moral Majority, Sigelman and Presser maintained that the Moral Majority could claim few adherents. In response, Simpson points out that some people may agree with the Moral Majority on issues of homosexuality, abortion, and school prayer, but may be forced to relax their views on the role of women in the workforce because of economic pressure to support the family. Thus, Simpson used the broader cutting point, "strongly agree" or "agree," to represent the Moral Majority perspective. The lesson for researchers is that the choice of cutting points can critically affect the outcome. In this case, shifting the point only slightly for one question changed the apparent support for the Moral Majority by more than threefold.

Don't Knows: Ignorance or Honesty?

Confronted by a pollster, no one wants to appear ignorant and thus may answer questions despite lack of knowledge. The extent of the problem is revealed in polling experiments that deliberately ask questions to which no one is likely to have an answer. For example, in 1978 the Survey Research Center asked about the Agricultural Trade Act, a bill so little known that the Survey Research Center presumed "virtually no respondents were familiar with its nature or contents." Even so, more than 30 percent reported an opinion—19 percent in favor, 11 percent opposed—whereas 70 percent were honest enough to admit that they did not know about the bill. Survey takers sometimes worsen the problem by asking questions that no one could reasonably be expected to answer. For example, both *Time* and the *Washington Post* asked respondents whether they thought President Reagan would have a recurrence of his 1985 cancer. Such questions deserved the honest answer, "No one knows, not even his physician." A more common example of unanswerable questions occurs in polls taken a long time before elections that ask citizens to make a choice before they know anything about most of the candidates.

One solution is to provide "don't know or no opinion" as a explicit choice. Typically this option increases the number who profess ignorance or uncertainty by about 20 percent over the number who spontaneously provide this response. For questions with a strong moral content, such as abortion, the "don't know" answer may be used by well-informed respondents who have a highly ambivalent response to the issue that cannot be pigeonholed as yes or no.

A second option is to ask respondents if they are familiar with a topic or are interested enough to have an opinion. The use of these "filter" questions raises additional problems of interpretation: will re-

Box 12.3. **The Gay Population**

Do people tell survey takers the truth about their behavior? In one survey, respondents claimed to be brushing their teeth at a rate that would consume three times as much toothpaste as was purchased in the United States. Thus it is not surprising that surveys produce conflicting results on questions as personal as sexual orientation. A survey released in 1993 conducted by the Battelle Human Affairs Research Center found that about 1 percent of men were exclusively gay and only 2.3 percent had sex with men in the past ten years. These figures contrasted with a 1993 Yankelovich Partners consumer survey in which 5.7 percent described themselves as "gay, homosexual or lesbian" and the 1948 Kinsey report finding of a 10 percent rate of homosexuality, measured as sexual relationships exclusively with men for three years. The low Battelle numbers led conservative policy advocate Phyllis Schafly to conclude: "It shows politicians they don't need to be worried about 1 percent of the population." Some gay leaders disputed the accuracy of these low estimates. The editor of the gay magazine *10 Percent,* pointed out by "their reasoning, there are about 2.5 million gay men in America. I guess we're all living in California."

Hidden in the debate were several statistical issues. The Battelle Institute interviewed only men aged 20 to 39, so little was learned about younger or older men. Even more problematic in the view of gay activists was the equating of sexual behavior with sexuality. In this view, men may be gay or have that propensity without explicit sexual behavior that they will admit in a survey. Data gathered by the National Opinion Research Center in 1992 found that 2.8 percent of men identified themselves as homosexuals, whereas 6 percent said they were attracted to other men and 9 percent of men reported having had at least one homosexual experience since puberty.

spondents vote for a candidate even though the filter suggests they do not have enough knowledge about the individual? Such an effect may have occurred in 1992 when voters knew little about candidate Ross Perot's positions on issues but nonetheless voted for him in unexpected numbers. Should we count only opinions of informed respondents, unfortunately often a small fraction of the population? Repeatedly, polls find that respondents will give an opinion on such national security issues as the U.S. intervention in Nicaragua in the 1980s, even though many people could not identify which side the U.S. government favored.

Similarly, polls on the Strategic Arms Limitation Treaties were of doubtful value because 77 percent of respondents could not correctly identify the two countries participating in the treaty—the United States and the Soviet Union—despite seven years of ongoing negotiations.

In the same way that election polling turns elections into horse-races, public opinion polling is criticized for turning public policy debates into popularity contests. For example, John Benson of the Roper Center and Everett Carl Ladd of the University of Connecticut point to the Persian Gulf War, during which polling organizations asked more than 2,000 questions on the war, typically surveying an ill-informed public that would have been better served by coverage of the issues involved rather than yet another poll.

Critics charge that the focus on polling serves those with political power by creating the image of consensus on issues. Just before President Nixon's invasion of Cambodia in 1970, only 7 percent of the U.S. public favored such a move; after the invasion, 50 percent thought Nixon was right. Columbia University political scientist Benjamin Ginsberg argues that polls create a false sense of unity because they ask citizens to respond passively to a preconceived set of issues. In his view, public protest and other forms of active participation more accurately gauge public opinion. At a minimum, researchers need to think about the timing of polls, assessing if they actually measure informed public opinion or if they simply reaffirm common prejudice that may be manipulated by political leaders.

What Do Women Want?

Many of the problems described in this chapter are encapsulated in a dispute about female sexuality that followed the publications of Shere Hite's books, two *Hite Reports* and *Women and Love*. Hite found that most women were unfulfilled in their sexuality and had sexual interests far more diverse than generally believed. An ABC/*Washington Post* survey conducted in 1987 produced entirely contradictory results:

	Hite	ABC/*Washington Post*
Percentage of women satisfied with their relationships	16	93
Percentage of women married 5 years having sex outside marriage	70	6

Who was right? Critics attacked Hite's methodology as unscientific because she distributed her surveys on a nonrandom basis to women's organizations and women's magazines. As in the *Literary Digest* case, Hite's network was large, including more than 100,000 surveys in one study, but the low 3 percent response rate led to an unrepresentative sample. Finally, contrary to standard polling practice, Hite changed her questions midway through one of her studies and encouraged respondents to answer whatever questions they liked. Whenever Hite equated her book with scientific studies, the critics were unrelenting, calling her results "garbage."

Unfortunately, this dispute about Hite's sampling method distracted attention from scholarly praise. In the tradition of *qualitative* research Hite uncovered depths of feelings and insights from women that would never be measured in the traditional ABC/*Washington Post* poll. Unquestionably the ABC/*Post* poll met standard polling criteria with a 1,505-person sample selected carefully as a cross-section of the country's age, education, and race. But did scientific method make the poll more accurate? Hite parodied its format: "Oh so you call people on the telephone, you don't know who's home with them, they don't know who you are, and then you say, 'Are you having extramarital sex?' and you expect them to tell you." It is remarkable that *anyone* answered yes under such circumstances. Independent evidence suggests that the ABC/*Post* poll significantly overstated marital bliss. For example, the Kinsey Institute survey found the rate of extramarital affairs to be double the ABC/*Post* count and a National Opinion Research Center Survey, published in 1994, found that 85 percent of married women 18 to 59 years old reported being faithful to their husbands.

The intensity of ABC's response was out of proportion to the importance of the scientific error in Hite's survey methodology. In fact, identical criticisms of nonrandom sampling were leveled at the television network itself for its equally invalid 900 telephone polls (see Box 12.2), commercial ventures that did not even purport to probe attitudes, as Hite did in her lengthy surveys. ABC and the *Washington Post* won the technical battle; even adjusting for the problems of telephone polling on private matters, their data were closer to the numerical truth about marital infidelity. If our goal is to understand social behavior, however, then Hite's research is more helpful. By limiting the debate

Box 12.4. **Teenage Sex: A Scientific Survey**

At the same time that Shere Hite and ABC/*Washington Post* disputed their questionable survey results, demographic experts were busy analyzing more reliable data on teenage sexual behavior. In a study published in the journal *Demography,* Joan Kahn, William Kalsbeek, and Sandra Hoffreth evaluated the National Surveys of Young Women by Temple University's Institute for Social Research and the National Survey of Family Growth (see chapter 4) and the National Longitudinal Survey (see chapter 5), both sponsored by the U.S. government. In their review article we learn precisely how the data had been collected and why the surveys measured different rates of sexual activity. For 19-year-olds, the three surveys were compatible, estimating the likelihood of first intercourse at more than 50 percent. But young teens reported significantly different levels of sexual activity in each survey, for example, ranging from 17 percent to 40 percent for 16-year-old black young women. The authors attribute such inconsistencies to several factors, including parental consent, which was required in order to take part in some surveys but not in others. Even though the authors were unable to account for all the differences in the three surveys, their evaluation contrasts favorably with the Hite–ABC dispute; it is a model of what we can learn when the data are analyzed carefully.

to numerical estimates on which Hite probably erred, the ABC/*Post* survey failed to look at women's perceptions, which were Hite's equally important research goals.

Summary

In summary, researchers face a daunting task in using public opinion data. Should we throw up our hands and dismiss poll results? As this book describes, data problems plague *all* social science statistics, and they are particularly bothersome when first learned by users unaccustomed to data-collection techniques. Just as we accept population counts, GDP, and crime rates despite their limitations, we should do the same with poll and survey data. We should join the experts who use these statistics to great advantage, albeit with appropriate caution.

Opinion polling is a well-developed science that has developed methodological standards to reduce the problems summarized in this chapter. Sampling error is the best-understood source of error, one that pollsters can control with reasonable sample sizes as long as non-response rates are not too high. Unfortunately, refusal rates appear to be increasing, and, unlike old-fashioned face-to-face interviewers, we often do not even know the basic demographic data about those who decline to participate.

Question wording is the most critical feature of opinion polling, one that is readily susceptible to purposeful or inadvertent manipulation. Poll research provides some guidelines about which words produce which response, but the examples in the text and the added complication of the order effect show that we must continuously watch for subtle complications. Pollsters are well aware of these limitations in their surveys, and national standards require that question wording be available when survey results are released. Nevertheless, it is often necessary for researchers to ask for such details directly from pollsters rather than rely on media reports.

Also troublesome is the problem of bias in polling. In addition to outright favoritism toward political candidates, opinion polling selects which questions will be asked and how they will be interpreted. Researchers need to be active social critics, thinking about why particular questions are used in surveys and why other questions are omitted. We need to speculate about what alternative surveys should be conducted. At times it may be possible to conduct our own local surveys; step-by-step procedures are outlined in a several guidebooks. But national surveys are too expensive for most independent researchers, so we are dependent on the resources of private pollsters and academic and government research centers. Fortunately, their data are largely open to scrutiny. Even when the media report only scant information about these surveys, far more detail is available from the poll takers themselves or the resource books listed in Where the Numbers Come From.

Case Study Questions

1. A study by psychologist Elizabeth Loftus asked respondents: Do you get headaches *frequently*, and if so, how often? Respondents reported on

average 2.2 headaches per week. To a slightly different question: Do you get headaches *occasionally*, and if so, how often?, respondents reported only 0.7 headaches per week. Explain this difference in response.

2. The 1986 U.S. Attorney General's Commission on Pornography reported the following poll results:

> 1970: During the past year have you seen or read a magazine which you regarded as pornographic? (20% yes)

> 1985: Have you ever read *Playboy* magazine or *Penthouse* magazine? (Two-thirds yes)

The commission noted the change in question wording, but concluded nonetheless that exposure to sexually explicit magazines increased from 1970 to 1985 because the second poll was "more specific in nature and therefore a more conservative estimate." Was this conclusion justified?

3. In 1992, the Ross Perot campaign used the following poll question: "Should laws be passed to eliminate all possibilities of special interests giving huge sums of money to candidates?" Ninety-nine percent of his followers agreed. How would you rewrite the question in order to gauge public opinion accurately?

4. Radio station KEMB in Emmetsburg, Iowa, conducts presidential polls by asking its listeners to flush their toilets when they hear the name of their favorite candidate. Support is measured at the sewage plant where the water level drops one inch for every 135 flushes. Although the radio station claims to be able to predict elections with this poll, what are the biases in this survey?

5. The General Social Survey asked two versions of a similar question: "Do you think the use of marijuana should be made legal or not?" and "Some people think the use of marijuana should be made legal. Other people think marijuana use should not be made legal. Which do you favor?"

Which question more accurately gauges public opinion? (In a 1978 survey, the second question form gained a 3.7 percent more favorable response.)

6. William the Conqueror's A.D. 1086 "Doomsday Survey" is one of the most valuable sources of data on life in medieval England. Design three survey questions for today's world that would be useful to social scientists in the year 3086.

Chapter 13

Conclusions

Students of statistics soon learn that there is a dazzling array of mathematical techniques for analyzing data, testing hypotheses, and estimating the probability of error. Nevertheless, the controversies reviewed in this book suggest that students and practitioners alike need to look more closely at the limitations of the data to which the sophisticated techniques are applied. Repeatedly, the origin of policy disputes can be traced to questions about the underlying data: Why are some data reported as fact to the exclusion of other equally reputable data? Why are only certain data collected? Why are the data organized into particular categories? And why do the data so often generate apparently conflicting statistics? In order to answer these questions, it is convenient to divide the controversies discussed in the previous chapters into five major groups: headline makers, truth by repetition, missing statistics, the "social" in statistics, and mathematical concepts.

Headline Makers

A few of the controversies involve egregious examples of misused statistics, the extreme of Disraeli's lies, damn lies, and statistics. In this category were statistics on the marriageability of older women, the "'list" of school problems, the number of missing children, the number of undocumented immigrants, and the income of divorced women. In each case, the controversies were started by eye-catching popular articles that carried alarming messages, although not ones supported by careful examination of the underlying data. Moreover, each example exploited fear: older women will not marry; today's youth are out of control; our children are likely to be abducted; and the United States is inundated with immigrants. Such reinforcement of stereotypical views is a tempting trap for newspapers and magazine writers who are looking for provocative headlines. Because articles that told the opposite side were published in academic journals, but not in the popular media, most readers learned only the original misleading statistics.

Part of the reason why the countervailing statistics received little attention was that those who might have publicized them were relatively powerless. In other words, the subjects of the articles, middle-aged women, children, and immigrants, had little access to the media that might have distributed alternative information. This situation of uncorrected statistical falsehood stands in contrast to disputed statistics involving corporate profits and wealthy individuals which prompted widely disseminated corrections to the original, ostensibly faulty, numbers. In general, we are likely to learn about disputed data when the issue involves the rich and powerful more often than when the controversies concern data involving the poor and powerless.

Truth by Repetition

A second group of statistical controversies were not actually incorrect, only misleading. The examples are numerous and include the personal savings rate, the number of homeless people, the illiteracy rate, GDP for poor countries, average family income, the Dow Jones Industrial Average, the *Fortune 500*, international test scores, productivity rates, small business job creation, and the cancer survival rate. In addition, there were statistics for which short-term changes were mistaken for long-term trends. Such examples included quarterly estimates of GDP, monthly trade statistics, annual SAT scores, yearly crime rates, monthly unemployment rates, and yearly educational attainment statistics.

These statistics were cited in popular and academic articles even though experts warned about their misleading characteristics. Readers may consult discussion in previous chapters for the reasons why these statistics are misleading. The question remains: why were the discredited statistics still used? The answer appears to be a situation similar to the problem with sensationalist statistics: the numbers tell a good story. It was far easier to lament the decline in personal savings, a rising crime rate, and the poor performance of U.S. school children on international tests, than to investigate the more complicated but truthful interpretation of these statistics. In an ironic twist, misleading statistics such as the Dow Jones averages and *Fortune 500* list have become important simply because they are perceived as important. Thus, the stock market responds to the Dow Jones, even though it is a poor measure of the overall stock market. And corporations take note of their status in the *Fortune 500*, even though accountants know it can be a misleading measure of corporate success.

This split between what the experts know and common usage of statistics has contributed to oversimplified analysis of policy issues. For example, in the study of illiteracy and of homelessness, popular accounts and even some research efforts focused on an attempt to reduce the social problem to a single number, thereby shifting discussion away from critical issues. There was more public debate about the precise illiteracy rate than about the more fundamental issue of what kind of literacy is necessary to function adequately in the United States. Similarly, there was a bitter dispute about the number of homeless people, without much understanding that homelessness was a transitory phase for a much larger number of individuals facing the problem of housing displacement. And finally, the apparently contradictory results in opinion polls make it appear that polls are meaningless because question wording or other manipulation of a survey can produce any desired result. Nevertheless, as polling experts are well aware, when properly interpreted, surveys can uncover subtleties in public opinion, as demonstrated by the studies of gun control and abortion.

A second problem with oversimplification is the likelihood that statistical reporting will be biased in favor of existing institutional arrangements. If complex analysis is sidestepped, then those who disseminate statistics can choose the simplification that benefits their interests. In the field of cancer research, experts understand the limitation of survival-rate statistics. Yet there is evidence that those who benefited from existing research budgets were willing to use oversimplified survival-rate statistics to lobby for additional research funds on ways to extend cancer survival at the expense of funding research on cancer prevention. In criminology, it is widely recognized that the predominant measures of crime overemphasize some crimes while overlooking others. But official reports on crime, usually put out by the same agencies that operate the criminal justice system, typically ignore these caveats that might question their funding priorities. Similarly, key economic variables such as GDP and unemployment are reported by government officials in a manner that supports the success of their economic policies, even though professional economists are well aware of the limitations of these statistics.

The lesson for researchers again is to be skeptical. Statistics that gain credence because of repeated use may not be so well regarded by experts who know the limitations of the underlying data.

What's Missing?

For some controversies, the problem was simply the absence of appropriate statistics. Researchers face a near dead-end in trying to study the extent of white-collar crime. For the study of individual wealth there are some sources of data, but as illustrated by the controversy about the interpretation of Federal Reserve Board survey data, these statistics are quite incomplete. Similarly, only partial information is available on corporate management, corporate ownership, and line-of-business reporting. All these cases involve data about those with power, and it does not require a conspiracy theory to argue that these individuals and groups are unwilling to participate in data-collection efforts in part out of a desire to protect their own status. From their perspective, little would be gained by sharing data on their position; on the contrary, social statistics might be used to argue that limits should be placed on their status.

The absence of other statistics can be traced to political conflict. During the 1980s, a number of statistical series were dropped by the U.S. government, including line-of-business reporting for diversified corporations, spendable weekly earnings as a measure of typical income, data on "small" strikes involving few workers, and education data on school busing and gender discrimination in teaching. The choice of which statistics were dropped seems to have been an obvious attempt to restrict research that took a certain point of view, in this instance statistics that were embarrassing to the administration in power at the time. In the case of AIDS and abortion statistics, the data are limited both because of unwillingness by those affected to take part in surveys and the federal government's reluctance to conduct relevant surveys.

From the other end of the economic and status ladder, the poor and the powerless are subject to considerable data-collection efforts. There are numerous studies of poverty, government income-maintenance programs, the homeless, and the unemployed, especially in comparison to the handful of studies of wealth and high incomes. The ability of the powerful to avoid statistical efforts raises the question of what interest the poor or middle-income groups have in complying with data collection. The controversies described in this book suggest that the numbers are beneficial for these groups. An accurate measure of the poverty rate can be used to argue for more poverty programs; a complete picture of housing inadequacy (not just homelessness) can be used to argue for new housing programs; a complete count of unemployment can be used to argue in favor of new jobs programs. Of course, alternative statistics have been used to argue against each of these programs. But, on balance, better numbers weigh in favor of those without other resources to present their case.

What's "Social" in Social Science Statistics?

The third and by far largest category reviewed in this book involves controversies in which there were at least two apparently contradictory statistics. Here the situation is more complex than the problem of trendy headlines, misleading statistics, or missing statistics. For most controversies, the numbers are not simply wrong or absent. Instead, apparently conflicting statistics occur because of the different ways in which the underlying data were organized into categories. This critical step of conceptualization is often overlooked, even though it is fundamental to all subsequent use of data.

Racial classification is an obvious instance in which there has been little recognition in research projects of the social construction of the categories. In retrospect, we can easily see the arbitrary and racist character of the 1790 U.S. Census three-fifths apportionment allocation for each black slave and the subsequent pseudo-scientific classification based on "quadroons" and "octoroons." But the current use of self-classification still reflects the older racist standard in the sense that partial black background usually means the individual is considered black. As a rebuttal to scientific racism, it is important to remember the social, not genetic, basis of the black and white racial categories.

The classification of Hispanics and Asians further demonstrates the arbitrary choice of which groups will be counted as separate "races" and the problems in defining the boundaries between these groups. As in the black–white dichotomy, the classification began from a white perspective in which all Hispanics and all Asians were grouped together, even though many individuals in the groups did not recognize such classification, typically preferring a country-of-origin label. Because of successful political efforts by Hispanic and Asian groups, these designations have changed with almost every census, which has been an inconvenience for research covering different time periods but is nonetheless an important reminder of the social origins of racial and ethnic designations.

For other controversies, there were similar, if less dramatic, problems in classifying the underlying data. In studying crime, for example, researchers must define which crimes will be counted as crime before there can be any consideration of the crime rate, the causes of crime, or the effectiveness of responses to crime. Most important, the manner in which white-collar crime is treated—or ignored—in official statistics causes entirely different analyses of who commits crimes and the efficacy of current allocation of resources to deal with crime. Specifically, if white-collar crime is counted, then much more crime is associated with high-income and high-status groups, and police resources aimed at white-collar crime are lacking compared with the amount spent to deal with traditionally defined crimes.

Polling is a unique interaction of social categories and their measurement. There is ample evidence that polls affect public opinion through the bandwagon and underdog effects. Equally troubling is the way in which public opinion polling sometimes undercuts thoughtful debate by asking for overly simplified answers from an underinformed public. For example, after the Persian Gulf War, some media polls focused more on what the public thought about the events than what actually had occurred. Researchers need to identify when surveys create opinion, rather than measure it. Finally, in election contests, coverage of poll results may replace substantive election campaigning so that "who is ahead" becomes more important than "who stands for what." Researchers may want to consider whether their projects foster "horserace journalism" instead of substantive analysis of the candidates and issues.

Many of the other statistical controversies were based on conceptual problems in economic theory. The clearest examples came from GDP statistics for which there are debates about how to account for pollution, resource depletion, the underground economy, and nonmarket production. Similarly, conceptual problems arose in accounting for housing: is it a consumption expense or an investment? Tax incidence required a number of theoretical assumptions about the ability of employers, landlords, and producers to pass the costs of taxes along to other groups. The measurement of the money supply involved complex issues of which kinds of assets serve as money. It is beyond the scope of this book to resolve any of these controversies in economic theory. Yet it is important for researchers to realize the degree to which economists dispute some of the most fundamental numbers used to describe the U.S. economy. The questionable accuracy of economic data may be humbling to economists, but it is often suggested within the profession as a necessary corrective to the advanced state of economic mathematical techniques. Without certainty about the underlying data, the most sophisticated economic model cannot be put to practical use.

The Mathematics of Social Science Statistics

The issue of conceptualization occurred for some statistics that one might consider free of theoretical decisions about social categories. Controversy about the inflation rate, for example, might be mistaken simply for a mathematical issue about how to take into account the effect of many products with changing prices. But this issue, called the *index number problem* by statisticians, in fact involves choices about how much each product will be counted in the inflation index. For example, different weights attached to different housing costs caused considerable variation in the official inflation rate during the early 1980s. The measurement of housing quality also was an index number problem based on a choice between different indicators of housing quality. Which of the housing problems were chosen—rats, leaking roofs, and so on—affected the measures of the trend in overall quality. The most extreme index number problem occurs in the *Places Rated* example, in which hundreds of cities could be ranked number one—or dead last—depending on the weights chosen for each factor. Estimates for the Crime Index, the level of Soviet military spending, the measurement of currency rates in different countries, and the measurement of productivity for an economy with a changing product mix also involved similar indexing problems for which there was no single correct solution.

A second mathematical issue that required conceptual decisions was the choice between absolute and relative statistics. In order to measure the extent of poverty, researchers must choose between various poverty lines, some of which are constant, or nearly so, in terms of the standard of living they represent, while others measure poverty as relative to current living standards, even if those standards have increased in terms of buying power. The debate about the trend in infant mortality also hinged on the distinction between absolute and relative change. Compared to high levels of the past, U.S. infant mortality has declined, an absolute improvement. But on a relative basis compared to other countries, U.S. infant mortality is a singular measure of health-care failure. Similarly, the trend in black college enrollment depends on whether we look at the number enrolled or the enrollment rate relative to improved high school achievement, by which standard college attendance is falling.

The issue of means and medians was critical for several statistical disputes discussed in this book: longevity for cancer patients, the distribution of income, the number of crimes per prison inmate, and the effect of the capital gains tax cut. These dissimilar social issues share the common problem of an asymmetric distribution in which there is a large cluster in the low end (short survival, low incomes, few crimes, low taxes), and a few individuals at the high end (long survival, high incomes, many crimes, high taxes). The resulting difference between the mean and median requires researchers to pay careful attention to which measure is appropriate for a particular project.

The statistical problem of whether to define categories at the start or the end of a time period affects two disputes, income mobility and small business job creation. In both cases, different conclusions were reached depending on whether individuals (or companies) were defined as rich (or large) at the beginning or at the end of the time period under analysis. Standard statistical practice requires that the outcome be reported using a variety of techniques to prove the robustness of the results. The failure of the initial investigators to do so led to suspicion about their conclusions.

Finally, the mathematical problem of projecting future statistics from current data was a controversial issue in several fields. Attempts to predict future crime incidence, the marriage rate of older women, and the future birthrate all suffered from the common problem of conservative assumptions in which current social conditions were assumed to continue. Too often these predictions carry the weight of mathematical certainty, when in fact society may change—indeed one purpose of social statistics can be to demonstrate precisely the need for those changes.

In summary, the mathematical complexities of social statistics also involve the problem of conceptualization. Thus, mathematical techniques —index numbers, means, medians, absolute and relative measures—all require the researcher to make choices about theoretical categories. Because of the complexities involved in learning the mathematical techniques, it is easy to overlook these underlying assumptions about how to organize the data, but they are critical for understanding precisely what is being measured and why there often are conflicting statistics for the same social issue.

What's a Researcher to Do?

The five major problems with social statistics—headline makers, error by repetition, missing statistics, lack of attention to social categories, and mathematical complications—all point to one remedy: data literacy. By better understanding the data used to create social statistics, we will be better equipped to understand complex social issues.

Ironically, the starting point for a critical view of the data may be an appreciation of the extensive data available to us. Many readers likely will share the amazement I felt in preparing this book at the sheer volume of U.S. social statistics. In addition to the well-known U.S. Census and Current Population Survey, there are large-scale U.S. surveys of housing, education, crime, crime victims, health, small business, large business, and a variety of demographic characteristics. Although some areas, such as health, enjoy larger and more complete surveys than, for example, education, nonetheless researchers in every field are confronted with ever-growing quantities of data, many of which are published by the government without further expert analysis. For social science students, there is little prospect that they will run out of numbers to examine; the challenge is to use them correctly.

A second step toward data literacy is an appreciation of why we have so many data. Without political pressure, few of the vast U.S. data resources would have been collected. For example, the U.S. Census, which we now take for granted, was not undertaken to provide a data set for researchers. Instead, the men who drafted the U.S. Constitution realized that the new democratic features of the government required statistics to determine the proportional representation from each state. Several methods were considered, including property values, before the concept of representation based on population was adopted (that is, except for slaves, who were counted as three-fifths of a person). Thus, although women, children, alien residents, and slaves could not vote, representational apportionment still required a complete population count.

Political pressure during the Progressive era on the dangers of U.S. workplaces provided the pressure for the first U.S. Bureau of Labor Statistics investigation and publication of workplace health and safety. In 1930, political leaders, who wanted statistical evidence of the severity of the depression, campaigned for better employment statistics in the census. Continued political lobbying led to the post–World War II Current Population Survey and its emphasis on employment statistics. Similarly, political pressure led to a major overhaul in the Department of Labor's Occupational Safety and Health statistics in the 1990s. In business statistics as well, it took pressure from those concerned about the power of large corporations to generate data used for antitrust enforcement and general research on the structure of markets in the U.S. economy.

These examples underscore the social nature of social science statistics. A society chooses what to measure—or better stated, groups within society struggle about what will be measured. On the one hand, the decisions to count all residents in the census, to document workplace hazards, to survey unemployment in great detail, and to measure how corporations dominate certain industries are all evidence that groups traditionally without power can use statistics as a resource to their advantage. On the other hand, the cutbacks in statistical efforts described earlier show how the numbers can be taken away as well. Overall, good statistics bring us closer to the truth, even when that truth undermines the authority of those in power.

A third step toward data literacy is an appreciation of the people behind the numbers. Among those who have traditionally fought for more and better social statistics are the men and women who collect and analyze the numbers for federal, state, and local governments. One might be tempted to respond that these individuals benefit personally from increased statistical collection, that is, the more numbers, the more jobs. But anyone who has consulted government statisticians is unlikely to take such a cynical view. The jobs are not well paid, the work is often tedious, and the rewards in terms of recognition are slim—unless a statistician makes an error.

Most of all, many of these individuals are eager to talk about the numbers to which they have dedicated their work lives. Certainly no one is better prepared to discuss problems in the data, and quite often it is government statisticians who warn outside users about the limits of the statistics for research and policy purposes. In other words, for the most part, government statisticians are not blind to errors in the numbers they carefully generate but tend to be advocates of careful scholarship and the appropriate use of statistics. Public opinion polling data are maintained by several university-affiliated groups. They, too, provide open access to the data, as well as freely given advice about its use.

Researchers can learn from these vital sources of knowledge. Many helpful reference works are published by statistical agencies, and it is often possible to consult directly with the government and university officials responsible for a particular data series. Unfortunately, the budget cutbacks of the 1980s hit hardest at the regional level, but there are still some offices for U.S. federal agencies outside Washington, D.C. State and local statistical information services vary greatly in quality, but in some locations, they equal federal authorities in terms of data collection and public access.

Data literacy is critical for playing the Data Game. By understanding what data are available, how they came to be collected, and who is responsible for their dissemination, we can begin to use social statistics to understand the society in which we live. Statistics alone will not provide a road map to a better world; they can only set a framework for our powers of analysis. But the more data literate we are, the more power we have to create a world of our own choosing.

Notes

CHAPTER 2: DEMOGRAPHY (6)

Data Sources (7)

U.S. Census (7)

History of U.S. Census in Patricia Cohen, *A Calculating People* (Chicago: University of Chicago Press, 1982); Margo J. Anderson, *The American Census: A Social History* (New Haven: Yale University Press, 1988); current U.S. Census methods in Bryant Robey, "Two Hundred Years and Counting: The 1990 Census," *Population Bulletin* 44 (April 1989); Hazard census data in U.S. Bureau of the Census, *Census of Population,* "General Social and Economic Characteristics," 1990-CP-2-19 Kentucky (Washington, D.C.: U.S. Government Printing Office, 1983), p. 45.

Vital Statistics (7)

Marriage and divorce statistics described in National Center for Health Statistics, *Vital Statistics of the United States, 1987,* vol. 3, *Marriage and Divorce* (Washington, D.C.: U.S. Government Printing Office, 1991), pp. 4-3–4-10; Donald J. Bogue, *Population of the United States* (New York: Free Press, 1985), pp. 165, 194–95; Larry L. Bumpass and James A. Sweet, *American Families and Households* (New York: Russell Sage Foundation, 1987), chaps. 2 and 5; data sample in National Center for Health Statistics, *Vital Statistics of the United States, 1987,* vol. 1, *Natality,* PHS-89-1100 (Washington, D.C.: U.S. Government Printing Office, 1989), p. 118.

Controversies (8)

The Population Undercount (8)

In-person enumeration in Robey, "Two Hundred Years," pp. 10–14. Undercount controversy in "Census Subject to Possible Correction," *Population Today* 17, no. 9 (September 1989): 3ff; Dudley Kirk, "Politics of Demography," *Society* 18 (January–February 1981): 22–25; "Census Mired in Dispute over Counting the Hidden," *Los Angeles Times,* March 15, 1989, p. 1; Reynolds Farley and Walter R. Allen, *The Color Line and the Quality of Life in America* (New York: Oxford University Press, 1987), pp. 420–38; cost to New York City in "Census Mired in Dispute," p. 19. Lawsuit in ibid. and "Accord on Census May Bring Change in Minority Data," *New York Times,* July 18, 1989, p. A1. "Decision was politically motivated," and "Commerce canned the project," in "Plan to Assess Census Undercounting Dropped," *Science* 239 (January 9, 1988): 456; Farley and Allen, *The Color Line,* pp. 424–25; summary of political dispute in Peter Skerry, "The Census Wars," *The Public Interest,* Winter 1992, pp. 17–32; on changes in spending because of adjustment, see Michael P. Murray, "Census Adjustment and the Distribution of Federal Spending," *Demography* 29, no. 3 (August 1992): 319–31; court cases on adjustment in "A Likely Long-Term Effect of Census Ruling More Litigation," *New York Times,* August 10, 1994, p. A8.

Box 2.1. Undercount in History (9)

Jefferson to Washington in Robey, "Two Hundred Years," p. 35; 1870 census in Anderson, *American Census,* p. 89.

Undocumented Immigrants (11)

Lawsuit in Frank D. Bean and Rodolfo O. de la Garza, "Illegal Aliens and Census Counts," *Society,* March/April 1988, pp. 48–53; "Lawsuit Challenges Census on Illegal Aliens," *New York Times,* February 18, 1988, p. A16. "Army of Russian troops," in "Census Is for Citizens Only," *Glendale News-Press,* June 2, 1989; 3 million in Michael Fix and Jeffrey S. Passel, *Immigration and Immigrants: Setting the Record Straight* (Washington, D.C.: Urban Institute, 1994), p. 24; and Robert Warren and Jeffrey S. Passel, "Count of the Uncountable: Estimates of Undocumented Aliens Counted in the 1980 United States Census," *Demography* 24, no. 3 (August 1987): 375–93. Estimation problems in Daniel Levine, Kenneth Hill, and Robert Warren, *Immigration Statistics: A Story of Neglect* (Washington, D.C.: National Academy Press, 1985), p. 88; Charles B. Keely, "Illegal Migration," *Scientific American* 246 (March 1982): 41–42; "Immigration Law Complicates Census Planning," *Los Angeles Times,* May 11, 1987, I, p. 4. Border crossing and yearly immigration in Fix, *Immigration,* p. 24; see also Katharine M. Donato, Jorge Durand, and Douglas S. Massey, "Stemming the Tide? Assessing the Deterrent Effects of the Immigration Reform and Control Act," *Demography* 29, no. 2 (May 1992): 139–57.

Costly Immigrants? (11)

Overuse in David Huddle, *The Cost of Immigration,* Carrying Capital Network, Washington, D.C., 1993; criticism in Jeffrey S. Passel, *Immigrants and Taxes: A Reappraisal of Huddle's "The Cost of Immigration"* (Washington, D.C.: Urban Institute, 1994); and Fix, *Immigration;* Texas study in "Stop Benefits for Aliens? It Wouldn't Be That Easy," *New York Times,* June 8, 1994, p. A1; Urban Institute researchers in Fix, *Immigration,* p. 62; summary of debate in Gregory Defreitas, "Fear of Foreigners," *Dollars and Sense,* January/February 1994, p. 8.

A Birth Dearth? (12)

Ben J. Wattenberg, *The Birth Dearth* (New York: Pharus Books, 1987). "Is it possible?" in Tony Kaye, "The Birth Dearth," *New Republic,* January 19, 1987, pp. 20–23. Front-cover news magazine coverage of book in "Are We Having Enough Babies?" *U.S. News and World Report,* January 22, 1987, pp. 56–63. Criticism of Wattenberg in Kaye, "The Birth Dearth," and Jonathan Lieberson, "Too Many People?" *New York Review of Books,* June 26, 1986, pp. 36–42. Criticism of Census projections in Dennis A. Ahlburg and James W. Vaupel, "Alternative Projections of the U.S. Population," *Demography* 27, no. 4 (November 1990): 641–50. Problems of prediction in "Census Bureau Demographer's Unqualified Prediction," *New York Times,* February 5, 1989, p. 30; 1945 estimate in Kaye, "The Birth Dearth," p. 21. Keyfitz in Nathan Keyfitz, "The Social and Political Context of Population Forecasting," in *The Politics of Numbers,* ed. William Alonso and Paul Starr (New York: Russell Sage Foundation, 1987), pp. 256–58.

Will You Still Feed Me? (13)

Example of projections in "What Will Happen When the Baby Boom Retires?" *USA Today Magazine of the American Scene,* August 1986, p. 15. Paul Craig Roberts in "Social Security Has Become a Giant Pyramid Scheme," *Business Week,* October 10, 1988, p. 28. Michael Boskin in *Too Many Promises: The Uncertain Future of Social Security* (Homewood, Ill: Dow-Jones Irwin, 1986). Bernstein in Merton C. Bernstein and Joan Brodshaug Bernstein, *Social Security: The System That Works* (New York: Basic Books, 1988), p. 72. Ackerman in *Hazardous to Our Wealth* (Boston: South End Press, 1984), p. 121. On federal expenditures for social security, see Phillip Longman, *Born to Pay* (Boston: Houghton Mifflin, 1987), pp. 8–10. "We must consider," ibid., p. 9. On confusing demographics with politics, see John Myles, "The Trillion Dollar Misunderstanding," *Working Papers for a New Society,* July/August 1981, pp. 23–31.

Race and Ethnicity (15)

Who Is Black? (15)

History of census questions in Ira S. Lowry, *The Science and Politics of Ethnic Enumeration* (Santa Monica, Calif.: Rand Corporation, 1980), pp. 8–9; and William Petersen, "Politics and the Measurement of Ethnicity," in Alonso and Starr, *The Politics of Numbers,* pp. 208–9; change in race designation and infant mortality in Robert A. Hahn, Joseph Mulinare, and Steven M. Teutsch, "Inconsistencies in Coding of Race and Ethnicity between Birth and Death in U.S. Infants," *Journal of the American Medical Association* 267, no. 2 (January 8, 1992): 259–79.

Box 2.2. Black "Insanity": An Argument for Slavery (16)

Patricia Cohen, *A Calculating People* (Chicago: University of Chicago Press, 1982), pp. 194–204; see also Anderson, *American Census,* pp. 29–31.

Who Is Asian? (16)

History of Asian enumeration in Lowry, *The Science and Politics,* pp. 7–10. Problem answers in "Simpler 1990 Census Form Upsets Asian-Americans," *Los Angeles Times,* April 12, 1988, I, p. 3; "Concerns Raised on the '90 Census," *New York Times,* April 17, 1988, p. 31; "Census Won't List Various Asian Groups," *Wall Street Journal,* May 23, 1988, p. 19. Limited space in census in "Scrambling to Be Counted in Census," *New York Times,* December 3, 1989, p. A17.

Box 2.3. Second Largest "Ethnic" Group: "No Response" (17)

Howard Wainer, "How Accurately Can We Assess Changes in Minority Performance on the SAT?" *American Psychologist* 43, no. 10 (October 1988): 774–78.

Who Is Hispanic? (17)

Change in census method in Joan Moore and Harry Pachon, *Hispanics in the United States* (Englewood Cliffs, N.J.: Prentice-Hall, 1985), p. 3; see also Nancy A. Denton and Douglas S. Massey, "Racial Identity among Caribbean Hispanics," *American Sociological Review* 54 (October 1989): 790–94. Respondent confusion in Lowry, *The Science and Politics,* p. 13. Los Angeles City Council in "L.A. Cases Seek Hispanic Gain," *New York Times,* July 10, 1989, p. A15.

Who Are My Ancestors? (19)

Ancestry in Reynolds Farley, "The New Census Question about Ancestry: What Did It Tell Us?" *Demography* 28, no. 3 (August 1991): 411–27.

Implications (19)

History of concept of race in J.C. King, *The Biology of Race* (Berkeley: University of California Press, 1981); see also Stephen J. Gould, *The Mismeasure of Man* (New York: Norton, 1981); and Ashley Montagu, *Man's Most Dangerous Myth: The Fallacy of Race* (New York: Oxford University Press, 1974). On the need for new categories, see *New York Review of Books*; "Should the Census Be Less Black and White?" *Business Week,* July 4, 1994, p. 40.

Box 2.4. If It's Tuesday, I'm Swedish (20)

Reynolds Farley, "The New Census Question about Ancestry: What Did It Tell Us?" *Demography* 28, no. 3 (August 1991): 421–23.

Households and Families (20)

Changing household characteristics in Nancy Folbre, *A Field Guide to the U.S. Economy* (New York: Pantheon, 1987), p. 3.9; and "Living Arrangements and Marital Status of Households and Families," *Family Economics Review* 2, no. 3, 1989, p. 16. Jencks in Christopher Jencks, "The Politics of Income Measurement," in Alonso and Starr, *The Politics of Numbers,* pp. 92–105.

"Oh No, I Forgot to Get Married!" (21)

"Too Late," in *Newsweek,* June 2, 1986, p. 54. Bennett–Bloom–Craig study described in Thomas Exter, "How to Figure Your Chances of Getting Married," *American Demographics,* June 1987, pp. 50–52; later published in Neil G. Bennett, David E. Bloom, and Patricia H. Craig, "The Divergence of Black and White Marriage Patterns" *American Journal of Sociology* 95, no. 3 (November 1989): 692–722. Christensen in Bryce J. Christensen, "The Costly Retreat from Marriage," *Public Interest* 91 (Spring 1988): 62–64. Census Bureau study in Jeanne E. Moorman, "The History and Future of the Relationship between Education and Marriage," March 1987, Marriage and Family Statistics Branch, U.S. Bureau of the Census, summarized in Exter, *How to Figure.* Comparison of two studies in ibid. and Susan Faludi, "The Marriage Trap," *Ms.,* July–August 1987, pp. 61ff. Comments on final Harvard–Yale article in "Study of Marriage Patterns Revised Omitting Impact of Women's Careers," *New York Times,* November 11, 1989, p. A9; Andrew Cherlin, "The Strange Career of the "Harvard–Yale Study," *Public Opinion Quarterly* 54 (1990): 117–24; and Susan Faludi, *Backlash: The Undeclared War against American Women* (New York: Crown, 1991):4–14.

Box 2.5. Head of Household (22)

Householder change in Sweet and Bumpass, *American Families,* pp. 336–37.

Box 2.6. Individuals Living Alone (22)

Data calculated from Sweet and Bumpass, *American Families,* pp. 344, 376. Debate over post-1987 change in "New Data Show Fewer People Living Alone," *Wall Street Journal,* August 18, 1987, p. 35.

Divorce (23)

Problems with divorce data in Sweet and Bumpass, *American Families,* chap. 5; Bogue, *Population of the United States,* pp. 194–97. Men's versus women's responses in Sweet and Bumpass, *American Families,* p. 210. Separation without divorce in "Two-thirds of Marriages Will Fail, Study Says," *Los Angeles Times,* March 13, 1989, p. A6. Data on trend in Arthur J. Norton and Jeanne E. Moorman, "Current Trends in Marriage and Divorce among American Women," *Journal of Marriage and the Family* 49 (February 1987): 3–14, and "Two-thirds of Marriages Will Fail." Harris in "One in Two? Not True," *Time,* July 13, 1987, p. 21; see also "Portrait of Divorce in America," *Newsweek,* February 2, 1987, p. 78. "It would be foolish," in "Two-thirds of Marriages Will Fail." Harris in "One in Two?" Census Bureau researchers in "Current Trends," p. 12; Martin and Bumpass in "Two-thirds of Marriages Will Fail."

Case Study Questions (26)

1. Harold Orlans, "The Politics of Minority Statistics," *Society* 26 (May–June 1989): 25.

2. Bumpass and Sweet in "Living Together," *Society* 25, no. 5 (July–August 1988): 3; and Koray Tanfer, "Patterns of Premarital Cohabitation among Never-Married Women in the United States," *Journal of Marriage and the Family* 49 (August 1987): 483–97.

3. Sweet and Bumpass, *American Families,* p. 210.

4. "Deciding What Counts in 1990," *Los Angeles Times,* March 14, 1989, p. 1; "Scrambling to be Counted," p. A17.

5. Margo J. Anderson, *The American Census: A Social History* (New Haven: Yale University Press, 1988), pp. 144–49.

6. Sweet and Bumpass, *American Families,* p. 38.

7. Peggy Lovell Webster and Jeffrey W. Dwyer, "The Cost of Being Non-white in Brazil," *Social Science Research* 72, no. 2 (January 1988): 136; and Carl N. Degler, *Neither Black nor White* (New York: Macmillan, 1971). On the Caribbean, see "Racial Identity among Caribbean Hispanics," pp. 791–93.

CHAPTER 3: HOUSING (28)

Data Sources (28)

U.S. Census (28)

History of housing surveys in John S. Adams, *Housing America in the 1980s* (New York: Russell Sage Foundation, 1987), pp. 4, 29–30; see also Joseph W. Duncan and William C. Shelton, *Revolution in United States Government Statistics* (Washington, D.C.: U.S. Government Printing Office, 1978), p. 39. On census form, see Bryant Robey, "Two Hundred Years and Counting: The 1990 Census," *Population Bulletin* 44, no. 1 (April 1989): 15–24. For advice on using census housing data, see U.S. Conference of Mayors, *Assessing Elderly Housing* (Washington, D.C.: American Association of Retired Persons, 1986). Data sample in Bureau of the Census, U.S. Department of Commerce, *1990 Census of Housing,* CH-2-29, "Detailed Housing Characteristics, Nebraska," p. 52.

American Housing Survey (29)

History in Adams, *Housing America in the 1980s,* pp. 33–36. Data sample in U.S. Department of Housing and Urban Development, *American Housing Survey for the Houston Metropolitan Area in 1991,* H-170-914-49, pp. 43, 46. On housing starts, see Norman Frumkin, *Guide to Economic Indicators* (Armonk, N.Y.: M.E. Sharpe, 1990), pp. 127–31. On economic surveys, see U.S. Department of Commerce, Bureau of the Census, *Characteristics of New Housing: 1986,* Construction Reports C25-86-13 (Washington, D.C.: U.S. Government Printing Office, 1987), p. 63. Dodge data in Cynthia Bansak and Anne Toohey, "Comparing Dodge's Construction Potentials Data and the Census Bureau's Building Permits Series," *Economic Review,* March/April 1994, pp. 23–37. Data sample in U.S. Department of Commerce, *Characteristics of New Housing, 1992,* p. 16.

Box 3.1. U.S. Census versus American Housing Survey (30)

Differences described in Adams, *Housing America in the 1980s,* pp. 34–37.

Price Data (31)

Shelter index in U.S. Department of Labor, Bureau of Labor Statistics, *Handbook of Labor Statistics* (Washington, D.C.: U.S. Government Printing Office, 1988), pp. 166–67.

Controversies (31)

Housing Quality (31)

Data in John C. Weicher, "Private Production: Has the Rising Tide Lifted All Boats?" in *Housing America's Poor,* ed. Peter D. Salins (Chapel Hill: University of North Carolina Press, 1987), p. 46. Dilapidated housing in Peter D. Salins, "America's Permanent Housing Problem," in Salins, *Housing America's Poor,* pp. 2–4. AHS quality measures in William C. Apgar, Jr., "The Leaky Boat: A Housing Problem Remains," in Salins, *Housing America's Poor,* pp. 67–89. Leaky roofs, rats, in ibid., p. 69. Moving target in Salins, "America's Permanent," pp. 2–9; "one reason," in ibid., p. 2.

Is There an Affordability Crisis? (32)

Experts on 25 percent in Adams, *Housing America in the 1980s,* p. 114. Spending data in Chester Hartman, "The Housing Crisis in Brief," in *America's Housing Crisis* (Boston: Routledge and Kegan Paul, 1983), pp. 17–18. Debate in ibid., pp. 17–25, and John I. Gilderbloom, "Trends in the Affordability of Rental Housing: 1970 to 1983," *Social Science Research* 70, no. 4 (July 1986): 301. Price index in U.S. Department of Commerce, *Characteristics of New Housing: 1986,* construction reports C25-86-13, p. 55. Affordability index in Glenn Crellin, "Housing Affordability Index—What It Is and Isn't," *Real Estate Issues,* Fall/ Winter 1988, pp. 50–51. Home prices in "Home Prices Rose Sharply in Southwest, Pacific Northwest in the Fourth Quarter," *Wall Street Journal,* February 10, 1993, p. A4; and "Southland Home Prices, Sales Drop," *Los Angeles Times*, May 5, 1994, p. D2. Housing squeeze in James D. Wright, "Address Unknown: Homelessness in Contemporary America," *Society* 26, no. 4 (September–October 1989): 52–53.

Government in the Housing Market? (35)

Rent-control advocate in Michael Mandel, "A Real Look at Rent Control," *Dollars and Sense,* January–February 1986, pp. 8–17. Eleven percent in Cushing N. Dolbeare, "The Low-Income Housing Crisis," in Hartman, *America's Housing Crisis,* p. 39. Bad effects of public housing in John C. Weicher, "Private Production: Has the Rising Tide Lifted All Boats?" in Salins, *Housing America's Poor,* pp. 58–59. Rent-control anathema in many conservative analyses; see, for example, B. Bruce-Briggs, "Rent Control Must Go," *New York Times Magazine,* April 18, 1976, pp. 19–31. Filtering in Weicher, "Private Production," pp. 53–63. Criticism in Michael E. Stone, "Housing and the Economic Crisis," in Hartman, *America's Housing Crisis,* pp. 99–150.

The Homeless (37)

HUD estimate discussed in Jon Erickson and Charles Wilhelm, *Housing the Homeless* (New Brunswick, N.J.: Center for Urban Policy Research, 1986), pp. 146–48. Communities estimate discussed in ibid., p. 129. Comparison in ibid., pp. 146–47. Freeman in Thomas J. Main, "What We Know about the Homeless," *Commentary,* May 1988, pp. 27–28. Burt in Martha Burt, *Over the Edge: The Growth of Homelessness in the 1980s* (New York: Russell Sage Foundation, 1992); Jencks in Christopher Jencks, *The Homeless* (Cambridge: Harvard University Press, 1994). "Never pin down" in Wright, "Address Unknown," pp. 52–53. Rand Corporation study in ibid., p. 48. Doubling up in ibid., and Neighborhood Reinvestment Corporation in "18 Million Homeless Seen by 2003," *Washington Post,* June 3, 1987, p. A8.

Geographic Units (40)

Origins of "tracts" in Duncan and Shelton, *Revolution,* p. 209; defined in Robey, "Two Hundred Years," p. 25. Definition of urban in James L. Newman, *Population Patterns, Dynamics and Prospects* (Englewood Cliffs, N.J.: Prentice-Hall, 1984), pp. 50–51. MSAs described in Adams, *Housing America in the 1980s,* pp. 31–32, 39; Buffalo in "Why Metro Numbers Are Meaning Less," *American Demographics,* March 1993, pp. 9–11; Standard Consolidated Areas described in ibid., p. 39.

Segregation (41)

"Our Nation," National Advisory Commission on Civil Disorders, *Report* (Washington, D.C.: U.S. Government Printing Office, 1968), p. 1. Nixon administration blocked in "Middle-Class Black Housing Still Largely Segregated," *Washington Post,* December 30, 1987, p. A4. On historical trend, see Reynolds Farley and Walter R. Allen, *The Color Line and the Quality of Life in America* (New York: Oxford University Press, 1987), pp. 139–57; see also Christine H. Rossell, "Does School Desegregation Policy Stimulate Residential Integration?" *Urban Education* 21, no. 4 (January 1987): 403. Suburban movement in John R. Logan and Mark Schneider, "Racial Segregation and Racial Change in American Suburbs," *American Journal of Sociology* 89 (January 1984): 46–57. Overall trend in Douglas S. Massey and Nancy Denton, "Trends in the Residential Segregation of Blacks, Hispanics and Asians: 1970–1980," *American Sociological Review* 52 (December 1987): 802–25. "Most blacks" in ibid., p. 823. On segregation indexes, see Michael J. White, "Segregation and Diversity Measures in Population Distribution," *Population Index* 52, no. 2 (Summer 1986): 198–221.

Is Seattle the Best Place to Live? (42)

Ratings in Richard Boyer and David Savageau, *Places Rated Almanac* (Englewood Cliffs, N.J.: Prentice-Hall, 1989), pp. 392–400; Bell Labs study in Richard A. Becker, Lorraine Denby, Robert McGill, and Allan R. Wilks, "Analysis of Data from the *Places Rated Almanac*," *The American Statistician* 41, no. 3 (August 1987): 169–86. Sophisticated approach in G.C. Blomquist, M.C. Berger, and J.P. Hoehn, "New Estimates of Quality of Life in Urban Areas," *American Economic Review* 78, no. 1 (March 1988): 89–107.

Case Study Questions (46)

1. Apgar,"The Leaky Boat," p. 73.
2. Adams, *Housing America in the 1980s,* p. 44.
3. "New Home Sales Fell a Steep 14.8% in March," *New York Times*, April 29, 1992, p. D6.
4. Brookes, "Surprise Home Buyers."
5. "Orange County Tops U.S.," *Los Angeles Times,* August 12, 1988, p. 22.
6. City of Pasadena, "The City of Pasadena Homeless Count," September 23, 1992," p. 15.

CHAPTER 4: HEALTH (48)

Data Sources (48)

NCHS in Nancy D. Pearce, *Data Systems of the National Center for Health Statistics,* Vital and Health Statistics, series 1, no. 16 (Washington, D.C.: U.S. Government Printing Office, 1982); on Current Population Survey, see chapter 9; other government surveys in National Center for Health Statistics, U.S. Department of Health and Human Services, *Facts at Your Fingertips* (Washington, D.C.: U.S. Government Printing Office, May 1981). Headaches in ibid., p. 67. WHO data in World Health Organization, *World Health Statistics Annual,* 1992, D82, D197.

Controversies (50)

Infant Mortality (50)

As a health indicator in C. Arden Miller, "Infant Mortality in the U.S.," *Scientific American* 253 (July 1985): 31–37. Soviet Union in "Getting Russia Well Again," *The Economist,* November 21, 1987, pp. 51–52. Historical data in Miller, "Infant Mortality in the U.S.," pp. 31–32. Data for 1988 in "Health Data Show Wide Gap," *New York Times,* March 23, 1990, p. A17; 1990 infant mortality in "Infant Deaths Drop but Black Babies Lag," *New York Times,* March 12, 1993, p. A17; measurement problems in Carl Haub and Machiko Yanagishita, "Infant Mortality: Who's Number One?" *Population Today,* March 1991, pp. 6–8; Schwartz in "Infant Death Rate Fell Again—Did You Hear?" *Wall Street Journal,* April 24, 1985, p. 30. For defense of U.S. health-care system, see also Harvey Sapolsky,

"The Numbers Are Awry on Infant Mortality," *Business Week,* August 15, 1988, p. 18. United States versus other countries in Miller, "Infant Mortality in the U.S." Swedish provinces in D. Rotstein, *The Paradox of Modern Medicine* (Cambridge: MIT Press, 1967), pp. 24–25. Heterogeneous population in Harry Schwartz, *The Case for Modern Medicine* (New York: McKay, 1972), p. 47. Data for whites and blacks in "Infant Deaths Drop but Black Babies Lag," *New York Times,* March 12, 1993, p. A17. Studies of reasons in Joel C. Kleinman and Samuel S. Kessel, "Racial Differences in Low Birth Weight," *New England Journal of Medicine* 317 (September 17, 1987): 749–53; and Jann L. Murray and Merton Bernfeld, "The Differential Effect of Prenatal Care," *New England Journal of Medicine* 319 (November 24, 1988): 1385–91. Infants saved in "Infant Mortality among Black Americans," *Journal of the American Medical Association* 257 (February 6, 1987): 599.

Box 4.1. Abortion (51)

Guttmacher data in *New York Times,* March 13, 1985, p. A1; August 25, 1987, p. A13; October 6, 1988, p. B18. Trends in "Study Finds Abortions Dropped in '92 to Lowest Level Since '79," *New York Times,* June 16, 1994, p. A1. Problems in measurement in Elise F. Jones and Jacqueline Darroch Forrest, "Underreporting of Abortions in Surveys in U.S. Women: 1976 to 1988," *Demography* 29, no. 1 (February 1992): 113–24.

Are We Living Longer? (53)

Life expectancy in "Life Expectancy Remains at Record Level," *Statistical Bulletin* 70, no. 3 (July–September 1989): 26–30. "Death Rate for Blacks Still High," *New York Times,* September 27, 1989, p. A14; see also "A Disturbing Decline in Black Life Expectancy," *Business Week,* February 27, 1989. Unreliable rates for extreme elderly in Ira Rosenwaike, Nurit Yaffe, and Phillip C. Sagi, "The Recent Decline in Mortality of the Extreme Aged," *American Journal of Public Health* 70 (October 1980): 1074–80. Who lies, in Kenneth C.W. Kammeyer and Helen L. Ginn, *An Introduction to Population* (Chicago: Dorsey Press, 1986), p. 71. Stephen Jay Gould, "The Median Isn't the Message," *Discover,* June 1985, pp. 40–42. U.S. mean life expectancy in "Other Industrial Nations Lead U.S. in Longevity," *Wall Street Journal,* August 19, 1992, p. B1; extrapolation in John M. Owen and James W. Vaupel, "An Exercise in Life Expectancy," *American Demographics,* November 1985, pp. 37–39. Walford in Roy L. Walford, *Maximum Life Span* (New York: Norton, 1983). Thomas McKeown, *The Role of Medicine: Dream, Mirage or Nemesis* (Princeton, N.J.: Princeton University Press, 1979). Debate summarized in John B. McKinlay and Sonja M. McKinlay, "The Questionable Contribution of Medical Measures to the Decline of Mortality in the United States in the Twentieth Century," *Health and Society,* Summer 1977, pp. 405–28; see also Kenneth C.W. Kammeyer and Helen L. Ginn, *An Introduction to Population* (Chicago: Dorsey Press, 1986), pp. 142–51. Optimistic appraisal also in Theodore J. Gordon, "Medical Breakthroughs," *The Futurist,* January–February 1987, pp. 15–17.

Box 4.2. The Oldest Person on Earth (56)

Roy L. Walford, *Maximum Life Span* (New York: Norton, 1983), pp. 12–15.

Cancer (56)

"Same kind of" in Ralph W. Moss, *The Cancer Syndrome* (New York: Grove Press, 1980), p. 16; see also Richard M. Nixon, "Acting against Cancer," *Saturday Evening Post,* July/August 1986, pp. 67–69. Halving U.S. mortality rate in J.C. Bailar III and Elaine M. Smith, "Progress against Cancer?" *New England Journal of Medicine* 314, no. 19 (May 8, 1986): 1226; and Tim Beardsley, "A War Not Won," *Scientific American,* January 1994, pp. 130–38; NCI versus critics in "Cancer: Illusory Progress?" *Scientific American,* June 1987, p. 29; "Cancer Stats Attacked as Misleading," *Science News* 131 (April 25, 1987): 260; "Cancer Stats: Gains and Losses," *Science News* 130 (December 13, 1986): 372; "Who's Got Cancer's Number?" *U.S. News and World Report,* December 15, 1986, p. 76; "Battling Cancer: Figures Can Say Anything," *U.S. News and World Report,* May 19, 1986; James E. Enstrom and Donald F. Austin, "Interpreting Cancer Survival Rates," *Science* 195 (March 4, 1977): 847–51. Cancer research funding in "Outspoken and Impatient Scientist Takes Charge of War on Cancer," *New York Times,* February 7, 1989, p. B7. Breast cancer detection in Bailar and Smith, "Progress against Cancer?" pp. 1229–30. Prostate cancer detection in ibid., p. 1230. Research use of incidence rates in ibid., p. 1228.

Box 4.3. Likelihood of Breast Cancer (58)

Richard R. Love, "The Risk of Breast Cancer in American Women," *Journal of the American Medical Association* 257 (March 20, 1987): 1470.

AIDS (59)

AIDS cases in U.S. Department of Health and Human Services, Centers for Disease Control, *Morbidity and Mortality Weekly Report,* February 11, 1994, p. 83. First survey in "U.S. Survey Finds 550,000 Are Infected With H.I.V. Outside Risk Groups," *New York Times,* December 14, 1993, p. B6; Asia and Africa in "The Numbers Debate," *World Press Review,* January 1994, p. 40.

Is Slower Safer? (60)

Drop in 1974 fatalities in "Official Report Says: Speed Doesn't Kill," *Consumers' Research,* December 1986, p. 30. Predicted increase in fatalities in "Does Speed Kill?" *Newsweek,* July 21, 1986, p. 16; and 1987 increase in fatalities in ibid., Burnley in "65 MPH Not Costing Lives," *New York Times,* May 4, 1988, p. A18. Critics' answer in "U.S. Issues Fatality Data on 65 MPH," *New York Times,* May 7, 1988, p. 36. Varying speeds in "Official Report Says," p. 29, and "Speeding, Coordination, and the 55-MPH Limit." Comments by Peter Asch, David T. Levy, Richard Fowles, Peter D. Loeb, Donald W. Snyder, and Charles A. Lave in *American Economic Review* 79, no. 4 (September 1989): 913–31.

Benefit–Cost Analysis (61)

For description of benefit–cost analysis, see James T. Campen, *Benefit, Cost and Beyond* (Cambridge, Mass.: Ballinger, 1986), or any of many textbooks such as Edward M. Gramlich, *Benefit–Cost Analysis of Government Programs* (Englewood Cliffs, N.J.: Prentice-Hall, 1981). Criticisms of value of human life in Mark Green and Norman Waitzman, "Cost, Benefit, and Class," *Working Papers for a New Society,* May/June 1980, pp. 39–51. $300,000 to $8 million in "What Is the Audited Value of Life?" *New York Times,* October 26, 1984, p. 24. $128 in Green and Waitzman, "Cost, Benefit and Class," p. 43. $400,000 in "What Is the Audited Value of Life?" Construction workers in ibid., Mark Green in Green and Waitzman, "Cost, Benefit and Class," pp. 48–49. Advocates of risk assessment in Mary Douglas and Aaron Wildavsky, *Risk and Culture: The Selection of Technical and Environmental Dangers* (Berkeley: University of California Press, 1982); see also Council of Economic Advisers, *Economic Report of the President 1987* (Washington, D.C.: U.S. Government Printing Office, 1987), pp. 179–207; Henry Fairlie, "Fear of Living," *The New Republic,* January 23, 1989, pp. 16–18. Criticism of risk assessment in William R. Freudenburg, "Perceived Risk, Real Risk: Social Science and the Art of Probabilistic Risk Assessment," *Science* 242 (October 7, 1988): 44–49; and Langdon Winner, "On Not Hitting the Tar-Baby: Risk Assessment and Conservatism," in Mary Gibson, *To Breathe Freely* (Totowa, N.J.: Rowman and Allanheld, 1985), pp. 269–84. Lawn mowers versus nuclear power in ibid., p. 277. Chernobyl in "Life's Risks: Balancing Fear against Reality of Statistics," *New York Times,* May 8, 1989, p. A1; "Genuinely puzzling" in Winner, "On Not Hitting the Tar-Baby," p. 275. William R. Freudenberg in "Perceived Risk," p. 47. Summary of the problem in *Benefit, Cost and Beyond,* pp. 52–55. Langdon Winner in "On Not Hitting the Tar-Baby," pp. 280–82.

Box 4.4. Cost of Tamper-proof Closures (62)

Paul W. MacAvoy, "FDA Regulation—At What Price?" *New York Times,* November 21, 1982, p. III-3.

Case Study Questions (65)

1. Richard J. David, "Did Low Birthweight among U.S. Blacks Really Increase?" *American Journal of Public Health* 76 (April 1986): 380–84.
2. R.D. Retherford, G.M. Mirza, M. Irfan, and I. Alam, "The Decline That Wasn't," *Population Today,* November 1989, pp. 6–9.
3. "Death Rate for Blacks Still High," *New York Times,* September 27, 1989, p. A14; and "U.S. Death Rates: Another Social Gap," *Business Week,* June 27, 1994, p. 18.
4. Utah in Myron Johnston, "Young and Alive," *American Demographics,* December 1986, p. 7. Cirrhosis of the liver in Victor Fuchs, *Who Shall Live?* (New York: Basic Books, 1974), pp. 52–54.
5. "Babies' Seats Are Air Safety Issue," *New York Times,* August 18, 1985, sec. 4, p. 23; and "Tighter Safety Rules Planned for Young Children in Planes," *New York Times,* November 4, 1989, p. A7.

CHAPTER 5: EDUCATION (67)

Data Sources (67)

Description of NCES data in U.S. Department of Education, National Center for Education Statistics, *Digest of Education Statistics* (Washington, D.C.: U.S. Government Printing Office, 1987), pp. 321–34; NCES data sample in U.S. Department of Education, *Digest,* 1993, p. 69. U.S. Census data sample in U.S. Bureau of the Census, *1990 Census of Population: Education in the United States,* CP-3-4 (Washington, D.C.: U.S. Government Printing Office, January 1994). National Longitudinal Survey data sample in U.S. Department of Education, *Digest,* 1993, p. 143.

Controversies (69)

Poor Data (69)

Summary of NCES problems in Charles Cooke, Alan Ginsburg, and Marshall Smith, "The Sorry State of Education Statisics," *Education Digest* 51, no. 4 (December 1985): 28–30; see also Janet A. Weiss and Judith Gruber, "The Managed Irrelevance of Federal Education Statistics," in William Alonso and Paul Starr, *The Politics of Numbers* (New York: Russell Sage Foundation, 1987). "Agency's Statistics Challenged," *New York Times,* March 11, 1986, p. C1; "Statistics Gap in Education," *Washington Post,* May 3, 1986, p. A25; and Anne C. Lewis, "New Data Collection System Raises New Questions," *Phi Delta Kappan,* June 1986, pp. 699–700. Achievement measurement discussed in John B. Carroll, "The National Assessments in Reading: Are We Misreading the Findings?" *Phi Delta Kappan,* February 1987, pp. 424–30.

High School Dropouts (70)

New York City in "Record Low Dropout Rate Is Greeted with Skepticism," *New York Times,* June 11, 1993, p. B16; U.S. estimates in Robert Kominski, "Estimating the National High School Dropout Rate," *Demography* 27, no. 2 (May 1990): 303–11; CPS in "New Education Legislation Defines Federal Role in Nation's Classrooms," *New York Times,* March 30, 1994, p. B7. 500,000 dropouts in Kominski, "Estimating," p. 309.

Box 5.1. Schools Are Only as Bad as We Think They Are (71)

Barry O'Neill, "The History of a Hoax," *New York Times Magazine,* March 6, 1994, pp. 46–49.

Illiteracy (72)

Rate of 0.5 percent in "Losing the War of Letters," *Time,* May 5, 1986, p. 68. Figures 33 percent and 60 million functional illiterates in Jonathan Kozol, *Illiterate America* (New York: Doubleday, 1985), p. 4. Census Bureau study publicity in "Losing the War of Letters." Critics in "Specialists Attack Report on U.S. Illiteracy Rate," *Washington Post,* May 3, 1986, p. A6. Educational Testing Service in Carroll, "The National Assessments." Literacy funding in Kozol, *Illiterate America,* p. 5; and "Illiteracy Seen as Threat to U.S. Economic Edge," *New York Times,* September 7, 1988, p. A23.

Black Educational Progress (73)

Progress in Reynolds Farley and Walter R. Allen, *The Color Line and the Quality of Life in America* (New York: Oxford University Press, 1987), p. 190. Quality of schools in ibid., pp. 203–8. Harrison and Gorham in "Even College Degrees Might Not Lift Blacks out of Poverty," *Business Week,* February 5, 1990, p. 18. Black enrollment in American Council on Education, *Minorities in Higher Education* (Washington, D.C., 1988); "Ranks of Black" in *New York Times,* February 5, 1989, p. A1; NCES and CPS enrollment data in Robert M. Hauser, "What Happens to Youth after High School?" *Focus* 13, no. 3 (Fall/Winter 1991): 1–13; "the NCES has" and "well designed" in Robert M. Hauser, "The Decline in College Entry among African Americans: Findings in Search of Explanations," in Paul M. Sniderman, Philip E. Tetlock, and Edward G. Carmines, *Prejudice, Politics and the American Dilemma* (Stanford, Calif.: Stanford University Press, 1993), p. 274; size of CPS in Hauser, "The Decline," p. 286; enrollment trends and rates in Daniel Koretz, *Trends in the Postsecondary Enrollment of Minorities* (Santa Monica, Calif.: Rand Corporation, 1990); explaining decline in Hauser, "The Decline," p. 305; NCES surveys in Hauser, "What Happens to Youth."

School Desegregation: What Has Happened? (75)

Orfield resignation in "Adviser to U.S. Desegregation Study Quits," *New York Times,* October 30, 1985, p. A12; and Ellen K. Coughlin, "When Research Comes up against Politics," *Chronicle of Higher Education,* November 27, 1985, p. 7. Commission report in "Desegregation Plans Said to Improve Race Balance," *New York Times,* May 20, 1987, p. A27. Orfield study in "Blacks Holding Ground, Hispanics Losing in Desegregation," *Phi Delta Kappan,* January 1987, p. 406. Welch debate in Finis Welch, "A Reconsideration of the Impact of School Desegregation Programs on Public School Enrollment of White Students, 1968–76," *Sociology of Education* 60 (October 1987): 215–21. Response in Franklin D. Wilson, "A Reply to Finis Welch," *Sociology of Education* 60 (October 1987): 222–23; see also Christine H. Rossell, "Does School Desegregation Policy Stimulate Residential Integration: A Critique of the Research," *Urban Education* 21, no. 4 (January 1987): 403–20. Wilson in "A Reply," p. 223.

Testing (76)

"An F" in "An F in World Competition," *Newsweek,* February 1992, p. 57; IAE and IAEP description and scores in National Center for Education Statistics, *International Mathematics and Science Assessments: What Have We Learned?* 92-011 (Washington, D.C.: U.S. Government Printing Office, 1992); summary of international testing controversy in Lawrence C. Stedman, "The Sandia Report and U.S. Achievement: An Assessment," *Journal of Educational Research* 87, no.

3 (January/February 1994): 133–46; China, Korea, and United States in Harold Stevenson and James W. Stigler, *The Learning Gap: Why Our Schools Are Failing and What We Can Learn about Japanese and Chinese Education* (New York: Summit Books, 1987); criticism in Gerald W. Bracey, "The Condition of Public Education," *Phi Delta Kappan,* October 1992, pp. 107–17. Early problems with IEA in Richard Wolf, "The NAEP and International Comparisons," *Phi Delta Kappan,* April 1988, pp. 580–82. "We should not cry" in Diane Ravitch, "U.S. Schools: The Bad News Is Right," *Washington Post,* November 17, 1991, p. C7; on governors' goals, see Iris Rotberg, "I Never Promised You First Place," *Phi Delta Kappan,* December 1990, pp. 296–303; Jaeger in Richard Jaeger, "Weak Measurement Serving Presumptive Policy," *Phi Delta Kappan,* October 1992, pp. 118–27.

Are Students Learning Less? (78)

Bush in Jaeger, "Weak Measurement," p. 119; SAT trend in Stedman, "The Sandia Report," pp. 135–37; number taking test since 1941 in Gerald W. Bracey, "Why Can't They Be Like We Were?" *Phi Delta Kappan,* October 1991, pp. 108–9; subgroups and "rather than castigate" in Jaeger, "Weak Measurement," p. 120. NAEP trend and "less than half" in Stedman, "The Sandia Report," pp. 137–40; debate on policy in Charles Murray and Richard Herrnstein, "What's Really behind the SAT-Score Decline?" *The Public Interest,* Winter 1992, pp. 32–56; and Jaeger, "Weak Measurement." "We know where" in Harold Hodgkinson, Letter to the Editor, *New York Times,* November 26, 1991, p. A20; see also Harold Hodgkinson, "American Education: The Good, the Bad, And the Task," *Phi Delta Kappan,* April 1993, pp. 619–23.

Case Study Questions (81)

1. Michael G. Bruce, "Higher Education: Taking Our Bearings," *Phi Delta Kappan,* November 1987, pp. 239–40; and Edward M. White and Ruediger Ahrens, "European vs. American Higher Education," *Change,* September/October 1989, pp. 53–55.

2. "The Misleading Concept of 'Average,' " *New York Times,* July 12, 1989, p. B7.

3. "Making the Grade," *American Demographics,* May 1987, p. 8.

4. Cooke, Ginsburg, and Smith, "The Sorry State of Education Statistics," p. 29.

CHAPTER 6: CRIME (83)

Data Sources (83)

Uniform Crime Reports (83)

UCR described in Federal Bureau of Investigation, U.S. Department of Justice, *Uniform Crime Reporting Handbook* (Washington, D.C.: U.S. Government Printing Office, 1984); and Federal Bureau of Investigation, U.S. Department of Justice, *Crime in the United States 1992* (Washington, D.C.: U.S. Government Printing Office, 1988), pp. 1–5. University of Georgia data in ibid., p. 160.

National Crime Survey (84)

National Crime Survey described in Bureau of Justice Statistics, U.S. Department of Justice, *Criminal Victimization in the United States* (Washington, D.C.: U.S. Department of Justice, 1992), pp. 1–2; reporting to police by income in ibid., p. 107.

Box 6.1. The Crime Index (85)

Crime clock in *Crime in the United States,* p. 4. Crime statistics in ibid., p. 58.

Controversies (85)

Is There a Crime Wave? (85)

Comparison of UCR and National Crime Survey in A.D. Biderman and J.P. Lynch, *Understanding Crime Incidence Statistics* (New York: Springer-Verlag, 1991). Improvements in NCS in Wesley G. Skogan, "The National Crime Survey Redesign," *Public Opinion Quarterly* 54 (1990): 256–72; UCR reporting improvements in Christopher Jencks, "Is Violent Crime Increasing?" *American Prospect,* Winter 1991, pp. 98–109. Misrepresentation of crime in New York City in Marvin E. Wolfgang, "Uniform Crime Reports: A Critical Reappraisal," in *Crime in America,* ed. Bruce J. Cohen (Itasca, Ill.: F.E. Peacock, 1985), p. 41; in Washington, D.C., in James P. Levine, Michael C. Musheno, and Dennis J. Palumbo, *Criminal Justice in America* (New York: Wiley, 1986), p. 99; in Indianapolis, in Harold E. Pepinsky and Paul Jesilow, *Myths That Cause Crime* (Cabin John, Md.: Seven Locks Press, 1985), p. 28. Problems with National Crime Survey in Stephen E. Brown and Thomas W. Wooley, "The National Crime Survey Program: Problems in Sample Selection and Data Analysis," *Social Science Quarterly* 66 (March 1985): 186–93. Debate about 1980 crime rates in "U.S. Study Group's Proposals Assailed by Council on Crime," *New York Times,* September 10, 1981, p. B10.

Box 6.2. Murder in Gotham (87)

Headlines in "Murder Rates Climbing on Main St., USA," *USA Today,* March 17, 1989, p. 1; "Number of Killings Soars in Big Cities Across U.S." *New York Times,* July 18, 1990, p. A1; big cities in Jencks, "Is Violent Crime Increasing?" pp. 99, 104; see also Christopher Jencks, *Rethinking Social Policy* (Cambridge: Harvard University Press, 1992), pp. 181–89.

Rape (89)

"How Justice Department Collected the Data for Its Rape Study," *New York Times,* May 24, 1985, p. A24; "Reporting Rape," *New York Times,* April 21, 1987, p. 22; Gilbert in Neil Gilbert, "Miscounting Social Ills," *Society,* March/

April 1994, p. 26; and Neil Gilbert, "The Phantom Epidemic of Sexual Assault," *The Public Interest,* Spring 1991, pp. 54–66. Rape statistics in Kathleen Maguire, Ann L. Pastore, and Timothy J. Flanagan, eds., *Sourcebook of Criminal Justice Statistics 1992* (Washington, D.C.: U.S. Department of Justice, Bureau of Justice Statistics, 1993), pp. 245, 257.

Box 6.3. A Worldwide Problem? (90)

Elliott Currie, *Confronting Crime: An American Challenge* (New York: Pantheon, 1985), pp. 24–35. Detroit murder rate in "Children Killing Children," *Washington Post,* December 4, 1986, p. A1. American men die, in Currie, *Confronting Crime,* p. 25.

Will You Be a Crime Victim? (90)

Bureau of Justice Statistics, U.S. Department of Justice, *Technical Report,* "Lifetime Likelihood of Victimization," March 1987; "83% to Be Victims of Crime Violence," *New York Times,* March 9, 1987, p. A13; criticism in James P. Lynch, "An Evaluation of Lifetime Likelihood of Victimization," *Public Opinion Quarterly* 53 (1989): 262–64.

Does Poverty Cause Crime? (91)

Crime rate in Highland Park and Grosse Point in *Crime in the United States,* p. 91. C.S. Tittle et al. research in Charles R. Tittle, Wayne J. Villemez, and Douglas A. Smith, "The Myth of Social Class and Criminality: An Empirical Assessment of the Empirical Evidence," *American Sociological Review* 43 (1978): 643–56. Criticisms in Gary Kleck, "On the Use of Self-report Data to Determine the Class Distribution of Criminal and Delinquent Behavior," *American Sociological Review* 47 (June 1982): 427–33. "American youths of all backgrounds" in Currie, *Confronting Crime,* p. 157. Behavioral Research Institute study in ibid., pp. 158–59; see also Richard McGahey, "Economic Conditions, Neighborhood Organization and Urban Crime," in M. Tonry and A. Reiss, Jr., eds., *Communities and Crime* (Chicago: University of Chicago Press, 1986), pp. 231–70.

Why Is the Black Crime Rate So High? (93)

Crime rates by sex, age, and race in Bureau of Justice Statistics, U.S. Department of Justice, *Report to the Nation on Crime and Justice* (Washington, D.C.: U.S. Department of Justice, 1988), p. 31. Black prison population in Andrew Hacker, "Black Crime, White Racism," *New York Review of Books,* March 3, 1988, p. 36. Hacker in ibid., pp. 36–41. Wright in Bruce Wright, *Black Robes, White Justice* (New York: Carol Publishing, 1987). Currie in Currie, *Confronting Crime,* pp. 152–59. "Genuine social disaster," in ibid., p. 160.

Does Prison Pay? (94)

Debate in Edwin W. Zedlewski, "When Have We Punished Enough?" *Public Administration Review* 45 (November 1985): 771–79; Franklin E. Zimring and

Gordon Hawkins, "The New Mathematics of Imprisonment," *Crime and Delinquency* 34 (October 1988): 425–36; Edwin Zedlewski, "New Mathematics of Imprisonment: A Reply to Zimring and Hawkins," *Crime and Delinquency* 35 (January 1989): 169–173. "To pen every" in Eugene H. Methvin, "Why Don't We Have the Prisons We Need?" *Reader's Digest,* November 1990, p. 71. Middle position in John J. DiIulio, Jr., and Anne Morrison Piehl, "Does Prison Pay? *The Brookings Review,* Fall 1991, pp. 28–35, and Anne Morrison Piehl and John J. DiIulio, Jr., "Does Prison Pay? Revisited," *The Brookings Review,* Winter 1995, pp. 21–25.

Does Capital Punishment Deter Murder? (95)

Isaac Ehrlich time series study in Isaac Ehrlich, "The Deterrent Effect of Capital Punishment: A Question of Life and Death," *American Economic Review,* June 1975, pp. 397–417. Use before Supreme Court in Richard M. McGahey, "Dr. Ehrlich's Magic Bullet: Economic Theory, Econometrics, and the Death Penalty," *Crime and Delinquency,* October 1980, p. 485. Criticisms of Ehrlich summarized in ibid., pp. 485–502; see also Jan Palmer, "Economic Analyses of the Deterrent Effect of Punishment: A Review," *Journal of Research in Crime and Deliquency,* January 1977, pp. 4–21; Peter Passell and John B. Taylor, "The Deterrent Effect of Capital Punishment: Another View," *American Economic Review,* June 1977, p. 445; and *Yale Law Journal* symposium, December 1975. Isaac Ehrlich cross-sectional study in "Capital Punishment and Deterrence: Some Further Thoughts and Additional Evidence," *Journal of Political Economy,* August 1977, pp. 741–88. Criticisms in McGahey, "Dr. Ehrlich's Magic Bullet," pp. 496–98; Franklin E. Zimring and Gordon Hawkins, *Capital Punishment and the American Agenda* (New York: Cambridge University Press, 1987), pp. 178–84. Very small deterrence in ibid., pp. 180–81. "There has been no spate of articles" in McGahey, "Dr. Ehrlich's Magic Bullet," p. 501.

Box 6.4. Missing Children—How Serious a Problem? (96)

On missing children, Peter Schneider, "Lost Innocents: The Myth of Missing Children," *Harper's,* February 1987, pp. 47–53; Ellen Goodman, "Missing Children: Facts and Fears," *Washington Post,* July 10, 1985, p. A19.

What about White-Collar Crime? (97)

Sutherland on white-collar crime in *White Collar Crime* (New York: Dryden Press, 1949). FBI white-collar crime data in "U.S. Reports 18% Rise in '85 in White-Collar Convictions," *New York Times,* September 29, 1987, p. A24. Broader definition of white-collar crime in Marshall B. Clinard and Peter C. Yeager, *Corporate Crime* (New York: Free Press, 1980); Russell Mokhiber, *Corporate Crime and Violence: Big Business Power and the Abuse of Public Trust* (San Francisco: Sierra Club Books, 1988); "Staying out of Prison Takes a Lot of Class," *Dollars and Sense,* no. 21 (November 1976); Pepinsky and Jesilow, *Myths That Cause Crime,* pp. 58–65. Green on white-collar crime in Mark Green and John F. Berry, "White-Collar Crime Is Big Business," *The Nation,* June 8, 1985, pp. 689ff. "Stealing $200 Billion the Respectable Way," *U.S. News and World Report,* May 20, 1985, pp. 83–86. Other estimates in J.W. Coleman, *The Criminal Elite* (New York: St. Martin's Press: 1985), pp. 2–11; Reiman on white-collar crime in Pepinsky and Jesilow, *Myths That Cause Crime,* p. 33.

Case Study Questions (99)

1. Data from U.S. Justice Department, *Crime in the United States* 1993, p. 41.
2. See references on accuracy of UCR and National Crime Survey.
3. See Albert Biderman and Albert J. Reiss, Jr., "On Exploring the 'Dark Figure' of Crime," *Annals of the American Academy of Political Science,* November 1967, pp. 1–15; and Gordon P. Waldo, *Measurement Issues in Criminal Justice* (New York: Sage, 1983).
4. See, "Sharp Decline in Crime Rates," *Washington Post,* October 26, 1986, p. A4.
5. See Philip J. Cook, "The Case of the Missing Victims: Gunshot Woundings in the National Crime Survey," *Journal of Quantitative Criminology* 1, no. 1 (1985): 91-102.
6. "The Plague of Crime," *Newsweek,* March 23, 1981, p. 46. The same week *Time* called it "The Curse of Violent Crime," *Time,* March 23, 1981, p. 17. Data from Bureau of Justice Statistics, U.S. Department of Justice, *Sourcebook of Criminal Justice Statistics, 1992,* pp. 245, 357.

CHAPTER 7: THE NATIONAL ECONOMY (101)

Data Sources (101)

U.S. Commerce Department (101)

History of national income and produce accounts summarized in Joseph W. Duncan and William C. Shelton, *Revolution in United States Government Statistics* (Washington, D.C.: U.S. Government Printing Office, 1978), pp. 74–107; and Mark Perlman, "Political Purpose and the National Accounts," in W. Alonso and P. Starr, *The Politics of Numbers* (New York: Russell Sage Foundation, 1987), pp. 135–51. GDP data in U.S. Department of Commerce, *Survey of Current Business,* February 1986, p. 18. Summary of NIPA in "National Income and Product Accounts Estimates," *Survey of Current Business,* January 1988, pp. 11–13. Official accounting methods in Bureau of Economic Analysis, U.S. Department of Commerce, *GNP: An Overview of Source Data and Estimating Methods,* BEA-MP-4 (Washington, D.C.: U.S. Government Printing Office, September 1987). Data sample in Council of Economic Advisers, *Economic Report of the President 1990* (Washington, D.C.: U.S. Government Printing Office, 1990), p. 294. Census of manufacturing described in Bureau of the Census, U.S. Department of Commerce, "1982 Census of Manufactures, Publications Order Form," MC82-1, August 1984; and *Statistical Policy Division, Office of Management and Budget, Statistical Services of the U.S. Government* (Washington, D.C.: U.S. Government Printing Office, 1975), pp. 125–43. Data sample in Bureau of the Census, U.S. Department of Commerce, "Industry Series, Newspapers, Periodicals, Books and Miscellaneous Publishing," *1982 Census of Manufactures,* MC87-I-27A (Washington, D.C.: U.S. Government Printing Office, 1982), p. 19. Trade statistics described in U.S. Department of Commerce, *Understanding U.S. Foreign Trade Data* (Washington, D.C.: U.S. Government Printing Office, August 1985). Data sample in U.S. Bureau of the Census, *U.S. Imports for Consumption and General Imports,* Report FT246/Annual 1987 (Washington, D.C.: U.S. Government Printing Office, 1988), pp. 1–37.

Box 7.1. The People behind the Numbers (103)

Women's dress shoes in U.S. Department of Commerce, "Tanning; Industrial Leather Goods; and Shoes," *1982 Census of Manufactures,* MC82-1-31A, p. 31. Manufacturing employment in U.S. Department of Labor, *Employment and Earnings* 36, no. 10 (October 1989): 77. GNP data in Council of Economic Advisers, *Economic Report of the President 1988* (Washington, D.C.: U.S. Government Printing Office, 1988), p. 250.

U.S. Labor Department (104)

Productivity measures described in Bureau of Labor Statistics, U.S. Department of Labor, *Handbook of Labor Statistics* (Washington, D.C.: U.S. Government Printing Office, 1985), pp. 226–27. Data sample in Bureau of Labor Statistics, U.S. Department of Labor, *Productivity Measures for Selected Industries and Government Services,* Bulletin 2406 (Washington, D.C.: U.S. Government Printing Office, April 1992), p. 86.

U.S. Federal Reserve Board (104)

U.S. Federal Reserve Board, "Introduction to Flow of Funds," 1980; "Recent Developments in Economic Statistics at the Federal Reserve: Part 1," *Business Economics,* October 1988, pp. 47–52; and Norman Frumkin, *Tracking America's Economy* (Armonk, N.Y.: M.E. Sharpe, 1987), pp. 114–35. Data sample in Board of Governors, Federal Reserve System, *Federal Reserve Bulletin* 79, no. 12 (December 1993): A39.

Private Sector (105)

On credit-reporting agencies, see chapter 11. On Bureau of Economic Analysis, see Duncan and Shelton, *Revolution in United States Government Statistics,* p. 107. Data sample in U.S. Small Business Administration, *State of Small Business* (Washington, D.C.: U.S. Government Printing Office, 1987), p. 25.

Controversies (105)

Which GDP? (105)

Revisions described in U.S. Department of Commerce, "Terminology for the Quarterly Estimates," *Survey of Current Business,* October 1993, p. 30. On GDP secrecy, see Allan H. Young, "Evaluation of GNP Estimates," *Survey of Current Business,* August 1987, p. 36; and "Sealed Lips, Locked Safes," *Business Week,* May 23, 1988, pp. 96–101. On GDP revisions, see Allan H. Young, "Reliability and Accuracy of the Quarterly Estimates of GDP," *Survey of Current Business,* October 1993, pp. 29–31; and Bureau of Economic Analysis, *The Use of National Income and Product Accounts,* Staff Paper 43 (Washington, D.C.: U.S. Government Printing Office, January 1986). Change in growth rate from 1982 to 1986 in Council of Economic Advisers, *Economic Report of the President 1990,* p. 282. For example of mistake in using unrevised data, see "Discounting 'Strong' Rates," *Wall Street Journal,* September 1, 1987, p. 31; and comments on Warren T. Brooks, "Hiding a Boom in a Statistical Bust," *Wall Street Journal,* August 6, 1987, p. 24.

Box 7.2. Forecasting (106)

Moore in "Economists Missing the Mark," *New York Times,* December 12, 1984, p. D1. Economic indicators described in Norman Frumkin, *Guide to Economic Indicators* (Armonk, N.Y.: M.E. Sharpe, 1990), pp. 163–72. Criticism in Lacy Hunt, "An Antiquated Irrelevant Index," *Wall Street Journal,* March 29, 1988, p. 30; "A Better Entrail," *The Economist,* February 10, 1990, p. 65.

Problems with GDP (107)

Kuznets's role is discussed in Duncan and Shelton, eds., *Revolution in United States Government Statistics,* p. 77. Critics of growth: Ezra J. Mishan, *The Costs of Economic Growth* (New York: Praeger, 1967); Kenneth Boulding, *Economics of Pollution* (New York: New York University Press, 1971). Measure of economic welfare in William Nordhaus and James Tobin, "Is Growth Obsolete?" in National Bureau for Economic Research, *Fiftieth Anniversary Colloquium V* (New York: Columbia University Press, 1972). On BEA nonacceptance of welfare measures, see "The Use of National Income and Product Accounts," p. 25. Alternative measures of welfare in Robert Eisner, "Extended Accounts for National Income and Product," *Journal of Economic Literature* 26, no. 4 (December 1988): 1611–84. Repetto in Robert Repetto, "Nature's Resources as Productive Assets," *Challenge,* September–October 1989, pp. 16–20. Green GDP in "Green Economics," *Scientific American,* July 1994, p. 102; Robert Eisner, *The Misunderstood Economy: What Counts and How to Count It* (Boston: Harvard University School Press, 1994).

Underground Economy (109)

Carol S. Carson, "The Underground Economy: An Introduction," *Survey of Current Business,* May 1984, pp. 21–27, and July 1984, pp. 106–18. GNP estimates in Peter M. Gutmann, "The Subterranean Economy," *Financial Analysts Journal,* November–December 1977, pp. 26ff; Edgar Feige, "How Big Is the Irregular Economy?" *Challenge,* November–December 1979, pp. 5–13; Philip Mattera, *Off the Books: The Rise of the Underground Economy* (London: Pluto Press, 1985). Already counted in GNP in Edward F. Denison, "Is U.S. Growth Understated

Because of the Underground Economy?" *Review of Economics and Income and Wealth,* March 1982, pp. 1–16. Unemployment and income data accuracy in Richard J. McDonald, "The 'Underground Economy' and BLS Statistical Data," *Monthly Labor Review,* January 1984, pp. 4–16. Housework estimates in Eisner, "Extended Accounts," pp. 1673–74. Effect on research in Robert Eisner, "The Total Incomes System of Accounts," *Survey of Current Business,* January 1985, pp. 32–34.

Intercountry Comparisons (110)

World Bank in The World Bank, *World Tables 1993* (Baltimore: Johns Hopkins University Press, 1993), pp. 2–5. Rostow in W.W. Rostow, *Politics and the Stages of Growth* (London: Cambridge University Press, 1971). For another example of GNP use, see Hollis Chenery and Moises Syrquin, *Patterns of Development* (London: Oxford University Press, 1975). World Bank loans in Raymond Vernon, "The Politics of Comparative Economic Statistics," in Starr, *The Politics of Statistics,* pp. 65–66.

Measuring Productivity (111)

"U.S. Productivity in Crisis," *Newsweek,* September 8, 1980, pp. 53ff. Magdoff in "The Economist's New Clothes," *The Nation,* March 27, 1982, pp. 355ff. Issue debated in Samuel Bowles, David M. Gordon, and Thomas E. Weisskopf, "At the Heart of Economic Decline," *The Nation,* July 10–17, 1982; and Harry Magdoff, "A Statistical Fiction," *The Nation,* July 10–17, 1982, pp. 44–48. Methodology summarized in U.S. Department of Labor, Bureau of Labor Statistics, *Handbook of Labor Statistics* (Washington, D.C.: U.S. Government Printing Office, 1988), chaps. 10 and 11.

Which Years? (112)

Importance of choice of years in Molly McUsic, "U.S. Manufacturing: Any Cause for Alarm?" *New England Economic Review,* January–February 1987, pp. 9–10. Misrepresentative choice of years in U.S. Chamber of Commerce, *Supply Side Economics* (Washington, D.C.: U.S. Government Printing Office, 1981), slide 10. Data showing increase in Council of Economic Advisers, *Economic Report of the President 1988,* p. 301.

Changing Products (113)

Changing products in Jerome A. Mark, "Problems Encountered in Measuring Single- and Multifactor Productivity," *Monthly Labor Review,* December 1986, pp. 4–6. On construction productivity, see Martin Neil Baily and Margaret M. Blair, "Productivity and American Management," in *American Living Standards,* ed. M. Baily et al. (Washington, D.C.: Brookings Institution, 1988), pp. 185–86; and Rosanne Cole, "Reviving the Federal Statistical System: A View from Industry," *American Economic Review* 80, no. 2 (May 1990): 334.

Services (113)

Service-sector problems are readily admitted by the BLS; see, for example, Mark, "Problems Encountered," pp. 3–11; Jerome A. Mark, "Measuring Productivity in Service Industries," *Monthly Labor Review,* June 1982, pp. 3–8; and Ronald E. Kutscher and Jerome A. Mark, "The Service-producing Sector: Some Common Perceptions Reviewed," *Monthly Labor Review,* April 1983, pp. 21–24. BLS in "Dubious Figures: Productivity Statistics for the Service Sector May Understate Gains," *Wall Street Journal,* August 12, 1992, p. A1.

The Savings Rate (114)

Joint Economic Committee in "Low Savings Rate Seen as Main U.S. Problem," *Los Angeles Times,* April 19, 1989, I, p. 12. Current savings rate in Council of Economic Advisers, *Economic Report of the President 1994* (Washington, D.C.: U.S. Government Printing Office, 1994), p. 300. Criticism of savings crisis in William E. Cullison, "Is Saving Too Low in the United States?" *Economic Review,* May/June 1990, pp. 20–34; Robert Kuttner, "America Is Saving More Now, Not Less—If You Count It Right," *Business Week,* April 13, 1992, p. 18; Dean Baker, *Conceptual and Accounting Issues in the Analysis of Saving, Investment and Macroeconomic Activity* (Washington, D.C.: Economic Policy Institute, 1994). Business saving in Susan Lee and Tatiana Pouschine, "Are We a Nation of Spendthrifts?" *Forbes,* December 16, 1985, pp. 128–34.

International Statistics (117)

Summary of problem in Robert E. Lipsey, "Reviving the Federal Statistical System: International Aspects," *American Economic Review* 80, no. 2 (May 1990): 337–40. On problems with short-term data, see Edwin A. Finn, Jr., "Of Apples, Oranges and Toyotas," *Forbes,* January 26, 1987, pp. 34–35; Taiwan and Japanese gold in "Trade Reports Sometimes Not What They Seem," *Los Angeles Times,* July 4, 1988, IV, p. 1. On uncounted exports see "Measuring the Service Economy," *New York Times,* October 27, 1985, p. F4; and "In a Maze of Numbers," *The Economist,* August 20, 1988, pp. 61–62. Freeman in "Measuring the Service Economy." Foreign production in William G. Shepard and Dexter Hutchins, "There's No Trade Deficit, Sam!" *Financial World,* February 23, 1988, pp. 28–35. Debt in Eisner, *Misunderstood Economy,* pp. 66–82. U.S. position in Council of Economic Advisers, *Economic Report of the President 1994,* p. 385.

Case Study Questions (121)

1. Eisner, *Misunderstood Economy,* p. 77.
2. Robert Eisner, "The Total Incomes System of Accounts," *Survey of Current Business,* January 1985, p. 33.
3. See Donald M. Fisk, "Measuring Productivity in State and Local Government," Bulletin 2166, U.S. Department of Labor, Bureau of Labor Statistics (Washington, D.C.: U.S. Government Printing Office, January 1984).

4. Marilyn Waring, *If Women Counted: A New Feminist Economics* (New York: Harper & Row, 1988).

5. See Kevin F. McCrohan and James D. Smith, "A Consumer Expenditure Approach to Estimating the Size of the Underground Economy," *Journal of Marketing* 50 (April 1986): 48–60.

CHAPTER 8: WEALTH, INCOME, AND POVERTY (122)

Data Sources (122)

Wealth (122)

Federal Reserve wealth survey in U.S. Federal Reserve Board, "1986 Survey of Consumer Finances," summarized in Robert B. Avery and Arthur B. Kennickell, "Rich Rewards," *American Demographics,* June 1989, pp. 19–22. Data sample in ibid., p. 20. Census Bureau wealth survey in U.S. Department of Commerce, "Household Wealth and Asset Ownership: 1984," Current Population Reports, series P-70, no. 7, summarized in Joe Schwartz, "Americans' Nest Eggs," *American Demographics,* December 1986, pp. 52–53. Survey discussed in nineteenth-century census described in Joseph W. Duncan and William C. Shelton, *Revolution in United States Government Statistics* (Washington, D.C.: U.S. Government Printing Office, 1978), p. 5. Data sample in Courtney Slater and Christopher Crane, "The Net Worth of Americans," *American Demographics,* July 1986, p. 5. Indirect estimates in James D. Smith and Stephen D. Franklin, "The Concentration of Personal Wealth," *American Economic Review* 64, no. 4 (May 1974): 162–67; James D. Smith, "Recent Trends in the Distribution of Wealth in the U.S.: Data, Research Problems, and Prospects," in *International Comparisons of the Distribution of Household Wealth,* ed. Edward N. Wolff (Oxford: Clarendon Press, 1987), pp. 72–89. Methods summarized in Lars Osberg, *Economic Inequality in the United States* (Armonk, N.Y.: M.E. Sharpe, 1984), pp. 38–45. Data sample in Edward W. Wolff and Marcia Marley, "Introduction and Overview," in Wolff, *International Comparisons,* p. 1.

Income (124)

U.S. Census data described in chapter 2. Data sample in U.S. Bureau of the Census, *State and Metropolitan Area Data Book* (Washington, D.C.: U.S. Government Printing Office, 1992), table 2, p. XLIV. CPS described in chapter 9. For critical commentary on CPS methodology, see Christopher Jencks, "The Politics of Income Measurement," in William Alonso and Paul Starr, eds., *The Politics of Numbers* (New York: Russell Sage Foundation, 1987), pp. 83–131. Data sample in *1990 Census Snapshot for All U.S. Places* (Milpitas, Calif.: Toucan Valley Publications, 1992), p. 510. Data sample in U.S. Labor Department, *Employment and Earnings,* May 1994, p. 111. PSID summarized in Greg J. Duncan, *Years of Poverty, Years of Plenty* (Ann Arbor: Institute for Social Research, University of Michigan, 1984). PSID compared with other sources in Christopher Jencks, *Who Gets Ahead: The Determinants of Economic Success in America* (New York: Basic Books, 1979), pp. 274–75.

Controversies (125)

Are the Rich Getting Richer? (125)

Federal reserve studies in *Federal Reserve Bulletin,* December 1984 and March 1986. JEC study in Smith and Franklin, "The Concentration of Personal Wealth." Controversy in "Scandal at the Fed?" *Dollars and Sense,* April 1987, pp. 10–22.

Box 8.1. I've Got a Secret (126)

Eugene P. Ericksen, "Estimating the Concentration of Wealth in America," *Public Opinion Quarterly* 52 (1988): 243–53.

What Is Wealth? (127)

Wealth data in Robert B. Avery and Arthur B. Kennickell, "Rich Rewards," *American Demographics,* June 1989, p. 20. Census Bureau data in Avery and Kennickell, "Rich Rewards," pp. 19–22. Financial net worth in "Where's the Wealth?" *Dollars and Sense,* April 1985, pp. 8–17. Retirement wealth in Martin Feldstein, "Social Security, Induced Retirement, and Aggregate Capital Accumulation," *Journal of Political Economy* 82 (September 1974): 905–26; and "Perceived Wealth in Bonds and Social Security: A Comment," *Journal of Political Economy* 84 (April 1976): 331–36; Edward N. Wolff, "Pensions and Social Security in the U.S.," in Wolff, *International Comparisons;* and " 'Superstar' Feldstein and His Little Mistake," *Dollars and Sense,* December 1980, pp. 8–9.

Box 8.2. Mean, Median, and Mode (128)

1980 data and discussion of U.S. Census Bureau use of mean and median in Jencks, "The Politics of Income Measurement," pp. 86–88.

Who Is the Richest of Them All? (128)

"The Forbes Four Hundred," *Forbes,* October 18, 1993, pp 112–13; and "The Billionaires," *Fortune,* September 7, 1992, p. 98. Discovery of Vogel in "The 400 Richest People in America," *Forbes,* October 26, 1987, p. 106. Crown discrepancy in "Billionaires," *Fortune,* October 12, 1987, p. 120; and "The 400 Richest People," pp. 116–17. Discussion of problems in measuring wealth in "What Lies behind the Numbers," *Fortune,* p. 129; and "The 400 Richest People," p. 112.

Are We Better Off? (129)

Income data in Council of Economic Advisers, *Economic Report of the President 1994* (Washington, D.C.: U.S. Government Printing Office, 1994), pp. 277, 320. Income per person data advocated in John E. Schwarz and Thomas J. Volgy, "The Myth of America's Economic Decline," *Harvard Business Review,* September–October 1985, pp. 101–2; Jerry Flint, "How Are We Doing?" *Forbes,* July 13, 1987, p. 94; and Charles Murray, *Losing Ground* (New York: Basic Books,

1984). Debate about data in Courtenay Slater, "Dollars That Count," *American Demographics,* January 1986, pp. 4–7. Spendable earnings data debate in Paul O. Flaim, "The Spendable Earnings Series: Has It Outlived Its Usefulness?" *Monthly Labor Review,* January 1982, pp. 3–9; Thomas E. Weisskopf, "Use of Hourly Earnings Proposed to Revive Spendable Earnings Series," *Monthly Labor Review,* November 1984, pp. 38–43; Paul O. Flaim, "Proposed Spending Earnings Series Retains Basic Faults of Earlier One," *Monthly Labor Review,* November 1984, pp. 43–44. Family income data in U.S. Bureau of the Census, "Money Income of Households, Families and Persons in the United States," series P-60. Limitations of data in Jencks, "The Politics of Income Measurement." Data in U.S. Census Bureau, *Statistical Abstract* (Washington, D.C.: U.S. Government Printing Office, 1989), p. 445. Size of families in U.S. Department of Commerce, "Household and Family Characteristics," *Current Population Reports,* P20-477, table A1.

Disappearing Middle Class (132)

"The Rich Get Richer, but the Question Is by How Much?" *New York Times,* July 20, 1992, p. C1; "However You Slice the Data the Richest Did Get Richer," *New York Times,* May 11, 1992, p. C1.

Mobility (133)

Mobility in Gary Solon, "Intergenerational Income Mobility in the United States," *American Economic Review* 82 (June 1992): 393–408; David J. Zimmerman, "Regression toward Mediocrity in Economic Stature," *American Economic Review* 82 (June 1992): 409–29; "The Born Wealthy or Poor Usually Stay So, Studies Say," *New York Times,* May 18, 1992, p. A1.

What Is Poverty? (135)

Political shaping of poverty line in Martin Rein, "Problems in the Definition and Measurement of Poverty," in *Poverty in America* (Ann Arbor: University of Michigan Press, 1968), p. 125; "The Hand That Shaped America's Poverty Line as the Realistic Index," *New York Times,* August 4, 1989, p. A12; Orshansky method described in Leonard Beeghley, "The Measurement of Poverty," *Social Problems* 31, no. 3 (February 1984): 322–33. Debate about poverty measures summarized in Isabel V. Sawhill, "Poverty in the U.S.: Why Is It So Persistent?" *Journal of Economic Literature* 26, no. 3 (September 1988): 1073–85. Poverty line is too low argued in Patricia Ruggles, *Drawing the Line: Alternative Poverty Measures and Their Implications for Public Policy* (Washington, D.C.: Urban Institute Press, 1990.); Osberg, *Economic Inequality,* pp. 63–73; Harrell R. Rodgers, Jr., "Hiding versus Ending Poverty," *Politics and Society* 8, no. 2 (1978): 253–66; and Patricia Ruggles, "The Poverty Line—Too Low for the 90s," *New York Times,* April 26, 1990, p. A23. Poverty line is too high argued in Rose Friedman, *Poverty: Definitions and Perspectives* (Washington, D.C.: American Enterprise Institute, 1965); June O'Neill, "Poverty: Programs and Policies," in *Thinking about America,* ed. Annelise Anderson and Dennis Bark (Stanford, Calif.: Hoover Institute, 1988); Gordon Tullock, *Economics of Income Redistribu-*

tion (Boston: Kluwer-Nijhoff, 1983), p. 2. Benefit programs and poverty line in "Poverty Estimates Lowered by Inclusion of Noncash Benefits," *Monthly Labor Review*, May 1984, pp. 46–47; Anderson in Beeghley, "The Measurement of Poverty," p. 331. Criticisms of market value approach in ibid.; and "Defining Away the Poor," *Dollars and Sense*, January/February 1987, p. 9.

Do the Poor Stay Poor? (137)

PSID results described in Sawhill, "Poverty in the U.S.," p. 1080. Conservative view in Mark Lilla, "Why the 'Income Distribution' Is So Misleading," *The Public Interest* 77 (Fall 1984): 68; and Charles Murray, *Losing Ground: American Social Policy 1950–1980* (New York: Basic Books, 1984). Liberal intepretation of PSID in Mary Jo Bane, "Household Composition and Poverty," in *Fighting Poverty: What Works and What Doesn't*, ed. Sheldon H. Danziger and Daniel H. Weinberg (Cambridge: Harvard University Press, 1986), pp. 209–31.

Box 8.3. The Economic Consequences of Divorce (138)

L. Weitzman, *The Divorce Revolution* (New York: Free Press, 1985); S.D. Hoffman and G.J. Duncan, "What *Are* the Economic Consequences of Divorce?" *Demography* 25, no. 4 (November 1988): 641–45. See also Susan Faludi, *Backlash: The Undeclared War against American Women* (New York: Crown, 1991): 19–27.

Case Study Questions (139)

1. Osberg, *Economic Inequality*, p. 25.
2. "Income Distribution," *Dollars and Sense*, February 1983, pp. 6–7.
3. Robert B. Hill, "The Black Middle Class Defined," *Ebony*, August 1987, p. 30; Andrew Brimmer, "Income and Wealth," *Ebony*, August 1987, p. 46; see also Gerald Jaynes and Robin Williams, *A Common Destiny: Blacks and American Society* (Washington, D.C.: National Academy Press, 1989).
4. Jencks, "The Politics of Income Measurement," pp. 92–105.
5. Suzanne M. Bianchi and Daphne Spain, *American Women in Transition* (New York: Russell Sage Foundation, 1986), pp. 170–73; Nancy F. Rytina, "Comparing Annual and Weekly Earnings from the Current Population Survey," *Monthly Labor Review* 106 (April 1983): 32–36; Randy Albelda, "Women's Income Not Up to Par," *Dollars and Sense*, July/August 1988, pp. 6–8.

CHAPTER 9: LABOR STATISTICS (141)

Data Sources (141)

U.S. Bureau of Labor Statistics (141)

A short summary of BLS data is U.S. Department of Labor, *Workers, Jobs, and Statistics* (Washington, D.C.: U.S. Government Printing Office; 1983). Detailed official descriptions in U.S. Department of Labor, *BLS Handbook of Methods,* vol. 1 (Washington, D.C.: U.S. Government Printing Office; 1982). Other descriptions in Norman Frumkin, *Tracking America's Economy* (Armonk, N.Y.: M.E. Sharpe, 1987), chap. 5; Albert T. Sommers and Lucie R. Blau, *The U.S. Economy Demystified* (Lexington, Mass.: D.C. Heath, 1988), pp. 78–80. Data sample in U.S. Labor Department, *Employment and Earnings* (Washington, D.C.: U.S. Government Printing Office, May 1994), p. 42.

U.S. Census Bureau (142)

On U.S. Census, see notes to chapter 2. Data sample in Bureau of the Census, U.S. Department of Commerce, *1980 Census of Population,* "Occupation by Industry," PC80-2-7C (Washington, D.C.: U.S. Government Printing Office, May 1984), pp. 148–49. On economic census, see U.S. Department of Commerce, Bureau of the Census, *Guide to the 1982 Economic Censuses and Related Statistics* (Washington, D.C.: U.S. Government Printing Office, 1984). Data sample in Bureau of the Census, U.S. Department of Commerce, *1982 Census of Governments,* "Compendium of Public Employment," GC87(3)-2 (Washington, D.C.: U.S. Government Printing Office, February 1991), p. 162.

Controversies (143)

Unemployment (143)

Measuring unemployment during the Great Depression, see William T. Moye and Joseph Goldberg, *The First Hundred Years of the Bureau of Labor Statistics* (Washington, D.C.: U.S. Government Printing Office, 1985), pp. 125–77; Margo J. Anderson, *The American Census: A Social History* (New Haven: Yale University Press, 1988), pp. 162–89. "The tide of employment" in Moye and Goldberg, *The First Hundred Years,* p. 130. History of Current Population Survey in John E. Bregger, "The Current Population Survey: A Historical Perspective and BLS's Role," *Monthly Labor Review,* June 1984, pp. 8–14.

Box 9.1. How to Survey the Unemployed (144)

New survey in "Jobless Rate Misstated: U.S. Cites Survey Bias," *New York Times,* November 17, 1993, p. A1; and "Labor Department Reports U.S. Unemployment Rate of 6.7%," *New York Times,* February 5, 1994, p. A1.

Undercount (144)

Unemployment underestimate debate discussed in David M. Gordon, *Problems in Political Economy* (Lexington, Mass.: D.C. Heath, 1977), pp. 70–75; and "Undercounting the Unemployed," *Dollars and Sense,* October 1986, pp. 18–19. BLS unemployment measures described in *BLS Handbook of Methods,* chap. 1; Norman Frumkin, *Tracking America's Economy* (Armonk, N.Y.: M.E. Sharpe, 1987), chap. 5. History of unemployment measure in Moye and Goldberg, *The First Hundred Years,* pp. 237–43; Brookings Institution study described in "Undercounting the Unemployed," p. 1.

Overcount (145)

Overcount in Peter Gutmann, "Statistical Illusions, Mistaken Policies," *Challenge,* November–December 1979, p. 17. Response to Gutmann in Richard J. McDonald, "The 'Underground Economy' and BLS Statistical Data," *Monthly Labor Review,* January 1984, pp. 11–15. On natural rate of unemployment debate, see, for example, Paul A. Samuelson and William D. Nordhaus, *Economics* (New York: McGraw-Hill, 1989), pp. 296–301.

Alternative Measures (146)

Alternative measures in Alexander Keyssar, *Out of Work: The First Century of Unemployment in Massachusetts* (New York: Cambridge University Press, 1986). Bush on 30 million jobs in *New York Times,* August 19, 1988, p. A1; backed away from in *New York Times,* August 24, 1988, p. A1. 1992 errors in "U.S. Increases Figures Showing Loss of Jobs," *New York Times,* June 4, 1992, p. C2; Virginia Carlson, Letters, *The Nation,* October 18, 1993, p. 410; and "New Data Shows State's Job Loss 6 Times Higher," *Los Angeles Times,* April 3, 1992, p. A1.

Better Jobs? (148)

Occupational data described in John Thompson, "BLS Job Cross-Classification System Relates Information from Six Sources," *Monthly Labor Review,* November 1981, pp. 40–44. Edwards's classification scheme in Alba Edwards, *Comparative Occupational Statistics for the United States* (Washington, D.C.: U.S. Bureau of the Census, 1943), pp. 175–76; and H. Anderson, *Occupational Trends in the United States* (Stanford, Calif.: Stanford University Press, 1940), p. 40. Criticisms in Margo Anderson Conk, *The United States Census and the New Jersey Urban Occupational Structure, 1870–1940* (Ann Arbor, Mich.: UMI Research Press, 1980); and Harry Braverman, *Labor and Monopoly Capital* (New York: Monthly Review Press, 1974), pp. 429–32. White collars in Peter M. Blau and Otis D. Duncan, *The American Occupational Structure* (New York: Wiley, 1967). Replicated in David L. Featherman and Robert M. Hauser, *Opportunity and Change* (New York: Academic Press, 1978). For summary of complex analysis based on occupational structures, see Dennis Gilbert and Joseph Kahl, *The American Class Structure* (Homewood, Ill.: Dorsey, 1982), chaps. 3 and 6. Criticism of white-collar, blue-collar distinction in Patrick H. Horan, "Is Status Attainment Research Atheoretical?" *American Sociological Review* 43 (August 1978): 534–41; and Sidney M. Willhelm, "Opportunities Are Diminishing," *Society,* March–April 1979, pp. 11–17. On 1980 reclassification, see Nancy F. Rytina and Suzanne M. Bianchi, "Occupational Reclassification and Changes in Distribution by Gender," *Monthly Labor Review,* March 1984, pp. 11–16.

Unions (150)

Union membership data described in Michael Goldfeld, *The Decline of Organized Labor in the United States* (Chicago: University of Chicago Press, 1987), pp.

8–25; Edward C. Kokkelenberg and Donna R. Sockell, "Union Membership in the United States, 1973–1981," *Industrial and Labor Relations Review* 38 (July 4, 1985): 497-533; Henry S. Farber, "The Recent Decline of Unionization in the United States," *Science*, November 13, 1987, pp. 915–20. Strike data described in U.S. Department of Labor, Bureau of Labor Statistics, *Monthly Labor Review*, January 1987, p. 78.

Is the Workplace Safe? (151)

History of BLS safety and health investigations in Moye and Goldberg, *The First Hundred Years*, pp. 58–61, 99–101, 132–33, 251–53. Safety and health data under OSHA described in Harvey J. Hilaski, "Understanding Statistics on Occupational Illnesses," *Monthly Labor Review*, March 1981, pp. 25–29. Debate about effectiveness of OSHA in Kenneth B. Noble, "For OSHA Balance Is Hard to Find," *New York Times*, January 10, 1988, p. E5. New OSHA surveys and data in U.S. Department of Labor, *Workplace Injuries and Illnesses in 1992*, USDL-93-55, (Washington, D.C.: U.S. Government Printing Office, 1993).

International Labor Statistics (152)

International labor statistics described in *BLS Handbook of Methods*, chap. 16; International Labor Office, *World Labor Report* (Geneva: International Labor Office, 1984). Definitions of labor force and unemployment in Patrick J. McMahon, "An International Comparison of Labor Force Participation," *Monthly Labor Review*, May 1986, pp. 3–12; Joyanna Moy, "An Analysis of Unemployment and Other Labor Market Indicators in 10 Countries," *Monthly Labor Review*, April 1988, "Appendix: Revisions in Comparative Statistics," pp. 48–50. BLS comparable data in Council of Economic Advisers, *Economic Report of the President*, Washington, D.C.: U.S. Government Printing Office, various years; and U.S. Department of Labor, Bureau of Labor Statistics, *Handbook of Labor Statistics* (Washington, D.C: U.S. Government Printing Office, 1989). Bush on job creation in *New York Times*, August 19, 1988, p. A1; backed away from in *New York Times*, August 24, 1988, p. A1. European workforce in McMahon, "An International Comparison of Labor Force Participation."

Case Study Questions (154)

1. Ben J. Wattenberg, *The Good News Is the Bad News Is Wrong* (New York: Simon and Schuster, 1984), pp. 231–33.

2. Gene Koretz, "Why U.S. Employment Numbers Can Be Hard to Read," *Business Week*, September 26, 1994, p. 24.

3. Council of Economic Advisers, *Economic Report of the President 1990* (Washington, D.C.: U.S. Government Printing Office, 1990), p. 340.

4. "Clippings," *Ms*, October 1993, p. 89.

5. Women in Japanese labor force in International Labor Office, *World Labor Report 1* (Geneva: International Labor Office, 1984), p. 54.

CHAPTER 10: BUSINESS STATISTICS (156)

Data Sources (156)

On number and types of businesses, see principles of economics textbooks, for example, Campbell R. McConnell, *Economics* (New York: McGraw-Hill, 1987), pp. 113–19.

Public Corporations (156)

On SEC, see Adolph G. Lurie, *How to Read Annual Reports—Intelligently* (Englewood Cliffs, N.J.: Prentice-Hall, 1984). List of companies reporting in U.S. Securities and Exchange Commission, *Companies Required to File Annual Reports* (Washington, D.C.: U.S. Government Printing Office, 1988). How to read annual reports in Fred C. Armstrong, *The Business of Economics* (St. Paul, Minn.: West, 1986), pp. 137–43. Annual reports criticized in "Curious about the Crash? Don't Read Your Annual Report," *Business Week,* April 11, 1988, p. 66. Data sample in General Motors 1988 Annual Report, pp. 2–3. Business handbooks include Moody's, Standard and Poor's, Dun and Bradstreet publications, and Ward's Business Directory. Data sample in *Fortune,* April 24, 1989, p. 354, and *The Business Week Top 1,000,* Special 1989 Issue, p. 166.

Privately Held Corporations (159)

Ranking and discussion of methods in "Behind the Green Door," *Forbes,* December 6, 1993, pp. 168–70. Comparative size of public corporations in "The Biggest Blowout Ever," *Fortune,* April 24, 1989, p. 347. See also *Macmillan Directory of Leading Private Companies* (Wilmette, Ill.: National Register Publishing, various years). Helpful resource is Gordon T. Law, Jr., and Michael E. Reilly, *A Guide to Information on Closely Held Corporations* (Buffalo: New York State School of Industrial and Labor Relations, 1986).

Small Businesses (159)

Number and revenue in U.S. Small Business Administration, *The State of Small Business 1987* (Washington, D.C.: U.S. Government Printing Office, 1987), p. 17. Data sample in Dun's Marketing Services, *Million Dollar Directory 1989* (Parsippany, N.J.: Dun's Marketing Services, 1989), p. 2886.

Aggregate Statistics (160)

Small Business Data Source described in U.S. Small Business Administration, *Handbook of Small Business Data* (Washington, D.C.: U.S. Government Printing Office, 1983). Data sample in U.S. Small Business Administration, *State of Small Business 1987,* p. 283.

Controversies (160)

Who Is the Biggest of Them All? (160)

Debate on use of *Fortune* sales data in letter to the editor by M.A. Adelman, *Fortune,* September 1955, p. 20; and F.M. Scherer, *Industrial Market Structure and Economic Performance,* 2d rev. ed. (Boston: Houghton Mifflin, 1980), p. 47.

Sara Lee in "The Fortune 500," *Fortune,* April 24, 1989, p. 354. Changes in list in "A New Era of Rapid Rise and Run," *Fortune,* April 24, 1989, p. 77. On problems of asset measurement in accounting textbooks, see for example, Belverd E. Needles, Jr., Henry R. Anderson, and James C. Caldwell, *Principles of Accounting* (Boston: Houghton-Mifflin, 1987), pp. 493–565. Market-value method defended in *The Business Week Top 1,000,* Special 1989 Issue, pp. 14–20. Comparison of all size measurements in S.S. Shalit and U. Sankar, "The Measurement of Firm Size," *Review of Economics and Statistics* 59 (August 1977): 290–98.

Box 10.1. Which Is Larger: GM or Switzerland? (162)

For use of list, see, for example, Robert J. Carbaugh, *International Economics* (Cambridge, Mass.: Winthrop, 1980), p. 219; and Bradley R. Schiller, *The Micro Economy Today* (New York: McGraw-Hill, 1994), p. 220.

Box 10.2. Top of the World (165)

Data and discussion in "The Global 1000," *Business Week,* July 11, 1994, pp. 55–56.

Are the Big Too Big? (165)

On history of antitrust, see Steven C. Salop, "Symposium on Mergers and Antitrust," *Journal of Economic Perspectives* 1, no. 2 (Fall 1987): 3–12; and Paul A. Samuelson and William D. Nordhaus, *Economics* (New York: McGraw-Hill, 1989), pp. 619–24. Market-share use in F.M. Scherer and David Ross, *Industrial Market Structure and Economic Performance,* 3d rev. ed. (Boston: Houghton Mifflin, 1990), pp. 72–96, 184–85. Critique of use of market share in Betty Bock, *Concentration, Oligopoly, and Profit* (New York: The Conference Board, 1972). HHI index described in Salop, "Symposium," p. 7; and "Herfindahl Index," *The New Palgrave: A Dictionary of Economics,* vol. 2 (New York: Stockton Press, 1987), p. 639. Policy of the 1980s debated in *Journal of Economic Perspectives* 1, no. 2 (Fall 1987): 3–54. Problems in defining market in Franklin M. Fisher, "Horizontal Mergers: Triage and Treatment," *Journal of Economic Perspectives* 1, no. 2 (Fall 1987), p. 26. Pabst and Blatz in Scherer, *Industrial Market Structure,* 2d rev. ed., p. 557. Northwest and Republic in Fisher, "Horizontal Mergers," pp. 32–35. Glass bottles in Scherer and Ross, *Industrial Market Structure,* 3d rev. ed., pp. 180–86. Trend in the 1980s in ibid., p. 191. IBM in ibid., pp. 459–62. History of antitrust enforcement in Richard G. Lipsey, Peter O. Steiner, and Douglas D. Purvis, *Economics* (New York: Harper & Row, 1987), p. 294. University of Chicago influence described in Stephen A. Rhoades, "The Decline and Possible Resurrection of Antitrust Policy toward Mergers," *Antitrust Law and Economic Review* 17, no. 4 (1985): 49–55. Shepard in William G. Shepherd, "Causes of Increased Competition in the U.S. Economy 1939–1980," *Review of Economics and Statistics,* November 1982, pp. 613–26; and William G. Shepherd, "Bust the Reagan Trustbusters," *Fortune,* August 4, 1986, pp. 225–27.

Box 10.3. The Herfindahl-Hirschman Index (166)

Scherer and Ross, *Industrial Market Structure,* 3d rev. ed., pp. 72–73, 185.

The Urge to Merge—Are the Big Getting Bigger? (169)

R.J. Reynolds–Nabisco buyout described in Bryan Burrough and John Helyar, *Barbarians at the Gate: The Fall of RJR Nabisco* (New York: Harper & Row, 1990). Trend in Scherer and Ross, *Industrial Market Structure,* 3d rev. ed., pp. 153–59. Early research in Adolf Berle and Gardiner Means, *The Modern Corporation and Private Property* (New York: Harcourt, Brace, 1968). Defense of takeovers in Council of Economic Advisers, *Economic Report of the President 1985* (Washington, D.C.: U.S. Government Printing Office, 1985), pp. 187–216. Increasing trend in manufacturing concentration in Samuelson and Nordhaus, *Economics* (1989), p. 622; Scherer and Ross, *Industrial Market Structure,* 3d rev. ed., pp. 59–61. In favor of merger controls, in Walter Adams and James W. Brock, *The Bigness Complex* (New York: Pantheon, 1986). See also symposium on takeovers, *Journal of Economic Perspectives* 2, no. 1 (Winter 1988).

Is Small Beautiful? (170)

Summary of debate in Bennett Harrison, *Lean and Mean: The Changing Landscape of Corporate Power in the Age of Flexibility* (New York: Basic Books, 1994); "Small businesses provide" in U.S. Small Business Administration, *Small Business Answer Card;* see also U.S. Small Business Administration, *State of Small Business;* Birch in David Birch, *Job Generation in America* (New York: Free Press, 1987); criticism in Catherine Armington and Marjorie Odle, "Small Business—How Many Jobs," *Brookings Review* 1 (Winter 1982): 14–17; Mark H. Maier "Is Small Beautiful? Small Business Job Creation," *Utne Reader: The Best of the Alternative Press* (August/September 1985); Douglas P. Handler, *Business Demographics* (New York: Economic Analysis Department, Dun & Bradstreet, 1989); Steven J. Davis, John Haltiwanger, and Scott Schuh, *Job Creation and Destruction in U.S. Manufacturing,* forthcoming. Birch errors in Harrison, *Lean and Mean,* chap. 2.

Line-of-Business Reporting (171)

Favor disclosure in Frederic M. Scherer, "Segmental Financial Reporting," in *Business Disclosure: Government's Need to Know,* ed. Harvey J. Goldschmid (New York: Columbia University Center for Law and Economic Studies, 1979), pp. 3–57. Opposing disclosure in George J. Bentson, "The FTC's Line of Business Program," in Goldschmid, *Business Disclosure,* pp. 58–140. History of issue in David J. Ravenscraft and Curtis L. Wagner III, "The Role of the FTC's Line of Business Data in Test and Expanding the Theory of the Firm," *Journal of Law and Economics* 34, (October 1991): 703–9; and "An innate fear of disclosure," *Forbes,* February 5, 1990, pp. 126–27.

Box 10.4. Standard Industrial Classification (173)

On specific codes, see Dun's Marketing Services, "Standard Industrial Classification Statistics." Use of codes in Scherer, *Industrial Market Structure,* 2d rev. ed., pp. 59–60; and Scherer and Ross, *Industrial Market Structure,* 3d rev. ed., p. 74.

On problems with SIC, see Rosanne Cole, "Reviving the Federal Statistical System: A View from Industry," *American Economic Review* 80, no. 2 (May 1990): 333–34.

How Much Profit? (173)

Chevron in "Chevron Energy Report," *New York Times*, November 18, 1980, p. A20; see also Richard C. Gerstenberg, former chair, General Motors, "The Profit System and America's Growth," *New York Times*, March 4, 1974, p. 29. Public estimate in James D. Gwartney and Richard Stroup, *Economics* (San Diego: Harcourt Brace Jovanovich, 1987), p. 493. On accounting losses accompanying high executive salaries, see "Pay Stubs of the Rich and Corporate," *Business Week*, May 7, 1990, p. 59. Accounting profits described in accounting textbooks; see, for example, Needles, Anderson, and Caldwell, *Principles of Accounting*, pp. 98–116. On interest payments, see "Are True Profits Falling or Rising?" *New York Times*, January 15, 1990, p. C2. Adjusted data described in "Corporate Profits: Reading between the Bottom Lines," *Business Week*, June 15, 1987, pp. 102–4, and August 23, 1987, p. F16.

How Now Dow? (175)

Dow described in Gary E. Clayton and Martin Gerhard Giesbrecht, *Everyday Statistics* (New York: McGraw-Hill, 1990), pp. 105–9. IBM and Exxon in "Dow 2500: Then and Now," *The Independent Investor* 5, no. 14 (July 26, 1989). Data sample in "When Scorpio Rises, Stocks Will Fall," *Business Week*, June 14, 1993, p. 106; and "Editor's Note," *Business Week*, August 16, 1993, p. 11.

Picking Stock Winners (175)

Comparing advisers example in "Four Pros Make Their Picks—and Two Take Their Lumps," *Business Week*, June 20, 1994, pp. 130–31. Mutual fund data in "And the Winners Are . . . ," *Business Week*, February 17, 1992; and "The Best Mutual Funds," *Business Week*, February 15, 1993. Hulbert in Mark Hulbert, *The Hulbert Guide to Financial Newsletters* (Chicago: Dearborn Financial Publishing, 1993), pp. 34–40; and "It's Hulbert-Bashing Time, Again," *New York Times*, August 15, 1993, p. F15; Malkiel in "Fund Managers are Brilliant, or Is the Record Being Misread?" *New York Times*, May 19, 1994, p. C2. Overview of research in Burton G. Malkiel, *A Random Walk Down Wall Street* (New York: Norton, 1992); and Peter Berstein, *Capital Ideas: The Improbable Origins of Modern Wall Street* (New York: Free Press, 1991).

Case Study Questions (179)

1. Frederic M. Scherer, "Segmental Financial Reporting," in Goldschmid, *Business Disclosure*, pp. 3–57.
2. See discussion and references on SIC above.
3. Council of Economic Advisers, *Economic Report of the President 1985* (Washington, D.C.: U.S. Government Printing Office, 1985), p. 200.

4. *New York Times*, October 1, 1994, p. B17.
5. Scherer, *Industrial Market Structure*, 2d rev. ed., pp. 39–41.
6. Ibid., p. 552–53.

CHAPTER 11: GOVERNMENT (181)

Data Sources (181)

U.S. budgets in *Budget of the United States Government* (Washington, D.C.: U.S. Government Printing Office). Budget process described in Joseph J. Minarik, *Making America's Budget Policy* (Armonk, N.Y.: M.E. Sharpe, 1989). U.S. Federal Reserve statistics described in "Recent Developments in Economic Statistics at the Federal Reserve: Part 2," *Business Economics,* July 1989, pp. 40–47; and Norman Frumkin, *Tracking America's Economy* (Armonk, N.Y.: M.E. Sharpe, 1987), chap. 17. Data sample in *Federal Reserve Bulletin* 80, no. 1 (January 1994): A14. Consumer and producer price indexes described in Bureau of Labor Statistics, U.S. Department of Labor, *Handbook of Labor Statistics* (Washington, D.C.: U.S. Government Printing Office, 1985), pp. 346–49. Commerce Department inflation adjustments in Allan H. Young, "Alternate Measures of Real GNP," *Survey of Current Business,* April 1989, pp. 27–34. On currency adjustments, see "Index of Weighted Average Exchange Values of the U.S. Dollar: Revisions," *Federal Reserve Bulletin,* August 1978, p. 700. Data sample in *Monthly Labor Review,* August 1994, p. 100.

Controversies (184)

How Much for the Military? (184)

U.S. 1995 military spending in *Budget of the United States Government 1995* (Washington, D.C.: U.S. Government Printing Office, 1995), p. 17. Omitted items in "Undercounting Military Spending," *Dollars and Sense,* September 1987; and Ethan B. Kapstein, "Military Expenditures in the Developing World: Assessing the Data," *Peace Economics, Peace Science and Public Policy* 1, no. 1 (1993): 7–13; Third World sources in Ethan Kapstein, *The Political Economy of National Security,* (Columbia: University of South Carolina Press, 1991); and Kapstein, "Military Expenditures." Soviet spending in Franklyn D. Holzman, "The CIA's Military Spending Estimates: Deceit and Its Costs," *Challenge,* May–June 1992, pp. 28–39.

How Much for Welfare? (186)

Murray in Charles Murray, *Losing Ground: American Social Policy 1950–1980* (New York: Basic Books, 1984). Critics in Christopher Jencks, "How Poor Are the Poor?" *New York Review of Books,* May 9, 1985, pp. 40–49. One-seventh in Sol Levitan, "The Evolving Welfare System," *Society* 23, 2 (January 2, 1986): 5. U.S. spending in "Comparing Social Paychecks," *Dollars and Sense,* October 1989, p. 23. Tullock in Gordon Tullock, *Economics of Income Redistribution* (Boston: Kluwer-Nijhoff, 1983), p. 2. Sweden in "Comparing Social Paychecks."

How Big Is the Deficit? (187)

"Asset management" in "Plan to Sell Surplus Property to Lower Deficit Hits Snags," *New York Times,* May 29, 1984, p. I-11. Conrail in "Uncle Sam's Loan Sale," *Business Week,* January 26, 1987, pp. 41–42. Shifting payday and off-budget in John Miller, "Washington's Magic Act," *Dollars and Sense,* January–February 1990, pp. 9–11; and "The Bottom Line: Gramm-Rudman Isn't Working," *Business Week,* April 10, 1989, p. 36. On off-budget items see Robert Eisner, *The Misunderstood Economy: What Counts and How to Count it* (Boston: Harvard Business School Press, 1994); and Robert Eisner, "Sense and Nonsense about Budget Deficits," *Harvard Business Review,* May–June 1993, pp. 99–111. On social security surplus, see "Budget: Dilemma Is How to Spend Surpluses," *Los Angeles Times,* May 22, 1988, p. A1.

A Debt Monster? (190)

Eisner position summarized in Robert Eisner, "The Federal Deficit: How Does It Matter?" *Science* 237 (September 25, 1987): 1577–82. Heilbroner summarized in Robert Heilbroner and Peter Bernstein, *The Debt and the Deficit* (New York: Norton, 1989). Capital accounting discussed in ibid., pp. 95–97; and Robert Eisner, "The Total Incomes System of Accounts," *Survey of Current Business,* January 1985, pp. 24–34. "The entire government" in Robert Eisner, "Budget Deficits: Rhetoric and Reality," *Journal of Economic Perspectives* 3, no. 2 (Spring 1989): 75. Criticism and other approaches in "Symposium," *Journal of Economic Perspectives* 3, no. 2 (Spring 1989). See also Letters, *New York Times,* March 12, 1989, IV, p. E24. Schultze in Charles L. Schultze, "Of Wolves, Termites, and Pussycats: Or, Why We Should Worry about the Budget Deficit," *Brookings Review,* Summer 1989, pp. 26–33; Aaron in Letters, *New York Times,* March 12, 1989, IV, p. E24. See also "Dual Federal Budgets Could Mislead," *Wall Street Journal,* December 16, 1986, p. 35. Heilbroner on public projects in Heilbroner and Bernstein, *The Debt,* pp. 106–9.

Taxes (192)

On 1980s tax cut, see Frank Ackerman, *Hazardous to Our Wealth: Economic Policies in the 1980s* (Boston: South End Press, 1984), pp. 33–48. Stockman in William Greider, "The Education of David Stockman," *Atlantic,* December 1981, pp. 46–47. On capital gains tax, see "Bush's Capital Gains Tax Plan Favors the Rich, Congressional Study Finds," *Wall Street Journal,* February 6, 1992, p. A3; Paul Craig Roberts, "Ditch the Capital-Gains Tax Once and for All," *Business Week,* April 3, 1989, p. 21; "Review and Outlook," *Wall Street Journal,* July 25, 1989, p. A18, and July 28, 1989, p. A10; Joseph A. Pechman, "Letters to the Editor," *Wall Street Journal,* August 1, 1989, p. A11; Robert S. McIntyre, "Tax Deform," *New Republic,* August 21, 1989, pp. 18–21. Tax burden in Joseph Pechman, *Who Paid the Taxes?* (Washington, D.C.: Brookings Institution, 1985); and Edgar K. Browning and William R. Johnson, *The Distribution of the Tax*

Burden (Washington, D.C.: American Enterprise Institute, 1979). Further debate in Edgar K. Browning, "Pechman's Tax Incidence Study: A Note on the Data," and Joseph A. Pechman, "Pechman's Tax Incidence Study: A Response," *American Economic Review* 76, no. 5 (December 1986): 1214–19, and Joseph A. Pechman, "The Future of the Income Tax," *American Economic Review* 80, no. 1 (March 1990): 1–20. See also Randy Albelda, "Let Them Pay Taxes," *Dollars and Sense,* April 1988, pp. 9-11.

Measuring Money (195)

Federal Reserve and measurement of money supply in many economics textbooks; see, for example, Paul A. Samuelson and William D. Nordhaus, *Economics* (New York: McGraw-Hill, 1989), chap. 11. Use of monetary targets summarized in Donald L. Kohn, "Policy Targets and Operating Procedures in the 1990s," *Federal Reserve Bulletin* 76, no. 1 (January 1990): 1–7; and Robert J. Gordon, *Macroeconomics* (Glenview, Ill.: Scott, Foresman, 1990), pp. 454–58. On missing currency see Case M. Sprinkle, "The Case of the Missing Currency," *Journal of Economic Perspectives* 7, no. 4 (Fall 1993): 175–84.

Inflation (197)

CPI versus PCE in Jack E. Tripleti, "Reconciling the CPI and the PCE Deflator," *Monthly Labor Review,* September 1981, pp. 3–15. Data in Council of Economic Advisers, *Economic Report of the President 1988* (Washington, D.C.: U.S. Government Printing Office, 1988), pp. 255, 317. Health-care costs in "Medical Costs Are in Orbit, Right? Well, Maybe," *Business Week,* April 1, 1991, p. 18; data since 1982 in Ana M. Aizcorbe and Patrick C. Jackman, "The Commodity Substitution Effect in CPI Data 1982–91," *Monthly Labor Review,* December 1993, pp. 25–33; and Mary Lynn Schmidt, "Effects of Updating the CPI Market Basket," *Monthly Labor Review,* December 1993, pp. 59–62; Pollin and Stone in Robert Pollin and Michael Stone, "The Illusion of an Improved CPI," *Challenge,* January–February 1991, pp. 53–57. Housing issue in U.S. Department of Labor, "Changing the Homeownership Component of the Consumer Price Index to Rental Equivalence," *CPI Detailed Report* (Washington, D.C.: U.S. Government Printing Office, January 1983). New poverty rate in Ronald Kwan, "Playing with Numbers," *Dollars and Sense,* May 1990, pp. 20–21.

Currency Rates (199)

Trade-weighted indexes in "The Buck Stops Where?" *Dollars and Sense,* March 1987, pp. 20–21. German well-being in "Comparing Wealth as Money Fluctuates," *New York Times,* August 23, 1988, p. IV-3. Purchasing power parity in Derek Blades, "International Statistics: An OECD View," *Business Economics,* July 1986, p. 42. PPP in "An Overdue Change in the Way Living Standards Are Compared," *New York Times,* May 27, 1993, p. C2; Big Mac in "Big Mac Currencies," *The Economist,* April 13, 1991, p. 78. China in Vaclav Smil, "How Rich Is China?" *Current History,* September 1993, pp. 265–69. East German currency in "The West German Mark May Soon Rule the East," *Business Week,* November 27, 1989, p. 65.

Box 11.1. CPI or PCE: Watch Out! (200)

On Harrison and Bluestone controversy, see Bennett Harrison and Barry Blue-stone, *The Great U-Turn: Corporate Restructuring and the Polarizing of America* (New York: Basic Books, 1988); and Marvin H. Kosters and Murray N. Ross, "A Shrinking Middle Class?" *The Public Interest* 90 (Winter 1980): 3–27. Deliberate deception in Warren T. Brookes, "Low-Pay Jobs: The Big Lie," *Wall Street Journal,* March 25, 1987, p. 32. Example of use of PCE in Frank Levy, "Incomes, Families, and Living Standards," in Robert E. Litan et al., *American Living Standards* (Washington, D.C.: Brookings Institution, 1988), pp. 108-53.

Case Study Questions (203)

1. "$180 Billion in U.S. Currency Eludes Tally; Is It Abroad?" *New York Times,* February 20, 1990, p. C1, and Phillip Mattera, *Off the Books* (London: Pluto Press, 1985), p. 44.
2. Randy Albelda, "Let Them Pay Taxes," *Dollars and Sense,* April 1988, pp. 9–11.
3. Capital accounts in Heilbroner and Bernstein, *The Debt;* and J. Richard Aronson and John L. Hilley, *Financing State and Local Governments* (Washington, D.C.: Brookings Institution, 1986).
4. Heilbroner and Bernstein, *The Debt;* Charles L. Schultze, "Of Wolves, Termites, and Pussycats: Or, Why We Should Worry about the Budget Deficit," *Brookings Review,* Summer 1989, pp. 26–33.
5. Robert J. Gordon, *Macroeconomics* (Glenview, Ill.: Scott, Foresman, 1990), pp. 53–54.
6. "The Changes behind the CPI's New Look," *Business Week,* March 2, 1987, p. 24; Charles Mason and Clifford Butler, "New Basket of Goods and Services Being Priced in Revised CPI," *Monthly Labor Review,* January 1987, pp. 3–22; Mary Lynn Schmidt, "Comparison of the Revised and Old CPI," *Monthly Labor Review,* November 1987, pp. 3–6.

CHAPTER 12: PUBLIC OPINION POLLING (205)

Data Sources (205)

Private Polling Organizations (205)

On political affiliation of pollsters see David W. Moore, *Superpollsters* (New York: Four Walls Eight Windows, 1992). Gallup data sample in George J. Gallup, Jr., and Frank Newport, "Almost Half of Americans Believe Biblical View of Creation," *The Gallup Poll Monthly* (November 1991), pp. 30–31.

Media Polls (206)

See Thomas E. Mann and Gary R. Orren, *Media Polls in American Politics* (Washington, D.C.: Brookings Institution, 1992). Roper Center study in Carl

Everett Ladd and John Benson, "The Growth of New Polls in American Politics," in Mann and Orren, *Media Polls,* p. 20.

Research Centers (207)

Survey Research Center data summarized in Philip E. Converse, *American Social Attitudes Data Sourcebook* (Cambridge: Harvard University Press, 1980). GSS data summarized in Richard G. Niemi, *Trends in Public Opinion: a Compendium of Survey Data* (Westport, Conn.: Greenwood Press, 1989). National Election Studies described in Warren E. Miller, *American National Election Studies Data Sourcebook* (Cambridge: Harvard University Press, 1989). ANES data sample in ibid., p. 85. GSS data sample in Tom W. Smith, "The Use of Public Opinion Data by the Attorney General's Commission on Pornography," *Public Opinion Quarterly* 51 (1987): 259.

Controversies (207)

Predicting Elections (207)

Literary Digest in Moore, *Superpollsters,* pp. 32–71; Peverill Squire, "Why the 1936 *Literary Digest* Poll Failed," *Public Opinion Quarterly* 52 (1988): 125–33; Don Cahalan, "The *Digest* Poll Rides Again!" *Public Opinion Quarterly* 53 (1989): 129–33. On Gallup in 1936, see Moore, *Superpollsters,* pp. 2–32; Gallup's own account in George Gallup and Saul Rae, *The Pulse of Democracy* (New York: Simon and Schuster, 1940), pp. 38–48. Truman/Dewey in Moore, *Superpollsters,* pp. 68–71.

Sampling in the 1990s (208)

Random dialing in Moore, *Superpollsters,* pp. 270–73; Rhodes versus Celeste in Herbert B. Asher, *Polling and the Public* (Washington, D.C.: CA Press, 1988), pp. 138–39. Summary of major media poll techniques in Asher, *Polling,* pp. 140–41; see also "Design of the Sample" in *The Gallup Poll Monthly;* refusal in Los Angeles in Moore, *Superpollsters,* pp. 320–21. Election margins of error in Michael R. Kagay, "Variability without Fault: Why Even Well-Designed Polls Can Disagree," in Mann and Orren, *Media Polls,* p. 105, and "Some Recent Polls," *New York Times,* November 7, 1988, p. B14, "Polls Say Clinton Keeps Lead," *New York Times,* November 1, 1992, p. A26. Telephone records in Brady and Orren, "Polling Pitfalls," pp. 63–64. *Columbus Dispatch* poll in Asher, *Polling,* pp. 138–39. Exit polling in Kathleen A. Frankovic, "Technology and the Changing Landscape of Media Polls," in Mann and Orren, *Media Polls,* pp. 34–40. Refusal rate in ibid., pp. 37–39.

Box 12.1. Black Candidates/White Voters (211)

Elections in Henry E. Brady and Gary R. Orren, "Polling Pitfalls: Sources of Error in Public Opinion Surveys," pp. 82–85; *Times* poll in *New York Times,* "Most Blacks Back Reagan, Poll Finds" January 5, 1986, p. 20; Asher, *Polling,* pp. 61–62.

Polling Standards (212)

Gallup explanation in Asher, *Polling,* p. 63. Standards in ibid., pp. 78–81. Goodell in Charles W. Roll and Albert H. Cantril, *Polls: Their Use and Misue in Politics* (New York: Basic Books), p. 13. On Nixon, see Moore, *Superpollsters,* p. 95; on Harris and Kennedys, see ibid., pp. 110–21.

Horserace Journalism (213)

Misreporting in Gerald C. Wright, "Errors in Measuring Vote Choice in the National Election Studies, 1952–1988," *American Journal of Political Science* 37 (February 1993): 291–316; and Gerald C. Wright, "Misreports of Vote Choice in the 1988 NES Senate Election Study," *Legislative Studies Quarterly* 55 (November 1990): 543–62. Rhodes victory in Asher, *Polling,* pp. 112–13; Mason-Dixon in "When Voters Tell Polls They're Undecided," Letter from J. Bradford Coker and Robert L. Joffee, *New York Times,* November 11, 1993, p. A18. Net effect in Larry J. Sabato, *The Rise of Political Consultants* (New York: Basic Books, 1981), p. 107. $500,000 study in Michael W. Traugott, "The Impact of Media Polls on the Public," in Mann and Orren, *Media Polls,* p. 138. Critical view in Todd Gitlin, "Blips, Bites and Savvy Talk," *Dissent,* Winter 1990, pp. 18–26; Goldwater in Thomas E. Mann and Gary R. Orren, "To Poll or Not to Poll . . . and Other Questions," in Mann and Orren, *Media Polls,* p. 5. Reagan and Jackson in E.J. Dionne, Jr., "Impact of Polls on Reporters and Democracy," in Mann and Orren, *Media Polls,* pp. 158–61. "Technology and the Changing Landscape of Media Polls," in ibid., pp. 52–53.

Question Wording (215)

Krosnick in Jon A. Krosnick, "Question Wording and Reports of Survey Results: The Case of Louis Harris and Associates and Aetna Life and Casualty," *Public Opinion Quarterly* 53 (1989): 107–13. Gun control in James D. Wright, "Public Opinion and Gun Control: A Comparison of Results from Two Recent National Surveys," *Annals, AAPSS* 455 (May 1981): 25–39. Abortion in Asher, *Polling,* p. 124; Kagay in Kagay, "Variability without Fault," p. 118. Rasinski in Kenneth A. Rasinski, "The Effect of Question Wording on Public Support for Government Spending," *Public Opinion Quarterly* 53 (1989): 388–94. Detroit study in Asher, *Polling,* p. 81.

Box 12.2 Dial 900 (216)

Moore, *Superpollsters* pp. 287–9; Kathleen A. Frankovic, "Technology and the Changing Landscape of Media Polls," in ibid., pp. 52–53.

Question Order (218)

Connecticut race in Irving Crespi and Dwight Morris, "Question Order Effect and the Measurement of Candidate Preference in the 1982 Connecticut Elections," *Public Opinion Quarterly* 48 (1984): 578–91; Perot in Brady and Orren, "Polling Pitfalls," p. 77; National Crime Survey in Howard Schuman and Stanley Presser,

Questions and Answers in Attitude Surveys (New York: Academic Press, 1981) p. 45; Hispanics in Elizabeth Martin, Theresa J. DeMaio, and Pamela C. Campanelli, "Context Effects for Census Measures of Race and Hispanic Origin," *Public Opinion Quarterly* 54 (1990): 551–66. Bush–Dukakis in Irving Crespi, *Public Opinion, Polls and Demcracy* (Boulder, Colo.: Westview Press, 1989), p. 69; SRC on housing in Schuman and Presser, *Questions,* p. 70.

Moral Majority: Agree or Strongly Agree? (220)

Debate about Moral Majority in Lee Sigelman and Stanley Presser, "Measuring Public Support for the New Christian Right," *Public Opinion Quarterly* 52 (1988): 325–37; and John H. Simpson, "A Reply to 'Measuring Public Support for the New Christian Right'," *Public Opinion Quarterly* 52 (1988): 338–41.

Don't Knows: Ignorance or Honesty? (221)

Agricultural Trade Act in Schuman and Presser, *Questions,* pp. 148–50; Reagan cancer in Asher, *Polling,* p. 3. Don't know and filters in Schuman and Presser, *Questions,* pp. 114–46. Nicaragua in Asher, *Polling,* pp. 125–26. SALT in Albert H. Cantril, *Polling on the Issues* (Cabin John, Md.: Seven Locks Press, 1980), p. 105. Roper Center study in Ladd, "The Growth of New Polls," p. 29. Nixon and Cambodia in Sabato, *The Rise of Political Consultants,* p. 82. Critical view in Benjamin Ginsberg, *The Captive Public* (New York: Basic Books, 1986).

Box 12.3. The Gay Population (222)

"A Sharper View of Gay Consumers," *New York Times,* June 9, 1994, p. C1; "Sex Surveys: Does Anyone Tell the Truth?" *American Demographics,* July 1993, p. 9; "Sex Survey of American Men Finds 1% Are Gay," *New York Times,* April 15, 1993, p. A1; Priscilla Painton, "The Shrinking Ten Percent," *Time,* April 26, 1993, pp. 27–29; "Polling on Sexual Issues Has Its Drawbacks," *New York Times,* April 25, 1993, p. A23; "Sex in America: Faithfulness in Marriage Thrives after All," *New York Times,* October 7, 1994, p. A1.

What Do Women Want? (223)

On Hite, see Shere Hite, *The Hite Report* (New York: Dell, 1977), and her other two books; on Hite/ABC controversy see Moore, *Superpollsters,* pp. 6–22. See also Susan Faludi, *Backlash: The Undeclared War against American Women* (New York: Crown, 1991), pp. 4–9; on NORC, see "Sex in America," p. A1.

Summary (225)

For summary of research on polling, see Graham R. Walden, *Public Opinion Polls and Survey Research: A Selective Annotated Bibliography of U.S. Guides and Studies from the 1980s* (New York: Garland, 1990). How to do your own survey in Celinda Lake, *Public Opinion Polling* (Washington, D.C.: Island Park Press, 1987); and Thomas I. Miller, *Citizen Surveys* (Washington, D.C.: International City Managers Association, 1991).

Box 12.4. Teenage Sex: A Scientific Survey (225)

Joan Kahn, William Kalsbeek, and Sandra Hoffreth, "National Estimates of Teenage Sexual Activity: Evaluating the Comparability of Three National Surveys," *Demography* 25, no. 2 (1988): 189–203.

Case Study Questions (226)

1. Herbert H. Clark, "Asking Questions and Influencing Answers," in Judith M. Tanur, *Questions about Questions: Inquiries into the Cognitive Bases of Surveys* (New York: Russell Sage Foundation, 1992), p. 21.
2. Smith, "The Use of Public Opinion Data by the Attorney General's Commission on Pornography," pp. 249–67.
3. "Pollsters Enlist Psychologists in Quest for Unbiased Results," *New York Times,* September 7, 1993, p. B5.
4. Mann and Orren, "To Poll or Not to Poll," p. 3.
5. Schuman and Presser, *Questions,* p. 183.

CHAPTER 13: CONCLUSIONS (229)

For an analysis of social and economic statistics, see John Irvine, Ian Miles, and Jeff Evans, *Demystifying Social Statistics* (London: Pluto Press, 1981); William Alonso and Paul Starr, *The Politics of Numbers* (New York: Russell Sage Foundation, 1987); and Lou Ferleger, " 'Truth' from Numbers: Sorting Out Statistics," *Socialist Review* 93, no. 4 (May–August 1987): 91–104. On assumptions used in government statistics, see Jerry Miron and Christina D. Romer, "Reviving the Federal Statistical System: The View from Academia," *American Economic Review* 80, no. 2 (May 1990): 329–36. On choices for U.S. enfranchisement, see Margo J. Anderson, *The American Census: A Social History* (New Haven: Yale University Press, 1988), pp. 11–12.

Index

Montagu, Ashley, 19
Monthly Labor Review, 29, 102, 142, 182
Monthly Vital Statistics Report, 7, 49
Moody's, 158
Moore, Geoffrey H., 106
Moorman, Jeanne E., 24
Moral Majority, public opinion polls on, 220–21
Morbidity and Mortality Weekly Report, 49
Morris, Dwight, 218
Morton, Oliver, 9
Mozambique, economic data of, 110
Murray, Charless, 186

Nader, Ralph, 62, 97
National Academy of Sciences, 9
National Advisory Commission on Civil Disorders, 41
National Assessment of Educational Progress (NAEP), 79–80
National Association of Home Builders, 31
National Association of Realtors, 31, 33, 34
National Bureau for Economic Research, 106, 170
National Cancer Act, 56–57
National Cancer Institute (NCI), 1, 49, 57, 58, 65
National Center for Education Statistics (NCES), 67, 68, 69–70, 74, 81
National Center for Health Statistics (NCHS), 7, 8, 48, 49, 52, 59, 65, 69
National Center for Missing and Exploited Children, 96
National Commission on Social Security Reform, 14
National Council on Public Polls, 212
National Crime Survey (NCS), 84, 85, 86–89, 90, 91, 97, 98, 99, 100, 219
National economy. *See* Economy, national

National Education Association (NEA), 68, 69, 70
National Election Studies, 207
National Highway Traffic and Safety Administration, 49
National Longitudinal Survey, 51, 69, 74, 134, 207, 225
National Opinion Research Center (NORC), 206, 207, 224
National Origins Act of 1924, 27
National Research Council, 60
National Rifle Association (NRA), 217
National Survey of Family Growth, 51, 225
National Surveys of Young Women, 225
Nation at Risk, A: The Imperative for Educational Reform, 70
NBC polls, 207, 209, 212
NCES. *See* National Center for Education Statistics
NCHS. *See* National Center for Health Statistics
NCI. *See* National Cancer Institute
Neighborhood Reinvestment Corporation, 39
Netherlands, unemployment in, 153
Newsweek, 21, 22, 71, 76, 205, 209
New York Stock Exchange, 175, 176, 179
New York Times polls, 206, 209, 211, 218, 219
900 telephone polls, 216, 224
Nixon, Richard, 41, 56, 88, 213, 223
NORC. *See* National Opinion Research Center
Nordhaus, William, 108, 110
Northwest Airlines, 167, 169
Norton, Arthur J., 24

Occupational Injuries and Illnesses, 142
Occupational Safety and Health Administration (OSHA), 62, 141, 151–52
Office of Management and Budget (OMB), 32, 40, 62, 173, 182
Official Summary of Security Transactions and Holdings, 157

About the Author

Mark H. Maier is Professor of Economics at Glendale College, Glendale, California. He is the author of *City Unions: Managing Discontent in New York City* (1987) and *Economics Live! Learning Economics the Collaborative Way* (with Diane Keenan, 1994). Dr. Maier received his Ph.D. in economics from the Graduate Faculty, New School for Social Research, in 1980.